Evaluating the Impact
of Manpower
Programs

Evaluating the Impact of Manpower Programs

Proceedings of a Conference Conducted June 15-17, 1971 at The Center for Human Resource Research, The Ohio State University

Edited by
Michael E. Borus
School of Labor and Industrial Relations
Michigan State University

Lexington Books
D.C. Heath and Company
Lexington, Massachusetts
Toronto   London

Abel

Table of Contents

Foreword

The conference from which these papers are drawn was the outgrowth of my experiences as a researcher conducting evaluations of manpower programs and as a Brookings Institution Economic Policy Fellow in the U.S. Department of Labor. Over the years, it has become obvious to me that evaluation of the impact of manpower programs is still in its infancy: there are many theoretical and technical problems which have to be resolved if the evaluations are to be really useful policy instruments. While in the Labor Department, William Tash and I tried to lay out the principles of evaluation in our *Measuring the Impact of Manpower Programs: A Primer*, but we found that many of the problems were beyond our abilities. It seemed desirable, therefore, to bring together all of the experts in the field of impact evaluation of manpower programs in an attempt to solve these problems. The Conference on the Evaluation of the Impact of Manpower Programs was the fruition of these efforts.

The Conference was jointly sponsored by the Office of Evaluation, Office of the Assistant Secretary for Policy, Evaluation and Research and the Division of Program Evaluation Studies, Manpower Administration, both in the U.S. Department of Labor, and the Center for Human Resource Research at The Ohio State University. I would like to acknowledge the support of these organizations and especially John Cheston, Director of the Office of Evaluation, S. Clifton Kelley, Director of the Center for Human Resource Research, Abraham Stahler, Chief of the Division of Program Evaluation Studies, and William Tash, Howard Vincent and Ralph Walker who served as Labor Department project officers. Finally, I would like to thank the secretarial staff of the Center for Human Resource Research, Kandy Bell, Mary Dombroviak, Dortha Gilbert, Cindi Gillen, Amalia Gomez, Gretchen Swartzlander, and Patty White, who took care of the voluminous paper work involved in an undertaking of this type and Charles Buntz who served as my research assistant. Without their help, the Conference could never have taken place.

Michael E. Borus

Introduction

Michael E. Borus[1]

May 1, 1971 marked the tenth anniversary of the passage of the Area Redevelopment Act (ARA), the modest beginning to the nation's manpower programs. In fiscal 1962, approximately 6,600 persons enrolled in this program; during fiscal 1970, 1,051,000 were enrolled in U.S. Department of Labor manpower programs. Just as the ARA has given way to much more sophisticated and extensive manpower programs, those of us who began conducting evaluation studies ten years ago tend now to look back sheepishly at the innocence of those early studies. We have come a long way in improving our evaluations—but there is a long road ahead before they may be used by policy-makers with certitude. The objectives of the Conference on the Evaluation of the Impact of Manpower Programs and this volume are to move us down this road.

This volume has two goals. First, the increased number of evaluations of manpower programs has prevented adequate communication among people working in this field. Common problems have had to be solved on an ad hoc basis by individual evaluators. One purpose of the papers in this volume is to bring together the techniques which have evolved for dealing with the practical problems involved in manpower program evaluation.

In addition, the technology of manpower program evaluation rests in large part on theoretical concepts of the social sciences. At present, the technology of program evaluation has pushed to the limit of existing theoretical knowledge. The second purpose of this volume is to provide a forum for ideas which attempt to push back this frontier—that is, to advance the theoretical foundations for program evaluation.

I think that many of the papers presented here will stimulate new techniques and thinking in manpower program evaluation. This can best be seen by turning to specific topic areas.

Designing an Evaluation System

Evaluations of manpower programs do not occur in a vacuum. They are intended to be used for making policy decisions. According to Peter Barth, however, past studies have had limited impact in the policy area, primarily because of their design. Most of the evaluation studies of manpower programs have been con-

---

[1] This paper was written while the author was a Research Associate of the Center for Human Resource Research and Visiting Associate Professor of Economics at The Ohio State University. He would like to thank Charles G. Buntz and John R. Shea for comments on an earlier version of this paper.

cerned with a single program and conducted on a one-shot basis. Due to the differing assumptions, control groups, data sources and estimation techniques which have been used in the individual studies, attempts to make cross-program comparisons have been almost meaningless. Yet, Barth argues cross-program comparisons are vital to making policy because (1) they present models of success for emulation in future programs; and (2) they demonstrate the relative trade-offs necessary to allocate the manpower budget between competing programs. He suggests that the supposed problems involved in cross-program analyses have been overstated and he discusses the most ambitious multiprogram evaluation conducted so far—the joint Office of Economic Opportunity-Department of Labor (OEO-DOL) four-program comparison—to illustrate how these problems may be overcome.

There has been no similar shift to the use of impact evaluation to compare intraprogram differences. Yet, to program operators, it is not sufficient for the evaluator to say that nationally a particular program yields high benefits. It is also necessary that the evaluator answer such questions as: "What components of the program are most effective?" and "Under what labor market conditions is this program most effective?" To answer these questions, the analysis must include as independent variables the interaction of program participation with specific components of the programs and characteristics of the labor market. In their paper, Edward Bryant and Morris Hansen present a plan for a continuing longitudinal sample survey which will provide the necessary data for such an analysis and cross-program comparisons.

In his comment, Paul Gayer notes that there are several additional benefits to the OEO-DOL cross-program comparison: it can be used to test longitudinal versus retrospective studies and to compare the various components of the different programs. He also points out that the Bryant-Hansen proposal for a continuing survey should vastly improve the data base for manpower programs by changing the incentives. John Cheston also discusses the advantages of interprogram comparisons, emphasizing that the need for control groups of nonparticipants may be reduced because there is a degree of randomness in assignment to programs which matches the program participants in terms of motivation and other factors.

Finally, John Scanlon, Joe Nay and Joseph Wholey lay out in considerable detail the type of information needed to conduct continuous interprogram and intraprogram evaluations. They make the point that much of the data already exist in Labor Department forms but that it is necessary to have an integrated evaluation design.

Choice of Appropriate Control Groups

While the use of control groups has been generally accepted, the choice of who shall serve as a control group has not been resolved. Einar Hardin notes the variety of techniques for choosing a control group which have been used. These include using (1) the program participants' own experience before training; (2) other individuals who are of the same age and economic status as the program participants, but who have not entered the program (selected from lists of youngsters at the same school at the same time as the program participants and persons applying at employment service offices); (3) individuals who apply to a program, are eligible to enter the program, meet the program entrance criteria, but who for one reason or another do not choose to participate; (4) the dropouts of manpower programs; and finally, (5) random assignment of individuals who sought to enter the program into two groups—one to be participants and the other control group members. Hardin argues that this last procedure should be attempted whenever possible, since it alone creates statistical equivalence between treatment and control groups. In each of the other cases, he hypothesizes differences in characteristics or motivation which would lead the control group to lack comparability with the program participants. If random assignment is not possible, however, he feels it advisable to use interested nonenrollees as the basic control group.

David Miller is generally skeptical about the use of control groups. He feels too little is known about the causes of the various effects of manpower programs and therefore it is difficult to say that matching on a selected number of characteristics establishes control. Miller also cites other problems of control group use including the interaction between experimental and control groups and nonrandom occurrences of extraneous effects which confound the experiment. Harold Nisselson, on the other hand, generally agrees with Hardin on the need for random assignment for evaluation purposes. He states, however, that greater emphasis should be placed on evaluating the impact of the programs on the universe of those in need rather than just on the participants. Finally, Abraham Stahler finds fault with the random assignment technique. He questions if manpower services should be denied to some persons solely for evaluative purposes.

Designing the Survey

Since most evaluations of manpower programs have been carried on by economists, these evaluations have concentrated on economic variables, in particular, the gains in income and employment. These are important variables and they should be measured. There are problems in their measurement, however; one of the most difficult is in selecting the method to collect data. In her paper, Marie Argana presents the results of two Census Bureau tests which indicate the value of unstructured work histories. She concludes, however, that the problems of data handling are severe with this format, and chronological questioning is probably to be preferred. In commenting on her paper, Gilbert Nestel suggests that these results be treated as tentative due to the size and choice of samples used in the tests.

Harold Sheppard also discusses the construction of questionnaires, but he argues for increased use of measures of attitudes both as independent and dependent variables. Among the measures he suggests are achievement motivation, achievement values, job-interview anxiety and various other social-psychological variables. He cites the use of these variables in his own studies to demonstrate their value for program evaluation. Sheppard's position is reinforced by the comments of Ralph Walker, although he questions the appropriateness of certain types of measures in mass surveys.

Measuring the Noneconomic Impacts of Manpower Programs

If we follow Sheppard's advice and move away from measuring only the economic impact of manpower programs, we find there are a host of social and psychological implications, which also should be examined in determining manpower programs' effectiveness. Such variables which may be affected by manpower programs and which should be measured are the effects upon education, health, crime, community power structure and political institutions, individual and job satisfaction, family life, social participation, housing, race relations, and social behavior. In many cases, these concepts are more difficult to measure than are dollars of income. Yet, in a period when alienation, crime, and racism are thought to be major problems of society, the effects of manpower programs in these areas may be more important than their economic effects. Furthermore, most of these variables have economic repercussions or dimensions. Therefore, four papers are devoted to the measurement of these impacts.

The paper by Stanislav Kasl examines six possible criteria for the measurement of health, broadly defined. Kasl also provides an extensive review of the scales available for measurement of these health criteria and a discussion of the merits of some specific measures he has used in a study of the effect of job loss. In commenting on this paper, Thomas Chirikos feels that the criteria and measures in the field of health are not sufficiently well defined to be used for evaluative research.

Gerald Somers and Ernst Stromsdorfer use several University of Wisconsin studies to demonstrate measures of the educational impact which manpower programs may have. These include the probabilities of attaining various educational levels and their interrelationships with labor market experience. Howard Rosen comments that many important variables have been ignored in the specifications of the models Somers and Stromsdorfer cite and further that they have not discovered the relationships which account for success or failure of programs.

The paper by John McDonnell reports on his attempts to measure recidivism among convicts who receive training. He cites a number of problems including defining recidivism, locating the participants and isolating the effects of various factors. This last factor is emphasized by Belton Fleisher in his comments.

Finally, Garth Mangum and R. Thayne Robson present many of the basic questions which must be answered to determine the impact of manpower programs on a community. These include how community institutions have changed, how many new jobs have been created, what the effects are on the aggregate labor force and employment and how to determine the secondary effects of manpower programs. James Hefner in his comments adds several other questions to this list and notes the need for a "community theory."

Finding the Hard-to-Locate

The collection of data on labor market experiences of program participants and control group members has been by far the most costly and time-consuming stage in the evaluation of manpower programs. There are two routes open to the manpower program evaluator: he can collect his own data or use the data collected by some other organization. The former permits the evaluator to collect all of the information which he deems relevant to his study. If he relies upon the data collected by others, he must first find the type of information which is available from the different sources. Furthermore, these data are often considerably limited because they are collected for purposes other than evaluation. In addition, the government agencies who usually are the source of these data place fairly strong restrictions on their availability and use by nongovernmental evaluators. The result has been that the majority of manpower program evaluations have relied upon data collected in surveys conducted by the evaluator.

The costs of these surveys, however, are tremendously high—in the neighborhood of $60 to $70 per respondent interviewed. More importantly from a methodological point of view, the response rates which are finally achieved are often very low and introduce a high probability of nonresponse bias. Obviously, there is a need to improve the response rates in manpower evaluation studies which rely on sample surveys.

Bryant and Hansen propose a method for preselecting individuals to be included in evaluation studies which should greatly alleviate the response problem. At the same time, however, it also is necessary to improve the practices of interviewing organizations in tracking, locating and interviewing the types of individuals who participate in manpower programs. Hilda Barnes in her paper stresses the importance of treating respondents as individuals in "a positive, friendly and enthusiastic manner"; that interviewer persistence, resourcefulness and motivation are more important than their demographic characteristics; and that the use of interpersonal contact is the best method for tracking. Celia Homans' paper complements that of Barnes. Her paper is more specific, detailing the administrative organization and the procedures for locating the hard to find for the OEO-DOL study NORC is conducting.

In contrast to the earlier papers which emphasize their own experiences finding the hard-to-locate, Morgan Lewis reviews the procedures used in a number of manpower studies. He suggests that indigenous interviewers are necessary, that a combination piece and hourly rate be used to pay these interviewers, that phone contact be limited and that the respondents be paid. Taken together the three papers provide the basic techniques to improve survey response rates.

Sources of Economic Data

Even with higher response rates, however, surveys may be prohibitively expensive and the evaluator may decide to turn to existing data files. To facilitate the use of such files, five data experts present papers in which they discuss the relative merits of some of the basic existent data sources and how access to them may be secured. John Fischer discusses the use of Internal Revenue Service data by the Job Corps; Robert Heller treats the use and availability of summary earnings records of the Social Security Administration; Dwight Kelley presents a brief rundown on unemployment insurance wage reports; Martin Koenig discusses the data files of the Manpower Administration; and Herbert Parnes and John Shea indicate the possible use of the National Longitudinal Surveys for control group purposes.

In their comments on these papers, Robert David, Edward Prescott and William Tash suggest a need to make these data sources more responsive to evaluation requirements at the local and regional levels, the need to integrate them and the need to make them more generally available to evaluators.

Measuring Secondary Labor Market Effects

Finally, we come to a theoretical issue which I believe seriously hinders the usefulness of evaluation findings. Manpower programs have as basic goals increasing national production and increasing the employment and earnings of particular groups of workers. To measure the extent that manpower programs achieve these goals requires knowledge not only of the effects of the programs on the participants in them but also on others who might be affected.

Sherwin Rosen seeks to determine if externalities exist in the training process. Following the work by Becker, he divides training into two forms, firm specific and general. Rosen feels that firm specific skills are probably relatively rare since most firms have competitors who operate with approximately the same production techniques. He suggests, however, that because workers interact on the job, they produce more as a team than they would as individuals. He argues further that personnel managers will choose workers who will work together to produce these externalities and that differential wage rates will reflect differences in the quality of work groups.

In the case of general training, Rosen argues that the individual should be willing to accept a lower wage in order to build up his skills (human capital) in a job that provides training. Problems arise here, however, due to imperfections in the capital market, market discrimination against some workers and wage rigidities, all of which would lead to externalities.

Finally, Rosen discusses the pecuniary externalities as manpower programs affect the supply of various types of labor. He shows that shifts in supply may affect the income of diverse groups throughout the economy, but he argues that these can be offset, if necessary, by transfer payments. The major concern he feels should be efficiency, the creation of more productive resources, which will be measured by the increment in income of the trainees.

Daniel Hamermesh, on the other hand, examines the short-run displacement within a firm which is caused by training subsidies. Whereas Rosen implicitly assumes full employment so that displaced workers are hired elsewhere, Hamermesh assumes implicitly that they will not be. On the basis of a simulation model where surplus labor is assumed, he finds that there will be less displacement in firms where the quit rate is high and the workers are relatively low skilled. He emphasizes the need, however, to concentrate on training to meet labor shortages.

Hamermesh also examines the effects of better labor market information processes which speed the man-job match. He points out that while the effect of such efforts is to lower the Phillips Curve, there may be less hoarding of labor by employers in periods of recession leading to greater fluctuations in employment. Finally, Hamermesh finds that training and labor market information programs may either increase or decrease the mobility of workers depending on the structure of the programs.

Glen Cain in his comments argues that neither Rosen nor Hamermesh provides a useful framework for estimating the secondary effects of manpower programs and objects strongly to Hamermesh's theoretical approach. His basic objection is that adjustments will occur which will absorb individuals who are displaced. He argues that generally demand curves for labor are downward sloping and that labor supply curves rise, so that while there are interindustry and interfirm shifts in supply as a result of manpower programs, they involve pecuniary and not technological changes. Losses suffered by the displaced are offset by gains for entrepreneurs or consumers.

Lester Thurow is more sympathetic to Hamermesh's approach. Thurow believes that there is a queue of workers with the bottom group unemployed. The size of this group he argues is determined by macroeconomic policies set in terms of target unemployment rates. Under these circumstances, he finds that for each trainee moved out of the unemployed and placed in a higher position in the queue, there is an offsetting displacement. On the other hand, Thurow believes that Rosen puts too strong an emphasis on the efficiency of the private labor market. He feels that time constraints, different amounts of natural human resources, the nonmarginal nature of manpower programs and nonrationality all lead to deviations from perfection in labor market operations.

Conclusion

In conclusion, this volume covers a range of topics over the entire spectrum of manpower program evaluation. In some cases, the papers present basic factual data essential to the evaluation process. In other papers are found new techniques which can markedly improve present practices. And, finally, several papers present theoretical and practical guidelines for the development of future evaluation methodology. I believe that they all should contribute significantly to the better formulation of manpower program evaluation and manpower policy decision-making.

Part One:
Designing an Evaluation
System

1 On Interprogram Manpower Studies

Peter S. Barth[1]

I have been asked to discuss the use of interprogram analysis in manpower evaluations, giving attention to a specific project that is now underway. Although the general subject would seem to fit perfectly into a volume such as this on manpower evaluation, the issue has rarely been dealt with even in a cursory fashion.

My intention is to divide the paper into the following parts: First, I want to discuss some of the reasons why interprogram studies can be so potentially valuable. Next, I shall indicate both some of the difficulties involved in undertaking such studies, and the associated reasons for the reluctance on the part of some agencies to do them. Then I intend to describe the scope and present status of a study now being carried out, and to conclude by indicating both some of the approaches that it can take, and the questions that I hope this study will enable us to answer.

The Value of Interprogram Studies

The basic purpose of evaluating any governmental program is to permit policy-makers to make better decisions. Obviously, there are other ends that evaluations can serve, such as the sparking of public controversy, to "make points" politically, and so on, but the clearest goal would appear to be to provide guidance to those who make the critical decisions about programs.

It is not unusual to find discussions or papers on evaluations that refer to decision-makers or policy-makers without ever elaborating on who these people are, the level of their authority or the scope of their power.[2] Yet important decisions within an agency like the Labor Department are made both at different levels and in different contexts. There are those policy-makers or planners who must formulate positions on major allocational questions, such as whether to begin or retain a program, the group to be serviced and so on. On the other hand, program managers and operators also need to make decisions—based upon information as to what aspects of their specific programs are relatively more suc-

---

[1] This paper was prepared while the author was on leave to the Office of Research and Development, Office of Policy, Evaluation and Research, U.S. Department of Labor and The Brookings Institution.

[2] An exception to this can be found in Cain and Hollister (1969a), p. 128.

3

cessful, what regions or locales are doing well, and a whole range of issues running from outreach techniques to the duration of a training course. Although certain elements of evaluations may be useful and of interest to both sets of decision-makers, it appears quite clear that the needs of either are generally different. For this reason, evaluations need to be prepared with a specific user in mind. Global evaluations that attempt to serve that nebulous entity—the decision-maker—may well turn out to serve no user at all.

The needs of program managers and operators largely can be classed as process evaluations. Here, the issues deal with elements of their program and the day-to-day operation of it. Interprogram evaluations can be useful if the evaluator demonstrates that (a) alternative practices used in other programs are more effective than current ones; and (b) these alternative techniques can be applied more widely. Even where rigidities develop in the system such that program managers become reluctant to adapt their techniques and practices, the usefulness of interprogram evaluations at this level is not lost, since new programs that are not so inflexible can be shaped more effectively.

A second relevant issue is that in order for an evaluation to make the desired impact, the decision-maker at any level must have (a) some discretion to make suggested or implied modifications; and (b) some feasible alternatives. The question of discretion may depend on the realities of politics. The matter of alternatives, however, is closely tied to the need for more interprogram work.[3] For without wandering too far into the domain of the political scientist, it appears that the budgetary process and the rewards system for most levels in the executive branch are stacked, so that decisions necessarily involve trade-offs, subject to the constraint that the total budget be spent. The only acceptable level of spending is one which fully uses the authorization and appropriation made by the Congress. Although one can find exceptions to this as in the recent case of the Job Opportunities in the Business Sector program (JOBS), the sums involved tend to be relatively small and/or the result of unintended errors in the system. The point is simply that an evaluation of a single program is of limited usefulness typically, because it does not offer a set of feasible alternatives for making trade-offs. An evaluation that is limited to the finding that a substantial net payoff exists for a specified program gives the planner no guide as to the other program that might be cut back. An absolutely inefficient program may not be reduced if no evidence is presented that some other program is an improvement over it. A related issue is the magnitude or degree to which good or bad programs are expanded or reduced. This question represents an enormous problem for the policy-maker, yet evaluators have neglected it almost entirely, and it is noted here only in passing.

The program managers or operators are just as dependent on comparative evidence as the planner is. In their case, however, although findings from other programs can be a guide as to potential areas or approaches to modify, *intra*program comparisons also can be suggestive of viable trade-offs that can be made. The

---

[3]A broader disc ssion of choice and alternatives (but without reference to interprogram comparisons) can oe found in Levine.

study that I shall be describing can provide both intraprogram and interprogram comparisons and both would appear to be of considerable potential use.

The need for interprogram and intraprogram evaluations does not require that various programs be analyzed simultaneously or even by the same individual. Still, the case for multiprogram evaluations is a compelling one when the tremendous heterogeneity of analysis and methodology in existing evaluations is observed. Variations begin with simple matters like the sample size and its selection procedure, region, control group choice, time frame, business cycle conditions, survey instrument if any, technique of analysis, and end up with fundamental differences in concepts such as the treatment of joint products, the length of time for which program benefits continue, the allocation of overhead costs, or the treatment of noneconomic benefits. In light of all these differences, and the problems of technical reconciliation that they pose for all potential users, the reluctance of policy-makers to be substantially moved thus far by such evaluation studies is hardly surprising or even regrettable. As more evaluations are undertaken that set out to compare alternatives that can be traded off, the probability that they will have a direct impact on decisions will almost surely increase.

A need exists for policy-makers to know more about almost all aspects of manpower programs and this extends well beyond the estimation of benefit-cost ratios. Basic phenomena and relationships must be analyzed and understood even before their full quantitative dimensions are agreed upon so that the effectiveness of programs eventually can be raised. Beyond this, when something is learned that may improve programs, alternatives must be presented to those in positions to effect change. On both of these scores interprogram evaluations offer some promise.

Problems of Interprogram Comparisons

It is not a closely guarded secret that interprogram evaluations have been received by some with the same sense that one learns that the Internal Revenue Service has selected him for an audit. The reactions may range from indifference to hostility, but there is a shared sense that it is all a troublesome waste of time that would be better left undone, since nothing is to be unearthed in any event. It is, to be sure, no simple task to jointly evaluate disparate programs. Yet, as long as they represent realistic alternative investment decisions by program planners, the programs must be thought of in a comparative sense. To the extent that decisions made within the Labor Department can affect relative budgetary shares for separate programs, it seems more than reasonable to compare program values explicitly. The arguments that have been made against comparing manpower programs are that the various programs serve a different clientele, that the program goals are different, and that the services rendered differ in length of time and in kind. Thus, from the economist's perspective, the inputs differ, the output is not the same, and the production processes are dissimilar. Each one of these, however, is only partially true and partially important. Do individuals entering different programs really come from separate classes or populations?

Although mean levels of educational attainment, age, job experience and so on may vary among some programs, there are individuals with comparable levels that can be drawn from various programs. Further, multiple regression permits us to estimate certain quantitative relationships while holding constant the effects on relevant dependent variables of other variables. Beyond this, it is not clear how substantial these differences are among program trainees, nor how many and to what degree similarities in other variables exist.

Do program goals differ? There are two significant considerations here. First, everyone evaluating manpower programs is soon struck by their vague, inarticulated aims. It would seem to matter little if we are considering interprogram comparisons or uniprogram evaluations if the evaluator cannot find a clear statement of program goals. To the extent that the evaluator exercises a best guess, he may as well do so for more than one program. Regardless of whether or not the ends are stated explicitly and precisely, the long-range goals of different manpower programs do not appear to be substantially different. Secondly, even where goals differ somewhat, one can at least determine how efficient various programs are in achieving these separate purposes. Thus, though Lockheed and Xerox produce vastly different product lines, and probably operate with substantially different time horizons, we can make some judgments about the relative efficiency of either company.

Another reason that may explain the aversion to comparative studies is the mistaken notion that only outcomes are subject to comparison. Thus, for example one hears that a certain manpower program should not be compared to another because the first tends to attract the harder-core cases. Since the more appropriate measure is not outcome but the change in outcome, the reluctance to accept interprogram analysis seems strange. One does not simply match employment rates of Job Corpsmen with Neighborhood Youth Corps (NYC) trainees at some fixed point after exit from the program. Rather, either you examine each in terms of suitable control groups—or you compare sets of outcomes for youth by classifying them according to similar socioeconomic characteristics at time of entry into each program. Thus, the degree to which one program works with the greater disadvantage ought not to prevent comparisons from being made.

A definite problem does exist, however, when comparing programs that are largely or exclusively for persons of different ages. One difficulty arises because some of the outcomes for youth may be socially desirable and economically rewarding only long after training ends. Thus, for example, a return to school or entry into the military will tend to depress benefit-cost ratios for youth unless adjustment is made for the eventual economic return associated with such choices. Comparing programs where trainees are of different ages highlights the importance of the choice of the discount rate, since programs for persons of the same age can be assumed to have their benefits accruing over basically comparable time horizons at similar rates.

We know very little about earnings patterns of trainees for considerable time periods after training, and even less about how these are functionally related to age. Yet, Regelson and others have pointed out how important our assumptions are regarding the longer-range impact of such programs on income differentials, how little is known about this impact, and how sensitive benefit-cost ratios are to varying assumptions about future earnings differentials.

In an evaluation such as the one I shall be describing, the problem of age differences is not particularly severe because (a) a significant number of trainees in the programs that are not specific to youth are young and could qualify for these other programs; and (b) there are two youth programs and two other programs in the evaluation, permitting at least two-way comparisons between both sets of programs.

A Description of a Current Evaluation
Study

The study is being funded under the joint sponsorship of the Labor Department and the Office of Economic Opportunity. The primary contractors are Operations Research Incorporated and National Opinion Research Corporation of the University of Chicago. The study began in late 1969 and data will continue to be collected at least until the end of 1971. Although the primary purpose of the study is to evaluate four specific manpower programs, the study will also yield a very rich store of data that can be used to examine basic relationships that can eventually lead to improved programs.

Basically, the study involves tracking approximately 7,000 entrants of four manpower programs. Because two of these programs, the Job Corps and the Neighborhood Youth Corps, are limited to youth, the size of each sample selected from these programs is approximately one-half the size of the samples drawn from MDTA Institutional and JOBS, where the latter two have both youth and adult enrollees. The sample group 16-21 in either MDTA or JOBS is about equal in size to the total sample in NYC or Job Corps. A control group of over 2,000 persons has also been selected—persons selected on the basis of age, income and residence.

The study is limited to a sample of urban areas—there are 10 cities selected on a probabilistic basis in the study. The sample was drawn from among cities where approximately 90 percent of all persons in the four programs, nationally, reside. Thus, although the findings are necessarily limited to urban enrollees, a great deal will still be known about these programs in general.

Several kinds of data are being collected on the program trainees that are being tracked. At the time an individual enters a program he is given a test that is designed to measure the trainee's level of educational achievement in vocabulary, spelling, reading, computational work, and problem solving. There are three levels of difficulty of this test and the appropriate one is administered on the basis of the respondent's stated level of educational attainment. Scores from the three tests can be linked on a continuous scale. The test is also administered at the time of exit from a program. Thus, some statements can be made about the change that occurs in educational achievement between the time of program entry and the point of exit. The control group is useful here since it will permit us to estimate the degree of improvement, if any, attributable to the passage of time, as well as to any learning that results from taking the test twice.

For a part of the sample, detailed data have been collected on the services made available to trainees during the course of the program. Weekly data are collected—not from the trainee but from the program operators, or in the case of JOBS from the employer—over the course of the training period. The information is collected in terms of the number of hours in that week that certain kinds of services (e.g., basic education, on-the-job training, counseling, child care, etc.) were rendered to a given trainee. There are several purposes here. First, these data will permit the kind of intraprogram analysis that was discussed earlier. It may, for example, allow us to isolate those program components that are correlated with success or failure in terms of program completion. Obviously, it shall also be examined in light of posttraining experience in terms of finding and keeping jobs, earnings levels and so on. Thus, for example, one conceivably can estimate the elasticity of a given program service (in terms of total hours used), *ceteris paribus*, with respect to the probability of finding (or keeping) a full-time job after training. Another important element in this sort of analysis is that it directly confronts the issue that the programs are continually being revised. Thus, for example, even if Job Corps is restructured or in fact is closed down, it may be possible to identify those elements within the program that have been more or less valuable. These findings can be helpful in the design of future programs.

Aside from the testing and the information on program services, data are being gathered both on costs and on local labor conditions. With both of these, we are relying primarily on secondary material available generally through the Department of Labor.

Finally, and really at the heart of this study, there are the data gathered through personal interviews of all the trainees and members of the household or control group. Four interviews are conducted per respondent. Trainees are interviewed at the time they enter the program. A second interview is administered at the time of exit from the program. Four months after that interview, a third one is taken. Wave IV is conducted eight months after Wave III, which is to say one year after exit from the program.

Wave I interviews were begun in December 1969 and continued through the summer of 1970. Interviews were staggered as persons entered programs at varying, and in some cases, unpredictable rates. Control group members were given Wave I interviews over this period too. The timing of Wave II interviews, with the exception of JOBS and the control group, depended upon the rates at which people dropped out of or graduated from programs. Thus, in some cases (most typically from the Job Corps group), Wave II might not be given for up to two years after Wave I. The customary experience, however, seems to have been people leaving programs early and, thus, most Wave II interviews, and in fact most Wave III interviews, already have been completed. In the case of JOBS, a maximum period of six months was set as the point of graduation. If the person left the employer before the six months ended, he was given a Wave II interview. Wave II interviews for the control group were staggered over the period after their Wave I interviews to match persons in the programs.

Although each of the four interviews differ, a number of questions are reiterated in two or more of them. Most questions are clustered about the following eleven subjects:

1. Job history, employment and income data are collected for one full year prior to the time of entry into the program. The identical information is collected then on each of the subsequent interviews for the intervening periods. The respondent is asked his occupation, salary, employer, how he found employment, reasons for not seeking work and so on.
2. The educational attainment of the trainee and his parents is asked. The type of education received is also obtained.
3. Family composition and status are obtained at the time of program entry until the fourth interview.
4. Purchasing patterns are examined and information is gathered on the trainee's debt position, before and following training.
5. Detailed information on income, including all transfer payments, is obtained on each of the four interviews.
6. Arrest records and experience with crime are traced.
7. Military experience and one's record in the military is secured from the respondent.
8. Attitudinal responses are obtained that may give us a clue as to the effect of programs on one's psychological state. Under this heading, I am also considering the respondent's answers to questions regarding how they liked the program, how useful it was, their recommendations, and so on.
9. The respondent is asked to tell us about services rendered to him by the program after he has left it. We also inquire into his perspective on the quality of those and other community services, e.g., legal aid, public health, policy protection, etc., and the quantity that he used.
10. Geographic mobility can be traced through these interviews.
11. The condition of the respondent's health is probed.

Analyses to be Undertaken

I have already indicated some of the kinds of analyses that can be undertaken with these data. There is a need to learn much more than simply that which the cost-benefit and cost-effectiveness analyses will provide although they must surely be done. There is a great need to acquire some basic understanding of how programs affect trainees. Generally, outcomes can be classed into intermediate ends or goals and longer-run or ultimate outcomes. Intermediate goals, such as work values acquired, form of exit from the program, test scores at completion of the program, geographic mobility and many other items are not actually ends in themselves, but serve only as indicators of later outcomes. The longer-run goals include such variables as employment stability, work-related income, health, the stability of the family, self-satisfaction, and arrest and conviction records. These are the variables that ultimately are of concern to users of evaluation studies. One of the reasons why a longitudinal study like this is so valuable is that it permits us to know how good the indicators really are in estimating long-run outcomes. Since the indicators can be acquired more cheaply, and because they serve to provide information to evaluators more quickly than long-run outcomes, it is important to learn how useful each of them is. Thus, for example, this study can test not simply the hypothesis that training leads to higher test scores, but that test scores are meaningfully correlated with some outcomes. Unfortunately, a large part of evaluation work has been devoted to examining these intermediate-range goals without testing how useful they are as indicators of long-range outcomes. And more importantly, some of these short-run outcomes eventually become the ultimate goals of the program operators, who believe that they have identified in them the solution to the problems of the disadvantaged. This study can test whether such beliefs are justified for each of the four programs examined. (For example, this study will permit testing not simply the hypothesis that counseling raises the probability of successful program completion, self-satisfaction and the like, but that such results are themselves correlated with long-run outcomes.)

A general framework for analyzing some of the relationships can be seen in the schematic illustration in Figure 1-1.

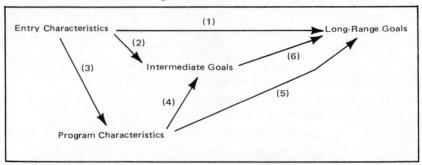

Figure 1-1

The following are examples of the kinds of hypotheses that will be tested within this framework, viewed across the four programs.

1. Matching entry characteristics to long-range goals—e.g., married trainees are more likely to have a higher gain in income one year after leaving the program than are unmarried trainees.
2. Examining entry characteristics and intermediate goals—e.g., controlling for educational attainment, race, etc.; those trainees who responded on Wave I that they felt their educational preparation was inadequate tend to stay longer in programs.
3. Analyzing entry characteristics and those of the program—e.g., there are no significant differences in the degree of disadvantage of youngsters in the NYC program and the Job Corps, as represented by arrest rates, educational attainment, and so on.
4. Studying entry and program characteristics as they relate to intermediate goals—e.g., the greater the amount of program time devoted to basic education, the higher the probability that the trainee will not have completed the program.
5. Examining entry and program characteristics and long-range goals—e.g., the unemployment rates for persons leaving their JOBS employer will be no different for blacks or whites one year after leaving.
6. Relating entry and intermediate goals and long-range goals—e.g., wage differentials that appear in Wave III interviews will favor the longer-term participants of Job Corps and NYC, but are washed out by the time of the Wave IV interview.

Outside of this framework, we can test the notion most explicitly expressed and used by Goldfarb, that ". . . income gains to trainees was the most measurable benefit of training programs and that many other important benefits increased as this benefit increased." [p. 77] The data should permit an analysis and correlation of a number of outcomes regressed upon earnings.

Conclusion

Interprogram studies are still oddities in the manpower field. Their scarcity has probably reduced the value of evaluation work from the standpoint of implementing any findings. Comparative studies offer the promise of being useful both to program managers and to program planners.

The OEO - Department of Labor study will yield a rich body of data that will be helpful in preparing both interprogram and intraprogram studies. Beyond simply the now familiar cost-benefit analysis, some basic relationships will be studied and evaluated. This should lead to improved methods of operation for existing programs and to better designed and planned future programs.

2 Methods for Cross-Program Comparisons

Edward C. Bryant and Morris H. Hansen

To make cross-program comparisons of manpower programs, typically, one is interested in some longitudinal comparison within each program that can then be compared across programs.[1] Such variables might be gain in income, change in retention rates, change in cost per trainee, change in attitudes, and so on. Unless some plan for measuring over time has been adopted, longitudinal comparisons must give way to retrospective inquiry with serious increases in biases. This concept of the planned longitudinal comparison forms the central theme of this paper. It is useful both for within program longitudinal comparisons and for cross-program comparisons.

The basic idea is that one can construct a continuing sample of participants in manpower programs. By continuing sample, we mean that every participant has a known probability of being included in the sample, regardless of the date of his enrollment and an interview would be conducted within a short time thereafter. Another interview would be conducted at the time of or shortly after completion of the program (or planned completion for dropouts). These times are appropriate for coordination of survey data with accounting and budgeting data on input and output.

Data on impact, however, can only be obtained by follow-up. Some further consideration needs to be given to selection of optimum time lapses for follow-up, but for discussion, we suggest the following: six months after termination, 18 months after termination, and three years after termination. Later follow-up could be optional.

The suggestion of six months after completion is motivated partly by the mobility factor. A job, if obtained, may cause the participant to change address and excessive time delay makes follow-up more difficult. Also, it is motivated by the need to know the job hunting activities undertaken by the participant and assistance provided by the government in support of the manpower program. These data need to be collected before the details have become blurred in the mind of the participant.

There is nothing magical about the proposed 18 month follow-up. It must be

[1]Generally, one is interested in making cross-sectional comparisons as well as longitudinal comparisons of manpower programs. The cross-sectional comparison matches programs or components within a relatively narrow time window. Retention rates in JOBS and in MDTA-OJT for 1970 would constitute such a comparison.

far enough removed from the training so that there can have been some impact. Perhaps two years would be better. If two years is used, then the next follow-up should be at four years rather than three. In any case, after the passage of some years, it becomes more and more difficult to attribute changes in economic status to the impact of any specific program. The reason for a possible follow-up beyond three or four years is to determine what tendency there is for trainees to regress to the pattern of employment they might have had if they had not been participants at an earlier time. It is obvious that conclusions in this area are risky.

What programs might be covered by such a continuing sample? There are no firm rules—only that the programs must have enough in common to make comparison meaningful. However, the past eight years of experience in manpower programs indicate that one does not really know what he will be comparing against in, say, two years. Thus, it is probably wise to err on the side of extensive coverage rather than selectivity. One might, for example, include MDTA, JOBS, NYC, Job Corps, and (possibly) Operation Mainstream. Whether vocational education should be included is a decision that might be based upon politics and policy rather than upon comparability of programs. Vocational education may be more comparable to MDTA than is Operation Mainstream, for example, yet vocational education and MDTA are the responsibility of different agencies. Also, the Department of Labor (DOL) and Office of Education share responsibility for the institutional training programs of MDTA. Clearly, some interagency cooperation is desirable, yet the system could operate effectively with only the manpower programs of the DOL.

What might be the structure of the sample? We envision a national probability sample similar to the one forming the basis for the Current Population Survey of the Bureau of the Census. That is, all of the geographic area of the United States could be put into 1,500 to 2,000 primary sample units (PSUs). Standard Metropolitan Statistical Areas (SMSAs) would be PSUs and would not be split up. They might be aggregated into Consolidated Metropolitan Areas (CMAs) where such areas have been defined. SMSAs are defined in terms of county and independent cities except in New England where counties are subdivided according to town boundaries. All PSUs then, with the special exception in the case of New England, would be counties or groups of contiguous counties not so great in area that they could not be controlled by a single field supervisor.[2] The boundaries of labor market areas could be taken into account in grouping contiguous counties.

The PSUs would be stratified into perhaps 100 strata, based upon geography, degree of urbanization, ethnicity, racial mix, principal industry, income and perhaps other factors. Grouping of PSUs into strata could be accomplished within

---

[2]The large-population PSUs might have more than one interviewer, however.

the manpower regions of the Department of Labor. The large SMSAs or CMAs would constitute entire strata, perhaps those with one million or more population would fall into this category. The single PSUs comprising these strata would, of course, come into the sample with certainty. From the remaining strata, one PSU would be drawn from each with probability proportional to some measure of size, say, 1970 population.

All projects in the 100 sample PSUs would be candidates for inclusion in the sample within the selected PSU. Note that all projects have some probability of inclusion because of their identification with some county, independent city or SMSA. Since every piece of geography has a known probability of inclusion, any project associated with that piece of geography has the same probability of inclusion.

Enrollees in projects in the sample PSUs would be subsampled at an overall rate designed to provide the reliability desired. Programs with small enrollments would be relatively more heavily sampled than programs with large enrollments. The total sample size would be determined on the basis of resources allocated to the project.

The general rule for allocation of the sample within programs to achieve a uniform overall probability of selection can be stated in the following terms.

Let P_{hi} = probability of selecting the ith PSU within the hth stratum (= 1 for PSUs drawn with certainty)

n = total desired annual intake to the sample from the specified program

N = total expected enrollment during the given year in the specified program

Then, the fraction of enrollees to be selected from each program within the sampled PSUs is

$$f_{hi} = \frac{n}{N \, P_{hi}}$$

This fraction equals n/N for the certainty PSUs and increases as the probability of selection, P_{hi}, decreases.[3]

If a program has a few dominating or very large projects, these should be included in the sample with certainty, whether or not they are located within the selected PSUs. Rules that yield an approximation to optimum sample design can be established for determining the size cut-offs for such projects.

---

[3] There are various ways of handling the problem that arises when f_{hi} is greater than 1.0, but they will not be presented here.

A set of rules must be specified for the identification of enrollees to be sampled. This choice cannot be left to the interviewer or to project management. We have done some experimentation with the use of alphabetic segments to define samples and feel that this approach has real merit. Conceptually, one divides the universe of names into, say, 1,000 segments, using about eight to ten alphabetic characters which identify last name, first name and middle initial (if any) in that sequence. One can use various sources of names to create the alphabetic segments. They need not be discussed here.

Each segment is defined with a starting point and continues up to (in the alphabetic sequence) but not including the lower boundary of the next alphabetic interval. For example, using 10 characters, an interval might be identified as HARRIS JAME up to (but not including) HULTZPETER. The number of segments to be drawn is dependent upon the sampling fraction desired. If the desired sampling fraction is three percent, then 30 of the 1,000 alphabetic segments would be drawn systematically within a random start. With a desired sampling fraction of 8.7 percent, one would select 87 segments from the 1,000 available, and so on.

An enrollee is either in the sample or not in the sample depending entirely upon whether or not his name falls in a selected segment. Note that the scheme is designed to achieve the overall *expected* sample size specified but that the proportion taken from any one project may depart substantially from expectation.

We are suggesting the use of alphabetic segments as a means of sampling because (1) the system is objective, easily audited, and leaves no room for personal biases in selection; and (2) most records are likely to be kept in alphabetic files, thus making operation simple.

The use of segments of social security numbers is another perfectly valid way of identifying sampled segments and it may be preferred if files are organized by social security number. It is not necessary to retain the same segments over time, or from one area to another.

How large a sample should be taken? Without substantially more information than we have concerning resources and needs, we can only speculate. However, examination of what one might achieve with modest sample sizes may be revealing.

Suppose there are five programs and that one decides arbitrarily to sample 400 participants annually from each at the enrollment stage. With a reasonable allowance for losses and with the follow-up schedule proposed above, one would interview, or attempt to interview, about 1,500 participants each year in each program, or 7,500 all together in the five programs. They would, of course, be reasonably uniformly distributed over the year because of the nature of their selection. This number amounts to an average workload of 75 interviews per PSU. However, the workload would vary considerably from PSU to PSU, although the method of selection of the sample outlined above will tend to equate the sizes of sample and workloads for the various PSUs, except for those that come into the sample with certainty. The workloads would be equal if the programs reached the same fraction of the population in each PSU. Also, if the total sample size were as small as suggested here, something like 50 strata might be used, rather than 100, to increase the efficiency of the field work. We are considering here a minimum program and will examine what kinds of comparisons can be made and with what accuracy.

The fact that the population is clustered into PSUs means that one loses some effectiveness as compared to a simple random sample of the entire United States. However, the clustered sample is feasible to operate while the simple random sample is not. Our experience leads us to believe that, in this particular case, the standard error of the clustered sample in estimating the proportion of enrollees having some characteristic might be something like 50 percent greater than that of a simple random sample. If so, then the standard error of a proportion possessing a characteristic (e.g., black male, completed program, is now employed, and so on) is approximately $1.5\sqrt{p(1-p/n)}$ where p is the proportion with the characteristic and n is the sample size. This factor of 1.5 will vary considerably from one statistic to another, but for many statistics of interest in comparisons between programs, and on this basis of theory and experience, we believe that the factor of 1.5 will provide a useful guide.

If our speculations about the effect of clustering are correct, an annual sample of 400 with a proportion, p, of 0.3 would have a standard error of about 3 percentage points, a level of accuracy that would be sufficient for many purposes. A desirable feature of the continuing sample is that two adjacent years can be aggregated to double the sample size and thus to cut the standard error. This may reduce the error by as much as 30 percent under favorable circumstances but ordinarily the reduction will be less. Thirty percent is the reduction that would be achieved by doubling the sample size through doubling the number of PSUs included in the sample as a way of doubling the overall sampling fraction.

Cross-program comparisons, under the same assumptions identified above, would have a standard error of $\sqrt{2} = 1.4$ times the above standard error. For a sample of 400, this is approximately five percentage points for a single-year comparison.

The continuing sample makes within-program longitudinal comparisons highly effective. The fact that the same individuals are being measured over time reduces the sampling error substantially. Even the sampling error of measures of change in the *program* (as contrasted to *individuals* in the program) is decreased by drawing observations on successive years from the same PSUs.

What about follow-up of changed addresses? We are proposing that intensive follow-up efforts be undertaken to locate persons who have changed their addresses

since last contact. Follow-up, however, may not be as costly as one might antici-
pate. About one-fifth of persons change addresses annually, but about twelve
percent move to another location in the same county, and a somewhat larger,
but unknown percent move to another address in the same SMSA. People who
move within the same county (or SMSA) are less costly to locate and interview
than those who move outside the sample PSUs. Also, since a 100 PSU sample
might cover about 50 percent of the population in the United States, one can
normally expect that about that fraction of movers outside the county or SMSA
will be found in other sample PSUs. Thus, there might be something like three or
four percent who, after location, would be expensive to interview.

The situation is worse with respect to manpower program enrollees, however,
since they typically are young, predominantly male, and more than proportion-
ately black. This is a highly mobile group, although there is strong evidence that
black persons tend to move within the same county or SMSA to a greater extent
than do whites.[4] In any case, the principles apply, although the levels may be
different.

What kinds of data should be collected? A look at the major evaluation efforts
conducted in the past or currently underway reveals strong similarities among
the data requirements. They all require demographic and economic background
on the participants. They all require an indication of whether the program was
completed by the participant and most require similar measures of impact.
Greater uniformity could be achieved with careful planning, and we feel that this
should be done.

The enrollment record is the first place where greater uniformity would be
helpful. There are strong similarities among Forms MA-101 (used in MDTA,
WIN, etc.), NYC-16 (used in NYC and New Careers) and MA-111 (used in
JOBS), but there are also major differences. Although additional information
could be obtained at the initial interview to accommodate the different enrollment forms, a greater similarity would be helpful. A standard set of data items
could be developed that, at enrollment time, would reflect the enrollee's job history, educational background, handicaps, economic status and job aspirations. If
as much of this as feasible were a part of the enrollment record, it could form a
data base to serve as a background against which to calibrate the sample.

At termination, the enrollee could be questioned about job plans, his acceptance of and adaptation to the training, and so on. The first follow-up would
concentrate heavily on his job history, the process used in obtaining employment, relatedness of job to training, job aspirations, and so on. Later follow-ups
would continue the same theme.

In a general purpose sample of the kind suggested here, it is not possible to
obtain all of the information that might be needed some time in the future. The
objective is to obtain a core of information, common to (or at least comparable

[4] See the paper in this volume by Celia Homans.

across) all programs, which will satisfy *most* evaluative needs. The continuing sample, of course, provides a vehicle for special studies that may be required from time to time and this is one of its principal advantages.

One can obtain data for special studies by adding specific questions or by thickening the sample for special projects of interest or by changing the interview cycle. The fact that a special national sample need not be drawn could provide substantial savings, both in dollar cost and in time lapse before usable data are available.

Note also that the Current Population Survey conducted by the Bureau of the Census provides data against which one can compare the sampled participants. A logical comparison group is the peer group of the participants, and the rate of approach toward or departure from that norm can be quite meaningful.

We assume that there is a continuing need to evaluate manpower programs and that funds will continue to be made available for that purpose. We also assume that a major portion of the data needs of the evaluator can be standardized and that the need for longitudinal data has been established. If these assumptions are correct, a continuing longitudinal sample will meet many of the evaluation needs at lower cost and with higher reliability than ad hoc studies planned individually. In this sense, our suggested approach is *nearer* the optimum. What the sample sizes should be, what the precise data elements should be, and what the follow-up intervals should be to more nearly optimize the system with respect to all of the evaluation objectives must be topics for further study.

Finally, while the topic of this paper is cross-program comparisons, it is impossible to avoid the issue of comparison groups. We do not want to spend much time discussing related issues, but a few remarks seem in order.

First, to the best of our knowledge, control groups, in the strict sense, have not been used in manpower program evaluations. Nor will they ever be unless, from a common pool of potential candidates, some individuals are selected at random to receive a service and some are selected at random and the service withheld from them. Alternatively, random selections might be made from a pool of persons who are eligible for each of two programs, some being assigned to one program on a random instead of a judgmental basis. Such methods are highly desirable, and we strongly urge their adoption in programs where feasible. However, in practice, we have usually found that the needs for evaluation have taken a subsidiary role to problems of implementation. It seems likely that this policy will continue in most situations, and that control groups, as we have defined them, will seldom be used. In any event, in frequent practice we will want to make comparisons between groups that do not constitute random samples of the same population.

We do feel that there may be more opportunity for random assignment of candidates to programs than has been exploited in the past. When the capacity of an experimental program is inadequate to accommodate all candidates, a randomization scheme is at least an unbiased way of making assignments. This process is being used successfully, for example, in selecting candidates for enrollment in Federal City College in Washington.

Because of the compromises one must make with the control concept, we probably should stop talking about control groups and adopt the terminology "comparison groups." Comparison groups can be formed from samples from various components of a single program (say, Neighborhood Youth Corps and Job Corps). Comparison groups can also be formed from samples of a given program and the general population, or some identifiable segment of it. Cross-program comparisons may use some or all of these concepts.

Designing an Evaluation System: Comment

John Cheston

Our interest in interprogram and intraprogram comparisons grows out of two concerns. One is positive in nature: such comparisons can be directed at important decisions which are actually made in the Department of Labor by top officials, as Peter Barth points out. The other is negative: the unlikelihood of ever actually being able to compare program impact on enrollees with what happens to controls *outside* of the programs.

We are interested in comparisons of program effect on like groups of people enrolled in different programs. Strictly speaking, such comparisons involve the use of controls, but in this case, the controls are chosen from within our programs rather than from outside our programs. We feel that this holds more promise, since the chances are that the nature and strength of motivation among two groups both enrolled in our programs is more likely to be similar than between a group inside and a group outside our programs.

And so we have reached a judgment (we in this case means the staff of the Evaluation Office of the Secretary) that interprogram and intraprogram comparisons hold sufficient promise to warrant substantial emphasis and attention. We think that they can be done. We agree with Peter Barth that there is sufficient overlap in the populations enrolled in various programs to provide opportunity for such comparisons. (There is, if you will, a great amount of innocent randomness of assignment among our programs.) Also, we agree with Barth that there is sufficient commonality of purpose among most of our programs to permit this kind of study.

At the same time, we are cautious of the limits of such comparisons, some of which have been pointed to by Barth, e.g., the difficulty of comparing programs which enroll essentially different age groups, and the difficulties in comparisons involving quite dissimilar types of programs.

We have some more specific comments on the two papers. First, on the Barth paper:

1. I have already indicated our basic agreement on the essential points in this paper.
2. We welcome the insights into the DOL's decision-making process, and ask for as much more as possible.
3. We wonder, though, if the design of the joint Labor-OEO study represents a form of overkill in cross-program comparison terms.
4. We wonder, also, whether those conducting the study feel confident that the use of the control group can yield reliable results.

21

5. We would like to hear more about the quality of the data being collected; i.e., the response rate from follow-up interviews, etc.

On the Edward Bryant and Morris Hansen paper, which goes mainly to the method of conducting cross-program comparisons, we would make the following points.

1. The suggested design calls for a continuing random sample. We ask why a continuing sample? Why select the sample in advance? Is it likely that studies would be conducted with such frequency as to require a continuously available sample? We also ask why a random sample? We wonder if problems of geographic dispersion and of wide variance in the characteristics of people enrolled in programs make this approach relatively inefficient. We would pose as a possibly more prudent and less expensive alternative an approach suited to a series of separate studies, using the method of matching cells of the populations from different programs.
2. We think that the difficulty and cost of conducting adequate follow-up interviews probably rules out the scheduling of follow-ups as long as 18 months after enrollment, as the authors suggest.
3. The authors suggest that the CPS can serve as a useful source of data for constructing norms as a basis for general comparison. We have explored that possibility and have generally been discouraged about the prospects, because of sample size in the CPS.

Designing an Evaluation
System: Comment

Paul D. Gayer

Let me begin by saying that I agree with most of what Professor Barth has said.[1] However, perhaps I can add to or amplify some of the things he covers.

First, I thoroughly agree with his reasoning on the value of cross-program studies. It is possible that Congress and the Administration might decide to end a manpower program entirely; it is most unlikely that they would be willing to do it on the basis of an evaluator's cost-benefit ratio. Much more likely are decisions to expand certain programs, cut back others—and these kinds of allocational decisions are the very ones for which cross-program studies can best meet the need for information to guide rational decision-making. While it is not, as he indicates, necessary that such studies be done simultaneously, or even by the same research team, the fact that seven or eight years of cost-benefit studies of manpower training programs have not led to a consensus on methodology makes it highly desirable. And a common time frame provides a modicum of defense against the charge of unfairness in comparing evolving programs.

I am no more persuaded than Professor Barth with the arguments that different manpower programs should not be compared because they have different goals, target population, and methodology. Besides the need to test these assertions, policy-makers must be able to decide whether in fact the programs *should* be serving different groups, or using different methods, or even striving for different goals. Comparison does not need to be invidious, nor does it imply any final ranking. At the same time, however, I am not as confident as he that we can judge the relative efficiency of programs where *goals* actually differ markedly. Lockheed and Xerox do have different product lines, but their goal is presumably the same; maximizing long-range profits (or should I say minimizing short-range losses).

Professor Barth's comment that the proper comparison is not outcomes, but change in outcomes, is most important, and has been ignored too often in single-program cost-benefit studies. To the extent that the entering population is homogeneous, it doesn't matter. I doubt, however, that sufficient homogeneity is likely for studies broader than the single local project.

I have little to add to his description of the specific study we have underway, except to point out that the study provides us with a comparison of broad approaches to manpower training. We have an institutional training program, MDTA; and an on-the-job program, JOBS. We have a youth program with high amounts of basic education, vocational training and counseling, the Job Corps;

---

[1]It would make both our jobs a great deal more difficult if I did not, as I am the OEO project manager on the same cross-program joint study he discusses, for which he is the Department of Labor project manager.

and a youth program which is primarily work experience, the Neighborhood Youth Corps. The Job Corps moves people to a new environment while training them; the other programs leave them in their old one. The opportunity for some cautious and qualified judgments about the relative merits of these approaches, with different groups, in different places, is there. The differences among the programs in recruiting, counseling, basic education, placement, and ancillary services (medical, legal, transportation, day-care assistance) also should permit us to point the way to possible improvements in present procedures.

The study will not only give us some indication of the relationship between proximate outcomes and longer-range benefits, it will also permit us to test whether retrospective studies are worthwhile, given their high proportion of non-response because people cannot be located. If our findings are identical to theirs (which I do not really expect), a careful longitudinal study which goes to great expense to keep track of a mobile population is probably not justified.

The study contains a wealth of information on the enrollee and his household, income, attitudes, abilities, training and education, and labor market experiences, along with the same information on a comparison group from a household sample. We intend to make these data available for further research by other scholars; however, such availability is some time away. We have just received the first tabulations from entrance interviews, and most outcome data are still a year away from being processed into usable form. Our experience with the Survey of Economic Opportunity data bank does not lead us to believe that the process of making the data available for other research will be quick or easy. In any case, we will complete our first analyses of the data before it is released.

One problem with our study is the timing. Most of our sample left training between April or May and December 1970—scarcely a good time to be entering the labor market. Given this, the longitudinal nature of our study becomes doubly important. Does manpower training which does not lead to fairly rapid job placement result in benefits to the trainee? Is his employability raised, or does the employer ignore training which the trainee got little chance to put into practice? As Professor Barth pointed out to me on another occasion, there may be strong grounds for training during economic slowdowns, as the opportunity cost of the time of an unemployed worker is very low; but such an argument depends on some permanent value to training, even when not immediately put into use.

The problem of selecting the proper time for a longitudinal study makes the proposal advanced by Dr. Bryant and Mr. Hansen doubly attractive. A continuing sample of manpower training enrollees would provide data for all time periods, it would permit analysis of the evolution of programs, and it might eliminate many of the problems of current management information systems.

One of the difficulties faced by anyone who has tried to use data from the various forms used by programs is the high proportion of them which are filled in inaccurately or not at all. The problem lies both with the amount and type of information we attempt to collect in this fashion and the incentive system for the person filling it out. Typically, such forms include some information necessary to process the enrollee at the local level. Because the person filling in the form knows of the need for this information, it is more likely to be filled in carefully—if the employee responsible does not do it, he'll hear about it, as an immediate check results when others attempt to use the information. On the other hand, information needed only at the national level is likely to be spottily spot-checked, if at all. And the pay, promotion, and job security of the form-filler-outer probably do not depend on his performance in this small facet of his job.

A continuing sample would permit at least two desirable changes in information collection. First, the sample survey could be geared to provide the information needed only or principally at the regional and national level, thus permitting management information (MI) items collected on everyone locally to be limited to those useful there. This would not only reduce the local paper work, but limit the information collected routinely in local offices to that which they have a direct interest in collecting accurately. Second, in a properly designed continuing survey, the pay and promotion of interviewers and field personnel could depend on their performance, and the result would be a higher quality of data, as well as more detail if desired for regional and national data.

In effect, we would be trading a large and unknown component of response error for a known sampling error, which could be made as small as we were willing to pay for. As Bryant and Hansen indicate, MI information could serve to calibrate the sample initially, and the result could be an accurate set of blow-up ratios using future MI information.

Incidentally, I'm not advocating that local program managers never see the sample survey results. Much of what would be collected they might find useful, particularly if some time and attention is spent on designing it to serve both local and national purposes, and if their advice is solicited. Even more, it is probable that an effort to demonstrate the usefulness to local managers of the sample survey information might be worthwhile.

I see more problems than do Bryant and Hansen, given the benefit of hindsight, with keeping such a study going. We have found it highly desirable to keep the same interviewers throughout the study; this requires a sufficient workload in one place to keep them busy. Seventy-five or even 150 per year is probably too low. We have also used almost entirely interviewers from the same race and socioeconomic background as the enrollees, and feel it has been very worthwhile. It has not been free, however; the interviewers have required extensive training and a highly competent field staff. The direct interviewer costs on our study are close to budget; the supervisory and field staff costs are much over.

Despite these problems, I still feel strongly that a continuing sample is the way to go. Unless we find that proximate outcomes are highly accurate indicators of long-range ones (which I do not expect), or that retrospective studies and MI data with half or more of the sample missing can be trusted (again, unlikely), the only feasible way to collect accurate data over time at a reasonable cost is a continuing sample.

3

An Evaluation System to Support a Decentralized, Comprehensive Manpower Program

John W. Scanlon, Joe N. Nay and
Joseph S. Wholey

Typically, federal programs are legislated and established with little forethought given to their evaluation. The Department of Labor has made a welcome departure from this practice in the case of the Administration-proposed Manpower Training legislation. In anticipation of its passage, the Urban Institute was asked to design an evaluation system suitable for implementation along with the decentralization and decategorization of programs that would take place. The study was later broadened to account for other legislative proposals that would also lead to a comprehensive manpower program planned and administered by area prime sponsors. The Urban Institute completed the evaluation design early this year [Scanlon, et al.].

Our purpose here is to highlight those changes we consider necessary in the Department of Labor's evaluation policy, as manpower programming is decentralized. The evaluation system recommended by the Urban Institute is quite different from current evaluation practices in the Department of Labor. While it is a different way of carrying out evaluation, there is nothing novel about the method or the supporting systems required. Nearly all the elements of the recommended system now exist in some form within the Department of Labor and its manpower programs. Two central themes will be stressed throughout our presentation.

First, the current evaluation activity in the Department of Labor will not provide the information needed in decentralized program planning and management; however, an appropriate evaluation system can be implemented through modification and utilization of existing systems and capabilities.

Second, evaluation should rely predominantly on continuous analysis of data reported from the local service delivery system. Information not readily available from the program reporting systems would be obtained by supplemental data collection on a sample basis.

We begin by discussing the limitations of current Department of Labor evaluation practices, go on to identify the type of information needed under decentralization, and then describe the components of the recommended evaluation system.

Where We Stand in Evaluation

Evaluation has come into its own over the past few years. There has been rather wide acknowledgement by public officials of the need to evaluate social programs. Legislation has called for it, money has been provided, evaluation staffs have been created or strengthened, and some major evaluation studies have been undertaken.

During this period, we have all learned that evaluation is difficult, takes a lot of time to carry out, and can be very expensive. We've discovered that the information generated is often incomplete, suspect, and unrelated to the problems at hand. We've found bureaucratic and organizational constraints so formidable that today, after investment of significant resources and effort, not one federal agency (including the Department of Labor) has an overall evaluation system and few programs are able to make any use of the evaluations produced. On the whole, federal evaluation efforts have not been cost-effective in terms of impact on policy or program development.

Since a change in approach to manpower program evaluation is being argued for, it will help to establish what is seen as limitations in the evaluation information currently available to decision-makers. The administrative levels of interest are the national policy-maker, the program manager, and the state and local project manager. Evaluations and evaluation-related activities of interest are those that have consumed the bulk of resources: the quantitative impact and cost-benefit studies, the national program management (or public administration) studies, and program information systems.

Program impact/cost-benefit studies are designed generally for national policy-makers. Our reviews have found them marked by certain design characteristics which severely restrict their reliability and usefulness.

(a) They have been one-shot, one-time efforts when we need continuous evaluation of program.
(b) They have been carried out in terms of program categories and are very weak on process data when we need analysis that gets at the underlying assumptions of these programs.
(c) They have been small sample studies working with gross averages, when we need studies large enough to allow analysis of the wide natural variations we know exist in costs and performance among projects within programs.

These studies have often been accompanied by conclusions and recommendations based on unsupportable or unmeasured assumptions and weak, and often confusing, data. Analysts who have resisted wild extrapolation usually find the data and scope of their study so limited that they have very little to say except to request that further research be done. To date, program impact and cost-benefit evaluations have not been available on a routine enough basis nor have they been rich enough in information to assist either strategic or operational planners.

Program management studies are designed for use by national program managers who need some form of timely feedback on conditions or special problems in the field. This type of study relies on collection of qualitative information on a number of projects picked to allow generalization. They are done quickly with little or no quantitative output data gathered. The result is a qualitative assessment of the program geared toward supporting changes in program regulations and guidelines by the National Office. This type of study will always be important. Nevertheless, without quantitative output data it is impossible to actually know whether projects (and the program as a whole) are failing or improving and whether program changes are effective. How much better it would be to mount program management studies on the basis of continuously developed evaluation data describing project performance. What is needed is measurement *and* interpretation of the variations in performance among projects and monitoring of project performance over time.

At the local level, the program operator has been viewed as more the object of evaluation than the user of it. We have found that the Department of Labor, in its program, has not satisfactorily provided for the evaluation information needs of state and local managers. For example, MDTA and the Employment Service are programs of significant scale and marked by considerable local control—and neither of these have an operational evaluation system providing continuous feedback for local planning and management. Although well-developed reporting systems exist for most manpower programs, the data are collected primarily for submission to Washington and not for local use.[1] Furthermore, the Department of Labor is not able to provide the kinds of information needed by local operators from its national evaluation programs. Rare is the program operator who has even seen a Labor-funded evaluation report.

In summary then, until now we've had narrow impact evaluation for the policy-maker, subjective public administration studies for the program manager, and purposeless data collection for the local operator. While methodological problems are significant, we believe that the limitations in design and low utility of evaluation result largely from two organizational factors—the lack of a management framework that ties evaluation directly to on-going administrative activities and the nature of the evaluation contracting process.

Administration of Evaluation

Evaluation is done to provide feedback from results to future decisions. The Department of Labor has not yet established the internal linkages between evaluation and operational and strategic decision-making. In other words, the Depart-

---

[1] A notable exception is the Concentrated Employment Program which has only recently developed and implemented a management control system for local project managers—the CEP Director Early Warning Light System.

ment of Labor isn't organized to produce or use evaluation in a systematic fashion.

Traditionally, evaluation planning and design has been guided by an unrealistic interpretation, or model, of both operational and strategic decision-making. At the strategic level, the budget process and paraphernalia of the Planning-Programming-Budgeting System have been seen as the vehicles through which evaluation would have impact. This process is viewed as a budget planner making marginal trade-offs among programs. Unfortunately, there is much more myth than substance to this view of the federal decision process. Its acceptance has lead to a demand for the Department of Labor to produce the impact/cost-benefit type of evaluations described above.

At the operating level, no consistent view—other than marginal trade-offs among projects—has emerged of what line managers or project operators do and what information can be provided to support them. Rarely, if ever, has a major evaluation effort on a program been preceded by an analysis of the planning-management-control process to be affected. Evaluation planning has failed to come to grips with the evaluation needs of the program itself, where most of the flexibility exists for improving the effectiveness and impact of programs over time.

We have been too quick to propose and accept neat conceptual decision-making models without doing the difficult job of modeling and accounting for the actual management process. If evaluation information is to be used, it must be made available in terms of the users' operational experience and resources. Determination of what that experience is should be part of evaluation planning and design.

Consider finally how evaluation plans are implemented. Agency evaluation staffs are small and consequently are dependent on contractor support. Every year a number of separate contract evaluations are carried out. When a contractor undertakes a study, he has to perform certain tasks: (1) modeling of the program process to establish measures; (2) data collection; (3) analysis of the data; and (4) translation of analysis into conclusions and recommendations. This effort has to be repeated in each study. When you stand back and look at the contracting process across all studies, you see an evaluation system being built piecemeal with every contractor doing his own thing on most bits and pieces.

After resources have been spent on a number of independent evaluations, what is the agency left with? The program models developed differ from study to study and have little operational meaning to program managers. The data collected are specialized and unique to each study. Differences in definition, sampling, technique, timing, and content make it impossible to relate the data of several independent collection efforts. Further analysis is often impossible. Therefore, the most expensive component of an evaluation effort—the data base developed—is lost to the Department of Labor. In the end, the agency is left with the contractors' written insights. Someone should be questioning whether these insights alone are worth the costs involved.

No matter what administrative or program structure emerges in the future, the Department of Labor has to move toward securing a multiple use data base for evaluation studies and exercising greater quality control over the validity and reliability of the data itself.

Steps have been taken over the past two years to alleviate these problems. Our study indicates, however, that one office acting alone cannot solve them. Simultaneous coordination and direction of several offices and staffs in the Manpower Administration is necessary for success. We have detailed in our report the steps we feel must be taken.

Decentralization and Decategorization—An Opportunity for Change

People in the field are already well aware of the limitations and problems of program evaluation. Today an opportunity for constructive change in evaluation policies is at hand. Decentralization and decategorization of programs will reduce many of the bureaucratic and organizational obstacles that have inhibited effective planning and execution of an overall manpower evaluation system.[2] Moreover, it is the conclusion of our study that a viable alternative to current evaluation practices is readily available—the appropriate evaluation system, which overcomes most of the objections raised earlier, can be implemented by modifying and utilizing existing capabilities and resources within the Department of Labor.

In our design, evaluation is defined by (1) measurements taken; (2) comparisons made; and (3) uses made of the information. The recommended evaluation system depends upon consideration of both methodological feasibility and the administrative functions requiring support from evaluation. We will first discuss the evaluation information needed in a decentralized program and, then, the most practical means of providing that information.

Information Needed in a Decentralized Manpower Program

The administrative structure and functions of a decentralized manpower system can be inferred from the various legislative proposals and from how business is carried out in the existing manpower programs. A key change will be the intervention of the local prime sponsor[3] in the project allocation process. Decentrali-

---

[2] For example: the categorical program structure; the instability of programs; multiple administrative channels; multiple management and data systems; the diffusion of program authority, responsibility and accountability.

[3] The term "local prime sponsor" refers to both state and city units of government.

zation gives local public officials control over a multimillion dollar program. State and local officials will make most of the allocation and day-to-day management decisions that will determine the program's ultimate degree of success. An appropriate first set of questions to be answered therefore is what evaluation information is needed by these prime sponsors acting as planners and as administrators.

We know that, at this point in time, a local sponsor's planning will be constrained by the lack of theory and the weak data base associated with the local labor markets. Given today's analytic capabilities, local planning and evaluation have to be done in terms of impact on the applicant. Success in local service delivery will be measured by process flow (e.g., completions, placements), changes in applicants' job-related characteristics (e.g., change in skill levels), and changes in the applicants' labor market experience (e.g., change in wage rate, income, job stability). The local labor market and economy must be considered an externality beyond the control or influence of the local manpower planner.

A major resource allocation question for local prime sponsors is this: given the type of local labor market and the type of applicants to be served, what can be expected to work best in his service delivery system? The necessary information can come from two sources: the prime sponsor's own experience in service delivery and the experience of other prime sponsors in service delivery. Therefore, the prime sponsor will need the capability (1) to measure the past performance of his delivery system and its various components in serving applicants; and (2) to determine how his performance compares with other individual projects operating in similar circumstances.

Once a plan of service has been established, the prime sponsor, as administrator, will require information on how well this plan is being implemented down to the individual project and subcontractor level. The only source of this information is data taken in the day-to-day operations and compared with time-phased projections in the plan. Here, the prime sponsor will require (1) a set of performance measures common to both his data collection system and his plan; and (2) the capability to process operational data on a weekly basis and compare such data with the plan.

Similarly, one must consider the responsibilities at *each* administrative level (local, state, regional office, national office) and identify the type of information needed, its content, the time-frame in which it is needed and potential sources. The operating responsibilities, and consequently the evaluation needed, depend on the particular type of decentralized system adopted.

For example, under all types of proposed decentralization, the Department of Labor is required to have a strong program development and technical assistance role. Each function can use particular types of evaluation information. For example, the capability to identify best practices is important to program development and the capability to identify prime sponsors, or parts of a prime sponsor's program, that may be in trouble is needed to channel technical assistance. Under some proposals, the Department of Labor would also be involved in resource allocation and be required to establish performance standards as apportionment criteria. The evaluation system would then have to produce ratings or rankings of prime sponsors on performance criteria.

An analysis of the administrative responsibilities that might be established in a decentralized system lead us to conclude that the overriding concern of evaluation should be with *relative program performance*, as measured by process flow, changes in applicant characteristics, and changes in applicant labor market experience. The evaluation system must first be able to capture a full description of the performance of the local service delivery system (without limiting its form and content), and then be capable of estimating relationships among performance measures and services provided, applicant characteristics, labor market descriptors and other explanatory variables.

Development of the Data Base

One basic program reporting system is seen as providing most of the data to support the evaluation analyses. To be workable, the reporting system and the prime sponsor plan must have a common definitional base which characterizes actual applicant flow through the service delivery system and into the labor market.

The Department of Labor already has the data system capability to carry out both types of priority evaluations using program-reported data and in several instances has demonstrated the feasibility of processing and using the data as recommended. The following three points are made in the study.

1) The recommended data will have to be collected at the prime sponsor level for his own use anyway, since it is essential for informed management of daily operations. During the site visits, we found that in many cases the data necessary for evaluation were being collected locally simply to run the service delivery operation. A significant increase in the amount of data reported is *not* being recommended.

2) The national evaluation program requires the further step of standardizing the prime sponsor planning format and reporting system. The maintenance and upgrading of the reporting system will be an ongoing effort of the Department of Labor.

3) The alternative—contractor collection of data outside the reporting system for relative effectiveness studies—would be difficult, expensive, untimely and, most likely, of little utility to the operating program. This has already been demonstrated by current and past evaluation efforts.

The recommended evaluation system will give the Department of Labor a basis for continuous and systematic improvement of the evaluation process. The data base should improve from year to year in terms of reliability and validity.

The Recommended Evaluation System

We have recommended a continuous evaluation process based in large part on analysis of reported program applicant and cost data. The highest priority evaluation designs are *relative effectiveness evaluation* and *plan vs. performance evaluation.*

> *Plan vs. Performance Evaluation:* comparison between estimates of input, process, and output levels in the comprehensive plan and the actual performance figures as the plan is being implemented.

> *Relative Effectiveness Evaluation:* estimates, using data from existing programs, of the functional relationships among types of applicants, types of labor markets, and types of service sequences as one set of variables, and costs and different measures of effectiveness as the other set.

The recommended evaluation system must be integrated with compatible planning, allocation, and control systems at the federal, regional, state, and local levels.[4] The elements of the evaluation system include (1) a definitional model of a comprehensive service delivery system; (2) a prime sponsor plan format based on the definitional model; (3) a reporting system (applicant and cost) that reports activity performed in the same terms as the plan; (4) local labor market data system; and (5) summary results of nationwide relative effectiveness evaluation disseminated from the national office to the field, using the same definitions and format as the plan and reporting system. Examples of the necessary elements are available in some form under the current categorical program structure. They are not now, however, utilized in evaluation as recommended. One should, therefore, consider the following cases which are illustrative of the elements required in the recommended evaluation system.

1) The CEP program comes closest to having a definitional model of the service delivery process and a compatible reporting system. The CEP Director Warning Light Report, an exception report on the service delivery process, is an example of the type of summary that can be made from the recommended plan vs. performance evaluation.
2) The MA-100 series reporting system, with some modification, can produce nearly all the types of applicant-based data required for the recommended evaluation. At present, reporting is not complete and not considered reliable.

---

[4]The flow diagram in Figure 3-1 is a simplified illustration of this evaluation philosophy applied to a decentralized, comprehensive manpower program. It shows the measures of the service delivery process to be obtained from the delivery of manpower services (left side of diagram); the comparisons and relationships to be made with these measures at each level of the manpower system (center of the diagram); and the planning, allocation, and control process that the evaluation information will support (right side of diagram).

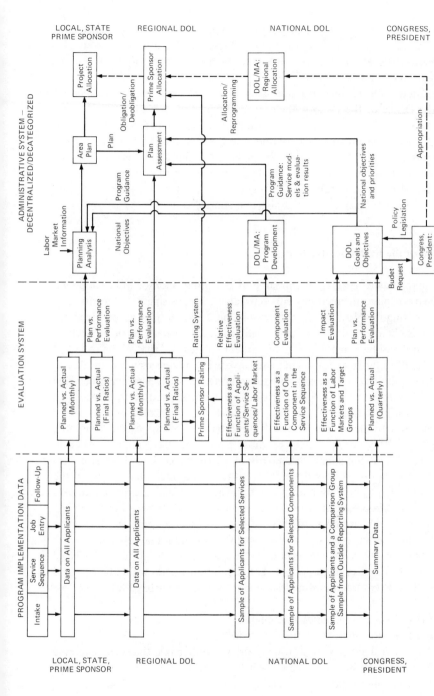

Figure 3-1. Schematic Diagram of Proposed DOL Evaluation System (Source: John W. Scanlon, et al., An Evaluation System to Support Planning, Allocation and Control in a Decentralized, Comprehensive Manpower Program (Washington, D.C.: The Urban Institute, 1971).

3) The Annual Manpower Planning Report, prepared for each labor area, provides an economic data base for the development of manpower planning information. Local labor market information has not generally been used in evaluation studies, however.

4) The Interim Operational Planning and Control System, being implemented by the Office of the Deputy Manpower Administrator, is a first step toward the type of planning and control system needed. (It extends only to the regions.) At the present time, neither the CAMPS, Plan of Service, nor the categorical program plans have the required definitional base, format, or respect to support the recommended plan vs. performance evaluation. Nor is relative effectiveness evaluation information being developed for dissemination to the field through the planning and control system.

Operation of the Evaluation System

Plan vs. performance evaluation will support the prime sponsor in developing a comprehensive plan, in managing subcontractors, in assessing components, and in implementing his plan. The critical requirement for the plan vs. performance evaluation is the capability to relate the applicant, the specific services provided the applicant, and his subsequent labor market experience. Data will be collected and reported locally from forms that also serve every day needs in the local service delivery units. Prime sponsors and Regional Offices will have the processing capability to compare actual local performance with planned performance on a weekly or monthly basis.

Relative effectiveness evaluation will support the prime sponsor in planning, the Regional Office in assessment of those plans, and the National Office in development of programs and "standards of performance." Relative effectiveness evaluation can be done more effectively at the national level because of the need to have a large population of service sequences and labor market conditions from which to choose, if statistically valid results are to be obtained. The National Office should have responsibility for the effort and disseminate the evaluation results in planning guidances to Regional Offices and prime sponsors.

The National Office would maintain the program data system as a basic building block for all evaluation data. The evaluation studies would be designed in-house. Outside contractors would be relied upon for specialized tasks, such as:

1) Studies of data system biases and reliability.
2) Special statistical analyses of the data tapes.
3) Supplemental data collection, usually on a sample basis, that can be related to the basic applicant file. These special collections would provide information not readily available from the program reporting system, such as long term follow-up, test score data, and real costs incurred by employers.

4) Case studies on samples of the most effective, average, and least effective projects in order to identify differences that might account for variations in performance.

There are two major problems facing the implementation of this system. The first is one of internal National Office management. It arises in part because of the need to integrate the efforts and outputs of many organizational units within the National Office when "carrying out evaluation"; and, in part, because of the need to account for the information needs (form and content) of several organizational units within the overall manpower system when "planning evaluation." These missing linkages have kept the full potential of present capabilities from being realized. There must be some single point of responsibility for the entire operational planning and evaluation system described if it is to function as an entity. Based on consideration of present Department of Labor organization, we concluded that, while the Office of Policy, Evaluation and Research (OPER) should continue to design and carry out evaluation studies, the most appropriate office to assume central responsibility for planning and directing the evaluation system is the Office of the Deputy Manpower Administrator (DMA). This would put responsibility for overall direction of the evaluation system in a central line management office (DMA) rather than a staff policy office (OPER).[5]

The second problem relates to establishing and assuring a continuous flow of reliable data from the service delivery system. Clearly, this is both a design and policy matter. But if we are right in stating that the prime sponsor needs at least the data described in our report to make sense of his own programs—and our field visits bear this out—the transmission of the data to Washington should be a manageable task. Failure to report should be amenable to correction through contractual agreements with prime sponsors, line item budget support for local collection and processing, incentives for complete reporting, technical assistance, and provision of a planning and control package useful to the prime sponsor. The reliability of the data can be maintained by special federal on-site assessment of project files, by processing the *individual* applicant data at each administrative level rather than using aggregate data supplied by the prime sponsor, and by comparing reported data with outside sources (such as social security data and sample surveys) to validate portions of the data.

Summary and Conclusions

How successful decentralization and decategorization are in improving program performance will depend greatly on the evaluation systems and evaluation information that the Department of Labor can provide State and local governments. The Urban Institute has analyzed and developed the major components

---

[5] This is discussed in detail in Chapter 8 of Scanlon, et al.

of an evaluation system in sufficient detail to make operational recommendations to the Department of Labor. We can summarize the major conclusions of
this effort in four points.

1) *National and local evaluations are required.* All forms of decentralization
   considered require a strong national evaluation effort (relative effectiveness)
   by the Department of Labor and a particular type of evaluation (plan vs.
   performance) at the local level.
2) *No evaluation "system" currently exists.* Evaluation activity in the Department of Labor does not now provide the information needed in decentralized program planning and management.
3) *Analysis using reported program data is recommended.* Most of the evaluation information required can be provided by two basic evaluation designs,
   using primarily data reported from the local service delivery system.
4) *Utilization of existing capabilities is being recommended.* The Department of
   Labor can implement the recommended evaluation system by more fully
   utilizing and integrating *existing* capabilities and designs. Decentralization
   and decategorization requires a different type of evaluation effort and a different type of internal planning and management of that effort by the Manpower Administration.

Moves to decentralize and decategorize mark a shift in federal policy from
innovative programs to innovation within programs. This will bring increased
pressure for the development of an evaluation system specifically geared to on-
going program and policy decision-making. Consequently, we are led to believe
that the real breakthroughs in evaluation development cannot be made in the
university or the research firm—but must be made instead in the program itself,
by evaluation staff who patiently work with operators to remove those obstacles
in procedure, ambiguities in definition and nonsense in analysis that turn policy-
makers against quantitative analysis, managers against information systems, and
people against programs.

**Part Two:
The Choice of Appropriate
Control Groups**

4 On the Choice of Control Groups

Einar Hardin

The impact of a manpower program upon outcome variables, whether these are economic, noneconomic, or mixed, is in principle not a matter of changes in variables over the course of time. Instead, it is a matter of differences in variables between two simultaneous, yet mutually exclusive states of affairs: when the program exists and when it does not exist, all other exogenous factors being held constant. A basic problem of measuring a manpower program impact is to obtain valid but necessarily indirect evidence on the magnitude of each outcome variable which would have emerged had the program not existed. The common solution to this problem is to attempt to observe a control group of persons who are statistically equivalent to the treatment group in all prior respects, except for not being treated.

This paper contains an examination of simple and patched-up before-after comparisons (which do not rely on control groups), and an analysis and appraisal of the choice of control groups in some published evaluations of manpower programs. When possible, the quantitative effects of alternative choices have been included. Recommendations as to practice and research concerning control groups are also presented.

Treatment Groups

An analysis of the choice of comparisons from which to calculate treatment effects must be preceded by a digression into the concept of treatment groups. A manpower program can be regarded as a treatment of a particular group of individuals. This group certainly includes the graduates who complete the treatment. It also includes dropouts who receive part but not all of the intended treatment. Finally, it might include persons who receive a number of auxiliary services in connection with recruitment and selection for the program but who do not enter the main program activity.

When the evaluator seeks to estimate the aggregate impact of the program, no distinction is necessary between graduates, dropouts, and screened nonenrollees. Disregard of the last two groups is justified only when it is known that benefits (positive and negative) after the treatment period arise from neither group and when the cost of incomplete treatment and auxiliary services is included with the cost of complete treatment.

41

A distinction between complete and incomplete treatment is appropriate, however, in analyses of gains from dropout rate reduction and in explanations of the magnitude of treatment effects. Inclusion of additional independent variables, representing the presence or degree of completion of treatment, makes the estimates of treatment effects contingent upon completion as compared with dropping out. Theoretically, such contingent estimates may be converted into aggregate effect estimates, but in practice, the forces governing the probability or degree of completion may be difficult to estimate with sufficient accuracy.

Simple Before-After Comparisons

The physical sciences do not always face a serious problem of estimating the values of outcome variables in the absence of treatment. Many physical objects have very stable characteristics, or at the least, the uncontrolled variations are minor compared with the impact of powerful forces applied in an experiment. When the characteristics are not fixed, there may exist a highly developed and well-tested theory useful in predicting variations. As a result, the impact of a treatment may frequently be inferred almost directly from the relationship between the after-treatment and before-treatment values of the outcome variable.

Human behavior in labor markets rarely exhibits such constancy. Theories are rudimentary and inaccurate. Treatments permissible for the program operators are likely to be much less powerful than environmental changes.

The level of aggregate economic activity varies periodically but not according to a fixed scheme, and different states or labor markets are affected in varying degrees and with unequal timing. Plants open and grow, contract and close. Hence, job opportunities change rapidly and far from predictably.

These environmental changes may seriously bias the simple before-after differences in earnings, employment, and other important variables which are measures of manpower program effectiveness. Whether the bias is positive or negative depends in part on the balance between expansive and contractive changes in the particular setting. Thus, except for many important contrary events in local labor markets, broad economic expansion in the middle and late 1960s could be expected to create a gross overstatement of the economic benefits from the nation's total manpower program when calculated from simple before-after comparisons. The reverse would be the case in a growing recession.

Adjustment to changes in job opportunities requires time. Persons who quit or lose their jobs in one period may not find new employment until one or several periods later, even if job opportunities exist at their termination; they may postpone job search for the purpose of leisure; or family duties or illness may keep them from accepting new employment. Ultimately, however, some return to work and resume earning wages. These adjustment phenomena probably lead to a strong positive bias in many simple before-after measures of manpower program effects. The unemployed and underemployed account for much enrollment. They include persons whose economic plight, in the period immediately preceding entry, was severe in comparison with their own past and who can be expected to gain employment even without additional manpower program services. Positive contributions of the program to employment and earnings growth in this group are magnified by natural recuperation. Since persons who have normal or above-normal employment and earnings are less likely to enter the program, regression toward the mean will produce more upward than downward effects on before-after changes in the enrollee group as a whole.

The presence of labor force entrants and reentrants among enrollees probably augments this upward bias in simple before-after measures. Naturally, the program may be a necessity for some persons to enter the labor force, so that their entire increase in employment and earnings is a program effect. However, when program participation is merely a reinforcement for persons who would have entered the labor force in any case and would have obtained at least limited employment and earnings, only part of their recorded before-after increase is attributable to participation. No significant offsetting influence can be expected from persons who, for training allowances or other special transfer payments or for future use, enroll in a manpower program on their way out of the labor force.

Regression toward the mean and bias from labor force entrants result in great part from changes in personal capabilities, needs, and desires, from delayed adjustments to job opportunities in an imperfect labor market, and from random changes in the economic environment which offset each other in the economic aggregates. Demonstrated stability of aggregate employment, earnings, and other variables in the local labor markets where manpower programs are conducted is no valid evidence against the existence of regression and labor force entry bias.[1]

A negative bias arises in the simple before-after comparison, when the economic status of program participants worsens permanently in the period covered by before-treatment data. When, for example, a specialized high-wage plant located in a depressed and geographically isolated area closes late in the before-treatment period, the pretreatment earnings of a laid-off person may overstate substantially his long-run earnings potential in the absence of treatment.

---

[1] The simple before-after comparisons suffer from many other weaknesses. One of these is vulnerability to poor data. If employment and earnings data are collected by personal interviews with treated persons after the end of treatment, the before-after difference may be overstated by greater omission of before-treatment than after-treatment earnings. Difficulties may also arise in use of social security and wage-reporting data on earnings before and after treatment: increases in coverage or ceiling and treatment-induced shifts of persons from noncovered to covered employment cause the simple before-after comparison to exaggerate the impact of treatment. For a useful discussion of a series of research designs which might be applicable to manpower program evaluation and of many of their weaknesses, see Campbell and Stanley. For discussions more directly applied to manpower programs, see Cain and Hollister (1969b) and Hardin. There is no need to catalog studies using the simple before-after design. For illustrations, see a largely operational report by the U.S. Department of Labor (1968) and an analysis of vocational rehabilitation by Conley.

The hazard of relying on simple before-after comparisons is vividly illustrated by data on Michigan nontrainees [Hardin and Borus (1971)]. Persons who qualified for occupational training, who had expressed a significant interest in training, but who did not enroll showed a $1,308 average increase in annual earnings from the year before the class for which they were considered to the year after the end of the same class; depending on class length, the average increase ranged from $657 to $2,108 per person. Unemployment benefits per nontrainee fell from $184 to $50, and annual welfare payments per nontrainee fell from $106 to $83. These changes for nontrainees are indicative of the gross overstatement of training impact which would have occurred had the authors used simple before-after differences for trainees as measures of program impact.

The Gibbard and Somers data on retraining in West Virginia present a seemingly different picture. Only 19 percent of their nontrainee sample had gains in average monthly earnings from the six months before the course to the six months after the course, 43 percent had no change, and the remaining 38 percent showed declines in monthly earnings, often by very substantial dollar amounts. Thus, the mean earnings gain of nontrainees was negative.

However, the studies differed not only in economic setting but also in selection of nontrainees. In contrast to the Hardin and Borus (1971) use of qualified interested nonenrollees, Gibbard and Somers used a random sample of persons having active or inactive job applications in the files of the state employment service. The presence of inactive or currently employed applicants can be expected to weaken regression toward the mean among the West Virginia nontrainees and to submerge the regression effect in the impact of environmental changes and exits from the labor force.

In sum, the simple before-after comparisons are dangerous sources of data on program effects. Because of probable biases, they cannot be used for ascertaining the magnitudes or the very existence of program effects.[2]

Patched Before-After Comparisons

One may attempt to reduce the bias of simple before-after comparisons by adjusting the before-treatment or after-treatment data according to observed regularities. In one approach, the outcome variables emerging on the assumption of no treatment might be extrapolated from trends observed before treatment. However, the fluctuations in before-treatment employment and earnings of manpower program enrollees and the difficulty of obtaining adequate time-series data make this approach unpromising.

---

[2] Some manpower program studies describe the status of treated persons after treatment without any reference to before-treatment or comparison-group status. In spite of their appearance of conveying objective information, they leave estimation of program effects entirely to the judgment and imagination of the reader.

Alternatively, one may adjust the outcome variables according to cross-sectional or time-series relationships with external variables. One such attempt was made by Scott in a study of on-the-job training of American Indians. Rejecting control group designs on the assertion that they probably fail to adjust for differences in motivation between experimental and control groups, he adjusted the observed change in monthly earnings and annual employment according to regression of these two variables for the trainees on age, marital status, and number of dependents and on average weekly earnings of Oklahoma manufacturing production workers and the nationwide nonwhite unemployment rate, respectively. The coefficients of the last two variables had signs opposite to reasonable expectations but were statistically nonsignificant. Among the demographic variables, only age (represented in linear form) was statistically significant, and it had positive coefficients.

Patching requires in principle the inclusion, among independent variables, of all those factors which govern earnings and employment at a given time and the prediction of the behavior of such factors to the end of the after-treatment period. It is obvious that Scott did not succeed in meeting this requirement and that our present scientific knowledge did not permit him to do it. When rejecting control-group designs in favor of a patched-up before-after design, Scott avoided the hypothetical bias of motivational differences at the price of very obvious biases from local environmental changes, regression toward the mean, and coincidental relationships between training and earnings growth.[3]

Types of Control Groups

The preceding discussion leads to the conclusion that inferences about program effects must be drawn from comparisons between persons who are treated and other persons who, except for not being treated, are as similar as one can find to the treated persons in all factors affecting the outcome variables. When employment and earnings are outcome variables, these background influences include demographic and other personal characteristics, labor force status and job opportunities prior to the start of treatment.

Many types of control groups have been used in published evaluation studies. These include samples of the target population, snowball samples, persons having common prior education, qualified program applicants who do not enroll, program dropouts, and enrollees or graduates in other programs. With one excep-

---

[3] Scott stated that two firms "indicated that if an Indian came to the firm looking for a job and if he appeared employable, the firm hired him and then contacted the local BIA office to determine if he was eligible for subsidy." He added that one trainee wrote that "he was working for a participating firm and one day was called into the office and informed that he was now a BIA trainee and his wage would be paid in part by the Bureau." This suggests that some employers merely accepted the subsidy of Indians whom they hired in any case, a practice which would introduce a strong upward bias in the estimate of OJT impact.

tion, these control groups are nonrandom in the sense that they have not been created by random assignment of persons between the control and treatment groups.

Control Groups from Target Population

One of the ultimate purposes of an evaluation study is to estimate how a manpower program affects the target population which it is to serve. If one may assume that the persons treated by the program are equivalent, in fact though not in process of selection, to a random sample of the target population, it becomes natural to draw the control group by sampling from the target population.

In evaluation of manpower training in West Virginia and Tennessee, the Somers group used as their main control groups active and inactive job applicants drawn from the files of local employment offices in counties where the training courses to be evaluated were located. The active files listed current claimants of unemployment compensation and other persons who in the previous thirty days had validated their job applications. The inactive files listed persons who had validated their job applications up to a year earlier but not in the previous thirty days and who had also not withdrawn them. Names were drawn at random in equal numbers from the two files. Those who were not known to be unemployed when a course was being set up or who had been bona fide applicants for training were replaced by the next eligible persons in the file.

Research data were obtained on enrollees and control group members in personal interviews. Like other field survey workers, the Somers group lost a substantial number of persons from the original sample because of inability to locate the intended respondents or to obtain useful information from them. The resulting sample of graduates was typically compared with the random sample drawn from employment service active and inactive files, the "nonapplicants" for training, but subsidiary comparisons of graduates were also made with dropouts and with persons who did not report for training although chosen or who were rejected by the employment service.

This procedure did not result in highly similar treatment and control groups. The nonapplicants and the rejects for training were substantially older than the graduates and the dropouts, had fewer years of formal schooling, and were more often black. In spite of the selection criteria, the nonapplicants were more often employed, somewhat less often out of the labor force, and noticeably less often unemployed one month before classes start than were the graduates and the dropouts. However, if unemployed at the time, they had more often been employed for 13-24 months and less often employed 4-12 months than had the graduates. Finally, the nonapplicants had more often had a regular occupation before training [Gibbard and Somers].

Fortunately, a degree of statistical control was generally applied in estimating the impact of training. In order to calculate the impact of training on employment and earnings during 18 months after the class, Stromsdorfer computed several linear regression equations from the West Virginia data. These equations contained sets of binary independent variables describing age, education, race, labor force experience, regular occupation, and several other demographic and labor market characteristics which could, and in many instances significantly did, affect employment and earnings. Gibbard and Somers made a similar regression analysis of employment during 12 months after class. Their calculations of impact on monthly earnings were based on comparisons of graduates and nonapplicants classified simultaneously by sex, age, and education, and this cross-tabulation doubtless reduced substantially the irrelevant influence of sex, age, and educational differences between graduates and nonapplicants. However, a lack of control for initial labor force status and a reduction in the size of the subsample used for cross-tabulation make it difficult for a reader to assess the comparability of experimental and control groups. These comments also apply to a related analysis by Cain and Stromsdorfer.

In his study of retraining in Tennessee, Solie followed a very similar procedure for control group selection. Like those of West Virginia, his nonapplicants were older and more poorly educated than the graduates. More were married, and more were unemployed for six months or longer at course start. However, the regression equations for weeks employed and weeks unemployed in a two-year period after the last class included a series of variables describing personal and labor market characteristics which eliminated some of the irrelevant background influences.

Although analysts of West Virginia and Tennessee training based their conclusions on comparisons between graduates and nonapplicants, they reported additional information bearing on the consequences of using other comparisons. This additional information, available only from regression equations, is summarized in Table 4-1.

The Stromsdorfer analysis indicated an earnings advantage of graduates ranging from $511 to $1,310 depending on the choice of control groups. Interestingly enough, the gains from graduation were largest when assessed by comparison with the gains of those who were admitted into training but did not report for class, a group which is often assumed to reject training because of good job opportunities. If dropouts are included with graduates in the experimental group according to the 30 percent dropout rate found by Gibbard and Somers, the annual earnings advantage of the experimental group is reduced by $154. However, there remains a substantial spread, $550, between the highest and lowest estimate of the impact of training on annual earnings.

The range of estimates of impact on employment is 2.8 weeks according to Stromsdorfer's calculations but 4.2 weeks according to Gibbard and Somers, and

Table 4-1
Summary of Regression Results Concerning Differences between Graduates and Other Respondent Groups in Earnings, Employment, or Unemployment, in West Virginia and Tennessee

Comparison Group for Graduates	Stromsdorfer, W. Va.		Gibbard and Somers, W. Va.	Solie, Tenn.	
	Earnings	Employment	Employment	Employment	Unemployment
Dropouts	−$ 511	− 4.2	− 2.7	−6.2	+2.5
Did Not Report	− 1310	− 13.9	−10.8	−3.9	+3.3
Rejected	− 959	− 13.5	−14.4	−6.5	+4.1
Nonapplicants	− 760	− 10.1	−15.0		

Note: Employment and unemployment are in weeks per year, and earnings are in dollars per year. These are calculated from results by Gibbard and Somers, p. 119; Stromsdorfer, p. 146; and Solie, pp. 201-202.

the ranking of comparison groups as to difference from graduates or enrollees is reversed between the two studies.[4]

Because dropouts are combined with those accepted but not reporting for training, the Solie analysis is not fully comparable with the other two. It is obvious that the choice between rejects and nonapplicants had more influence on the estimate of employment than unemployment impact.[5]

Control Group by Snowball Technique

In a nationwide study of MDTA occupational institutional training described by Main, the National Opinion Research Corporation (NORC) obtained a control group by partial matching. Starting with a national probability sample of MDTA trainees, the NORC interviewers asked each trainee to "provide the names and addresses of up to about three friends, neighbors, or relatives who were unemployed about the time his training course started," with attempts made to ensure these were of same sex as the trainee. When personal referral failed to yield an eligible nontrainee, the interviewer "began canvassing in the block where the trainee lived looking for a person who was unemployed about the time the trainee's course was started."

This procedure, which NORC terms "snowball," led to a control group one-third of which had been found by canvassing after trainee nominations were exhausted. The control group showed only limited differences from the trainee group in demographic and economic characteristics, and statistical control by binary variables in the regression equations further reduced irrelevant influences.

There is no obvious evidence that this technique for control group selection has strong biases not removable by statistical control. However, since the control group members are chosen without regard to their desires and qualifications for training, there may exist strong trainee-nontrainee differences in psychological traits affecting employment and earnings. One may also wonder whether there are subtle psychological biases in nomination decisions of trainees and whether controls obtained by canvassing differ from nominees in their degree of resemblance to the corresponding trainees.

---

[4] The Stromsdorfer analysis covered 18 months as compared with 12-month coverage by Gibbard and Somers. The analyses also differed in sample size and in the set of independent variables. These factors probably explain the differences in results.

[5] Rejected applicants fared better than nonapplicants according to Solie but not according to Stromsdorfer or Gibbard and Somers. The common notion that rejects have poorer job prospects than the general target population should be tempered with a realization that these rejects are perhaps merely the less desirable applicants for training and that they can be superior to the general pool of active and inactive job seekers if recruitment for manpower programs is sufficiently selective.

Matched Control Groups from Common
High Schools

When program participants are drawn from a clearly delineated pool of persons who have a common educational experience which is required for the program and when abundant data exist on the members of the pool, adequate control groups may be assembled from among the other pool members. Such an approach has been used by Carroll and Ihnen and by Bowlby and Schriver.

Carroll and Ihnen selected a treatment group of persons who graduated in 1959 and 1960 from a two-year technical school (Gaston Tech) with only white male enrollment, who were graduates of North Carolina high schools, and who met certain requirements as to mobility, employment, lack of permanent disabilities affecting employment opportunities, and absence of other training or education after high school. For each Gaston Tech graduate, the analysts selected a control group member from persons who had been in the same high school graduating class, who had comparable academic high school records, who also were white males, who had no training or education after high school, and who met the same requirements as to mobility, employment, and permanent disabilities. After eliminating unmatched treatment and control group members, the authors ran multiple regression analyses on earnings of the remaining 90 persons, holding constant several background variables.

Bowlby and Schriver selected a sample from an initial list of 1,701 former Tennessee Area Vocational-Technical School (AVTS) students, visited each of the Tennessee high schools from which these had graduated, and selected a panel of six potential matches (same sex, race, and grade point average). Each panel was narrowed to three persons resembling the corresponding AVTS student in IQ score, father's occupation (professional-managerial vs. lower-skilled), and high school curriculum. Mail questionnaires sent to 872 persons yielded 129 matched pairs, but after further analysis of postsecondary education, mobility, and marital status, the final sample was reduced to 58 pairs. Cross-tabulations by training status (AVTS or not) separately against sex, urban-rural residence, and marital status were used for calculating the impact of training on unemployment, nonwork, labor force participation, and occupational mobility.

These studies clearly demonstrate one of the central consequences of matching: a pronounced loss of observations which, although probably enhancing the comparability of the specific treatment and control groups, casts serious doubts on the applicability of the results to the original population of treated persons.

Control Groups from Dropouts

It is occasionally suggested that dropouts might be used as controls for those completing a manpower program. However, except for those few who leave the program in the first few days, the dropouts normally are exposed to a significant amount of treatment. Some entrants into training courses learn the critical skills quickly and see no merit in continuing the course after that time. Some may be forced by illness or family circumstances to leave the course but have already learned useful skills. Experiencing renewed educational failure, others may become demoralized and less employable from the program. In any of these cases, program participation does not leave the dropout unaffected. Unless such cases can first be removed accurately—a most difficult task—the theoretically questionable use of dropouts as control groups practically becomes a source of serious bias in estimates of program impact.

Control Groups from Qualified, Interested Nonenrollees

If qualifications and desire for enrollment in a manpower program are factors which also influence a person's job and earnings opportunities in the absence of participation and which are not fully reflected in demographic and economic control variables, the long-run labor market prospects of enrollees are not identical with those of the target population and are not measured, even with statistical control, by the actual labor market performance of the target population after the end of the program period. Persons who are known to have qualifications and desire for participation in a manpower program, such as a training course, but who do not actually enter may then be a better source of control group members.

It should be recognized that the reasons why qualified and interested persons actually do not enroll may be systematically related to the values of the outcome variables and that, accordingly, the estimate of program impact may be biased. However, systematic reasons may have little bearing on labor market prospects, and some nonenrollment may arise randomly. Qualified, interested persons may be judged slightly less qualified or, conversely, slightly overqualified as compared with those actually entering the program, but these judgments may be defective and erratic. Some selected persons may happen not to receive notices of selection or may be slow or temporarily unable to accept. Some may fear the program or think it will not help them after all. Some may happen to land jobs or, being declared ineligible for allowances or other program support, may be forced to take their chances on the labor market.

Qualified, interested nonenrollees may have a second weakness as control group members. All persons receiving consideration for training come to the attention of counselors and job placement officers more than do the ordinary job applicants. The additional informational and psychological services they receive may help improve their employment and earnings. Program impact computed from the difference between the two groups is understated by an amount equal to the impact of any such extra services to qualified and interested nonenrollees.

In a study of MDTA and ARA institutional occupational training in Michigan, Hardin and Borus [1971] chose as control groups those persons who had met the applicable basic qualifications for training in a particular course (formal schooling, work experience, GATB scores, sex, etc.), who had expressed a clear interest in enrolling in the course, but who for a variety of reasons did not enroll. Control group members and trainees were selected from the same set of courses, since the authors expected and subsequently found that the earnings of nontrainees varied with the course for which they were considered and since the study put heavy stress on estimating the variations in training effects according to course and labor market characteristics. Since each course was designed for a specific occupation, there was a great deal of similarity between trainees and nontrainees in personal as well as labor market characteristics. Statistical control was employed to increase further the comparability of trainees and nontrainees.

Qualified, interested nonenrollees were also used as control groups in the Borus, Brennan and Rosen study of the Neighborhood Youth Corps out-of-school program in Indiana. Statistical control was again employed to reduce the effects of the relatively small differences between treatment and control groups.

Additional restrictions. Some authors have imposed additional restrictions on the selection of nontrainees as well as trainees. In his study of Connecticut training, Borus [1964] separated his sample of enrollees and qualified, interested nonenrollees into six categories according to whether they (1) utilized their training; (2) completed their course but either did not utilize their training or were not placed because of having learned new skills; (3) withdrew from training for employment reasons; (4) withdrew from training without employment; (5) refused training for employment reasons; or (6) refused training without employment. In estimating the private economic benefits from training, he compared group (1) primarily with group (2) but also with groups (4) and (6).[6]

Such an approach is clearly based on the assumption that only technical vocational skills are carriers of benefits from training: the definition of the first group is "workers who, as a consequence of having taken the retraining course, were placed in jobs which utilized skills learned in the retraining course" [Borus (1964) p. 374]. There are good reasons to believe that a training course may also teach cleanliness, orderliness, and punctuality; may expose the trainee to the full range of diagnostic, counseling, and job placement services of the public employment service; and may give him a badge of approval valuable in the eyes of employers. Without offering evidence, Solie states that "many of the trainees experienced a restoration of their self-confidence as a result of completing the pro-

---

[6]Because he assumed the existence of a pure vacuum effect, he used no control groups when estimating the impact on the national product and inferred this impact instead from the average annual earnings after training of group (1), workers who utlized their training. For discussions of vacuum and displacement effects, see Borus (1964), Hardin and Borus (1966, 1971), and Ribich.

gram. Thus, some who had previously given up all but half-hearted attempts to find jobs once again began an aggressive, active search for employment—a search which was rewarded in almost every case." The difference between those who utilize their skills and those who graduate but, in a narrow sense, do not utilize their skills may well understate substantially the benefits from training.

The use of additional conditions may also lead to difficult data problems. How does one find out what skills are learned in a course and which of these are used on a particular job? What norms are to be applied in judging whether enough is used to warrant saying the job utilizes these skills? Can one accept the individual person's interpretation as to whether he is hired because of having learned new skills and whether he quits or refuses training because he has found employment? What role do work experience and attitudes toward training play in replies given long after the event?

It is likely that these additional restrictions affect considerably the estimates of training impact. Borus reports that the workers who utilized their training (graduates and dropouts combined) had annual wages $424 higher than graduates who did not use their training, $1,176 higher than those who withdrew without employment, and $1,033 higher than those who refused training without having employment. However, the users earned only $3 and $10 more per year, respectively, than workers who for employment reasons either refused training or withdrew from it.

Comparisons with Other Treatment Groups

When nontreatment is eliminated from admissible choices by prior considerations and the analysis is undertaken for guidance in choice among two or more treatments of a common target population, there is no need for explicit control groups. The magnitudes of outcome variables for a nontreatment control group will cancel out when differences among treatments are calculated. It remains essential, however, to ensure that the treatment groups have mutually equivalent before-treatment characteristics after any application of statistical control.

The Hu, Lee, Stromsdorfer and Kaufman study of vocational education illustrates this approach. Five high school curricula are compared in terms of the earnings, employment, and voting participation of their graduates, with sample selection control for age and for education after high school and with statistical control for city, sex, IQ, race, marital status, and father's education. However, socioeconomic family background can be expected to influence earnings, employment, and voting habits of recent graduates directly and not only through curriculum choice. Although father's education may be the single most important indicator of such background, father's occupation and parental voting patterns—two variables not used in the study—might also have been valuable in statistical control.

Control Groups by Random Assignment of
Qualified Interested Persons

The procedure of randomization has long been of immense value to research in agriculture, biological sciences, and psychology. If properly employed, it may have equal value in studies of the impact of manpower programs. In this procedure, as it would be applied to manpower programs, each qualified and interested person is assigned to receive treatment or not to receive treatment according to random chance based on a predetermined probability. Observations on the outcome variables (earnings, employment, etc.) are collected for both treatment and control groups covering a common period of time.

Randomization creates very useful statistical similarities between treatment and control groups. Except for sampling variations, which increasingly offset each other with growing sample size or with repeated experiments, the control group has the same mean values of independent variables and the same relationship of dependent to independent variables (except for treatment) as does the treatment group. Thus, unless the experimenter uses faulty experimental techniques, a feature which would equally invalidate comparisons based on nonrandom groups, the treatment effect is measured directly by the difference between the mean values of the outcome variable for the two groups.

Statistical control in a nonrandom setting becomes adequate only when all important variables affecting the dependent variable are properly measured and are included in tables or equations in proper mathematical form. Adequate control by randomization requires, in contrast, neither measurement and mathematical specification of such variables nor even knowledge of their existence. In particular, when randomization is attained, there is no need to identify and measure psychological variables which may affect both program participation and labor market success, nor is it important to obtain before-treatment data in order to measure gains.[7]

Randomization is equally useful when there is more than one treatment for which there are interested and qualified persons. Following a set of predetermined probabilities, the experimenter assigns each person to one of the treatment groups or to the sole control group.

The selection probabilities may differ for subgroups or persons defined by objective prior characteristics, such as age, sex, race, formal schooling, and prior work experience. If a treatment effect is estimated for each subgroup, the overall effect can be calculated as the weighted sum of subgroup effects. However, the probabilities must in all instances be independent of unrecorded subjective assessments of the likely success of the person either in the program or in his

---

[7]Although not important for avoidance of bias, additional independent variables in a random-assignment design increase statistical efficiency and permit detection of interactions with the treatment variable, a task which should be assigned higher priority than is done in most current evaluation studies.

subsequent work. Otherwise, selection becomes subject to nonrandom influences for which statistical control cannot correct, and the results become difficult to interpret.

The choice of selection probabilities influences the sampling variability of the estimate of treatment effect, and guidance should be sought from texts or specialists on sampling. Equal subgroup sizes may perhaps be advisable in evaluations of small enrollment programs which are to be treated as separate phenomena. However, since sampling variability declines with increased sample size, very high selection probabilities may yield satisfactory control groups, when one evaluates large enrollment programs.

Random assignment does not prevent a program operator from recruiting, screening, and selecting applicants, since randomization is introduced only after he has prepared a list of acceptable persons eligible and willing to enter the program. However, he is affected in four ways. First, he must make efforts to ensure that all persons on the final list will enter the program if invited. Failure to obtain entry weakens the design, since statistical equivalence of treatment and control groups is no longer guaranteed. Second, he must obtain a longer list of eligible and willing candidates than are to be enrolled, so that the program remains suitably full after control group members are removed from the treatment group by random selection. If the selection probability is high, finding the additional eligible and willing persons may not be burdensome. Third, in order to create a sufficiently long after-treatment period of observation on both groups, he must normally arrange to bar those randomly selected for no treatment from entering substitute manpower programs for a specified length of time. Fourth, he must prepare and file a written record of his list before randomization, his randomization procedure, and his final list.

The program budget approved by the funding agency should specify the selection probability (or probabilities) to be used, the randomization device to be applied, and the permanent record to be prepared and filed. The listing of persons in the permanent record should contain all information available to the program operator which may help locate the individuals personally or in wage-reporting, Social Security, or other government data files. The permanent record should also contain enough detail on the randomization procedure to permit an assessment of its quality: the source of random numbers, the series actually drawn, and the decision rule. The budget should include an adequate item for the extra cost of randomization which the program operator incurs.

The response of the target population or the general public may influence the future use of random assignment. Little opposition is likely to arise when the benefits to the individual are somewhat uncertain, when persons excluded from the program do not long remain barred, when random assignment is only among forms of treatment and treatment of some kind is offered to everyone, or when there are more well-qualified applicants than program vacancies. In opposite circumstances, randomization may be unfeasible. Carefully designed and managed efforts to build randomization into a selected set of programs may alone be able to tell us how the target population and the general public will react.

An evaluation study by Robin gives us reason not to reject randomization as being an entirely unfeasible approach but also illustrates some of the difficulties. In Cincinnati's summer-only Neighborhood Youth Corps (NYC) program (which was part of the In-School NYC program), there was, at the start of summer 1966, an initial waiting list of 351 youths who had applied for the program, had been found eligible, and had not worked in the program earlier. These people were separated at random into an experimental group of 176 and a control group of 175 persons. The local NYC staff agreed to terminate the experimental group at the end of summer 1966 and to bar both groups from any other NYC participation until all after-treatment data had been collected in March and April 1967. The report does not indicate any opposition to this arrangement.

The difficulties of maintaining strict experimental control are illustrated by the events occurring after this promising start. First, the analysts learned that 36 persons selected for the treatment group actually did not enter the summer program. Second, they were unable to obtain interviews with 38 persons selected for the control group. Imperfect assignment and loss of observations might have introduced biases in comparisons between remaining treatment and control groups. Although very similar in terms of sex, age, and educational attainment, the two groups differed in presence of police record and of father at home and in vocational-curriculum enrollment.

The general conclusion of the Robin study was that summer-only NYC enrollment affected neither educational and occupational attitudes nor educational performance. Until information is available on the relationship, if any, of police record, father's presence, and vocational-curriculum enrollment to attitudes and to trends in educational performance, it is not possible to say whether an actual program impact was hidden by selective losses of observations.[8]

Recommendations

Several implications for the choice of control groups can be collected from the preceding discussion. Some of these have a bearing on evaluation practice, others lead to further research.

1. The choice of control groups can affect the impact estimates far more than can be tolerated. Statistical control can help to alleviate the problem but is currently unable to resolve it.

---

[8] Robin also analyzed the NYC summer-only program in Detroit. Because all applicants were admitted, he used a nonrandom control group of financially ineligible applicants. Substantial differences between treatment and control groups were found in personal background. This analysis also failed to show any program impact on educational and occupational variables.

2. Simple before-after comparisons of treatment groups create substantial biases in impact estimates. Such comparisons may be worse than no evaluation at all.

3. Patched before-after comparisons have not yet improved greatly on the simple before-after comparisons. However, as we develop better theories of the outcome variables, patching may become more effective.

4. Dropouts from manpower programs are frequently affected by their incomplete treatment. Such effects should not be disregarded in analyses of aggregate impact. Dropouts are inappropriate as control groups for those completing treatment.

5. Random assignment of qualified, interested persons to be treated or not to be treated creates statistical equivalence between treatment and control groups. Randomization should be attempted in a number of manpower programs, and detailed provisions for randomization should be included in program budgets.

6. Better theoretical understanding and statistical estimation of forces governing typical outcome variables are necessary for improved control group selection when randomization is not used and for improved statistical control in random as well as nonrandom assignments.

7. Research is needed on personality, motivational, and other psychological factors to assess their influences on selective enrollment in manpower programs and on subsequent earnings, employment, and other outcome variables. It may be particularly fruitful in guiding the choice between target population samples and samples of qualified, interested nonenrollees as nonrandom control groups.

8. Until new results emerge, qualified and interested nonenrollees seem to be more appropriate control groups than does the general target population.

On the Choice of
Control Groups: Comment

David A. Miller

Impact of a manpower program may be *defined* as the difference in effect between the presence and absence of a program; but it does not follow, necessarily, that impact may be *measured* by the difference observed in effect between a group of enrollees and a group of nonenrollees. Where studies of impact or effect are to be based on the measured difference between an experimental group and a test group—in other words, a control group—very strict conditions must be met. This discussion will argue that, far from meeting such conditions, control group methodology has been and probably will continue to be deficient in providing a firm basis for evaluating manpower programs, and that, in fact, studies entailing control groups are in many ways worse measures of impact than the simple before-and-after studies which have been subject to such criticism.

There are two major limitations in control group studies of manpower or broad-based behavioral programs: formal statistical restrictions and programmatic limitations. The former pertain to the satisfaction of statistical conditions needed to justify the use of control groups, and the latter pertain to practical, though no less serious, restrictions.

In designing control groups, use is often made of statistical matching on demographics. Researchers have tried to define matching groups on the basis of factors which, in the aggregate, have shown some relationship with such economic variables as length of employment, wage level, etc. But, there is no evidence that members of the matched pairs would behave similarly under the effect of treatment, or, for that matter, nontreatment. This approach, however, requires statistical matching as opposed to simple group matching. If this condition is not met—and the research has to supply the burden of proof *a priori* that it is—unwarranted conclusions may well result. In the case of matching on demographics, the evidence is either missing or contradictory. In some cases, such factors as race, age, and sex seem to be outcome determinants; in others, education or skill level, and so on. Certainly, too little is known about the behavior of demographically defined groups under the restricted conditions of manpower programs to justify control group selection on the basis of matched pairs. This problem, though, can be overcome by random assignment. The question then arises, would a control group selection by random assignment result in an adequate methodology? Probably not.

Far more serious than the problem of matching is the problem of confounding, or combining the results of treatment with extraneous factors, as Snedecor points out in describing control group methodology in agriculture.

In these circumstances, statistical evidence that the population averages are different may have little bearing on the problem of possible treatment effects. Although the statistics may lead correctly to rejection of the null hypothesis, and although this hypothesis may, in fact, be untrue, yet the treatments themselves may have no effects, or may tend to cause a difference opposite to that in the sample. [p. 90]

These confounding effects cannot easily be eliminated from even the simplest study, and the influence of undefined causes in broad studies of such complex and interactive efforts as manpower programs can be so overwhelming as to cast doubt on any study, random or not. Researchers in the experimental sciences have been long aware of the subtleties involved in the use of control groups, as may be evidenced from a simple study by Oswald of the effects of a sleep-producing drug.

After describing an experiment in which a sleep-inducing drug and a control pill, identical in appearance but with no soporific qualities, are alternated in patients under the most carefully controlled conditions, Oswald introduces his conclusions only after a strong caution about the limitations inherent in control group methodology. He frets about variables not controllable in the laboratory: the weather, road noise, differences in beds (and even bed linens). Oswald quite properly realizes that such unaccounted-for factors can bias outcome—yet his problem is quite simple and straightforward compared with the Pandora's box of uncontrollables and unknowns in the manpower training area. Considering the compromises which must be made in control group design, in fact, it is unreasonable even to speak of control groups in manpower research. Rather, one should be dealing with comparison groups, which provide a more flexible means for observing similarities and differences.[1] Moreover, there is some question as to whether a program experience is a legitimate statistical event. Programs are complex combinations of different treatments of different qualities and different durations.

Finally, one additional condition must be satisfied for control groups—a condition which the study of manpower programs cannot meet: independence. The effects of a manpower program are not limited to enrollees. They interact with the entire community and with any individuals selected as controls. The program opens up new training and service options which would not otherwise have been available—increasing resources and allowing those not in the program to avail themselves of services similar to those rendered by the program, becoming in effect ghost program enrollees. Knowledge of the program is itself an effect and may cause the control population to behave differently. Feedback between the enrollees and control population may further weaken the study. If the study involves contacting the control group, then an additional extraneous factor has been introduced, and interactive effects must be assumed. The problem of un-

---

[1] A similar contention is made in the paper in this volume by E. Bryant and M. Hansen, and was used to modify the design of the longitudinal impact study of Work Incentive Program enrollees.

controlled interactive effects may be illustrated by a simple analogy in agricultural experimentation. Suppose in testing a new fertilizer the experimenter arranges the plants in such a way that the experimental plants—as they grow—tend to shade the control plants. Then, the induced effects—having nothing to do with treatment—may decide the outcome.

Leaving formal considerations, let us look at some of the problems in designing, carrying out and interpreting impact studies using control groups. First, as has been noted, we would have to restrict such studies to random assignment of enrollees and nonenrollees. Such an approach poses ethical, if not legal, problems. Can anyone justify the arbitrary exclusion from a program of persons desiring service solely to satisfy the demands of research? In addition, there may be clear-cut legal barriers. The Work Incentive Program, for example, is required by the enabling legislation to enroll certain welfare recipients on a priority basis—thus assuring that the program universe and the residual universe will be different. And even if one were not constrained by these ethical or practical considerations, how could the research isolate the elements of treatment for the experimental population and isolate the control group from similar elements? We are dealing, after all, with human beings in highly dynamic and largely uncontrolled circumstances.

Finally, assume that somehow all the previous problems have been overcome. What would the results mean? Suppose that the outcomes of the test group and program group do show similarities or differences—does this really have anything to do with impact? If the unemployment rate in an area increases considerably and no one is employed (control or experimental group), does this imply that the program had no impact? (It would be unreasonable for an agricultural researcher to assume that some plant nutrient had no effect because during his study both the experimental and control fields were destroyed by blight.) In fact, the insistence for control groups may have overlooked the purpose of impact evaluation: to assess the effectiveness of programs so that informed decisions can be made about the usefulness of an approach, the relative merits of alternative strategies, or the implementation of structural or procedural changes. Overall, the reason for evaluation is to optimize the effectiveness of manpower policy.

The emphasis on purely economic measures in the discussion of control groups implies that impact can be defined by simple employment, retention, and wage indicators, and that levels of such indicators must be used to justify the worth of a program. But, impact may be observable only over the longer run, produced by program effects best determined through before-and-after measures. The insistence upon control group methodology may reflect more of a dogmatic assumption that true research must follow certain paths than a thoughtful analysis of the need for policy data and a consideration of the most appropriate and effective ways of meeting that need. The evolution of control group methodology may in the end produce statistical ways to produce answers of no applicability. Why, after all, does much academic research seem to be structured to avoid the intrusion of human interpretation into the analysis and evaluation of program impact?

On the Choice of
Control Groups: Comment

Harold Nisselson

Professor Hardin has given us a wide-ranging and stimulating review of technical and other problems involved in the choice of appropriate control groups for evaluating the impact of manpower training programs, and the limitations in available statistical techniques for analysis. His paper illustrates graphically how sophisticated a view has been developed of the problems of evaluation. I would like to use the opportunity given me to discuss his paper to point up some of the questions which he was not able to fully develop within the time allotted to him.

First, let me say that I am in complete agreement with him as to the need to start building randomization designs into the evaluation of social programs. I say social rather than manpower training programs since, for example, the evaluation of education programs is in no better state in this regard. Current evidence at the national level on the impact of Title I compensatory education programs on the academic and personal skills of pupils, for example, derives exclusively from nonrandom ex post facto studies [e.g., Glass].

I'm not quite sure what to make of Professor Hardin's discussion of target group samples. In fact I'm not sure that he didn't include it as a strawman. My problem basically is that his conclusion that ". . . qualified and interested non-enrollees seem to be more appropriate control groups than does the general target population" seems to lack a reference to the purpose of the evaluation study in mind. There surely are some studies for which his conclusion is applicable and others for which it is not.

To examine this point in somewhat more detail, I would like to start with Professor Hardin's statement that "one of the ultimate purposes of an evaluation study is to estimate how a manpower program affects the target population which it is to serve." This cannot be done by ignoring those members of the target population who the programs are not serving. I would propose that his statement be amended to refer to a program of evaluation studies. In such a program, a large variety of evaluation studies will be of interest, aimed at one or more components of a manpower training program from outreach and recruiting to postprogram services. Each of these components, of course, can be the subject of study through randomized experiments.

I would go further than Professor Hardin and suggest that *the* ultimate purpose of an evaluation *program* (not merely one of the ultimate purposes) is to measure target population impacts in order to provide predictions for program planners and administrators as to the impact that changes in a manpower training program might be expected to have on the target populations involved. I say this because I believe that trade-off analysis is perhaps the most critical function of planning. Thus, the argument for drawing comparison data from samples of the target population does not rest on the hypothetical assumption cited by Professor Hardin "... that the persons treated by the program are equivalent ... to a random sample of the target population ... " but, rather, on the need to find out just who the programs are and are not treating if the evaluation program is to serve its ultimate purpose. Hopefully, from the measures of impact observed for those treated, one could synthesize measures for types of persons in the target population not observed, and for mixes of types different than found to be in the program. If the recruiting, screening, and selection processes were made the subject of randomized experiments, one would have the further refinement of determining who the programs could and could not treat. Of course, as Professor Hardin indicates, one would not be content to just make simple comparisons between the program enrollees and the target population. It is of interest that in the evaluation of federal aid to education programs, the assessment of who the programs are reaching and who they are not is generally viewed as among the items in the first order of business for program evaluation—if only because it is a good bit easier to determine than is impact on those aided.

If we assume that Professor Hardin's evaluation study had the purpose of assessing impact on those aided rather than the target population to be served, his proposal to use "qualified, interested" persons as a control group seems reasonable but subject to caveats as to the implied sampling process involved, and the meaning of the terms "qualified" and "interested." In point of fact, these terms have only an operational definition referring to the processes of recruitment, screening, and selection, as well as to the individual. Professor Hardin, properly I believe, argues that program dropouts should be included in measures of program impact (with the exceptions he specifies). Yet the difference between an early dropout and a no show or refuser can get to be very fuzzy operationally, and may merely be an artifact of the persuasiveness and other characteristics of program recruiters. Similarly, when dealing with the disadvantaged, the definition of "qualified" is not at all clean. The restriction of impact measures to "qualified, interested" persons, while it may be a best compromise, inevitably reflects any bias arising from these artifacts.

Turning to the problems of analysis with nonrandom observational studies, Professor Hardin has made it clear that the acceptability of a nonrandom control group depends on having available the analytics to deal with the potential biases to be faced. He has ample warning of the biases which may come from the influence of outside events and from the phenomenon of regression toward the mean. He points out that "statistical control in a nonrandom setting becomes adequate only when all important variables affecting the dependent variable are properly measured and are included in tables or equations in proper mathematical form." Considering the limitations in current knowledge and the finiteness of the resources for any one evaluation study, this is a powerful argument for making a start on randomized experiments for evaluation.

Finally, in connection with his reference to "equations in proper mathematical form," I would like to bring to your attention the question of the appropriate analysis of sets of data when the independent variables are subject to error. In educational evaluation, this problem is intimately bound up with the unreliability of tests which may be administered to pupils and used in covariance analysis. In the analysis of manpower programs, apart from the obvious parallels of achievement tests, I believe that a number of variables commonly treated as independent variates measured without error should more properly be treated as sample observations subject to error. Examples of such variables are mobility or unemployment during a specified reference period. In such cases, single equation regression methods can be expected to produce biased estimates of the regression coefficients used to measure impact. One approach to this problem is the structural equation methods developed by the econometricians.[1] There needs to be a great deal more work done to develop useful analytic tools and to identify the circumstances under which they are appropriate.

---

[1] See Johnston, Lord (1959, 1960), and Mandansky.

On the Choice of
Control Group: Comment

Abraham Stahler

One of the most controversial, debated, and uncertain areas of impact evaluation is the choice and use of appropriate control groups as a source for measuring the effects of manpower programs.

The need for control groups—or comparison groups—is widely accepted in many types of impact studies. Dr. Hardin states the need well when he says, "A basic problem of measuring a manpower program impact is to obtain valid but necessarily indirect evidence of the magnitude of each outcome variable which would have emerged, had the program not existed. The common solution to this problem is to attempt to observe a control group of persons who are statistically equivalent to the treatment group of persons in all prior respects, except for not being treated." Dr. Hardin gives us a good rundown and appraisal of a variety of control groups as reflected in published evaluations of manpower programs. In general, he points out convincingly the shortcomings of the groups he assesses.

His major conclusion is that "evaluation studies of manpower programs have made little use of the procedure of randomization." And he proceeds to recommend that control groups be chosen which represent a random assignment of qualified, interested persons. To quote Dr. Hardin, "In this procedure, as it would be applied to manpower programs, each qualified and interested person is assigned to receive treatment or not to receive treatment according to random chance. . . . Observations on the outcome variables . . . are collected for both treatment and control groups covering a common period of time." He further recommends that "in order to create a sufficiently long aftertreatment period of observation on both groups, he (the program operator) must normally arrange to bar those randomly selected for no treatment from entering substitute programs for a specified length of time."

In essence, Dr. Hardin recommends accepting or denying entrance into a suitable manpower program those needing such services, based on whether they happen to fall randomly into one group or another, and, moreover, to bar those in the control group from receiving the benefits of any manpower services for an extended period of time.

Unfortunately, Dr. Hardin, while pointing out, from a research standpoint, an appropriate method for use in establishing control groups, fails to answer a crucial question that needs to be answered in the real world in which manpower programs are designed to operate. Since manpower programs are operated to assist disadvantaged and others of our population to prepare them for self-supporting employment, how can one (1) publicize the availability of the manpower program and services, and even recruit enrollees through out-reach methods; (2) interview them in depth and determine their eligibility and need for assistance through such program; (3) then deliberately deny them the needed service in order that they may serve in a control group; and (4) *subsequently*, enter others into the program, often neighbors, friends, or relatives, who have no more interest or need in receiving services than those denied service?

What do you tell individuals selected to be members of the control group as to why they cannot enter into the program when their means for a decent livelihood may have well depended upon the help that they came for? Surely, one cannot give such individual a placebo pill to make him feel he received the assistance he needs and came for. When one realizes that manpower programs have been established primarily to assist usually discouraged and disadvantaged individuals to better their lot rather than for research purposes, how can one deny them service that they need and applied for? Moreover, how can one continue to deny them services over a period of time despite their urgent need and interest? These are questions that are extremely difficult to answer.

One can accept the application of Dr. Hardin's recommendations to a highly controlled experimental program. For example, the United States Employment Service conducted a study some time ago designed to develop and test more effective methods for providing services to unemployed older workers (45 plus). The study was carried out through selected local offices of the Employment Service in seven areas. As older workers came into the office seeking job-finding assistance during the study, those with selected last digits in their social security number were referred for intensive counseling and placement services, utilizing a variety of newly installed techniques, and those with other last digist were referred for services customarily provided to all job seekers.

Follow-up was subsequently made to determine the comparative results from intensive service and from the usual services. The characteristics of both groups, as one would expect from this random selection, were very similar. Results from the newly installed intensive services were so much better than the customary services that the agency was encouraged to proceed with the installation of those services on a wide scale. In this type of situation, where something new is being tried, the control randomized group works extremely well. Even those denied the new services are still given assistance.

But how does one go about applying the randomized control group method in an on-going, widespread manpower program, especially after the applicant has knowledge of the training and other services available to him and wants and needs those services to help him earn a livelihood for himself and family?

Evidently, there is further need to search out and try other means of establishing a sound and acceptable comparison group, approximately as good as a randomized control group but in which there is no necessity to deny services to those seeking and in need of them (let alone deny those services for an extended period). Hopefully, further research will be done in this area.

**Part Three:
Designing Survey Instrument**

5

Methods of Collecting Work History Information

Marie G. Argana

The collection of work history information has been a subject of discussion for many years. There are several factors involved in collecting these data. Obviously, the first problem is that of questionnaire design so as to obtain the kind of information needed. A second and perhaps more important problem is how to manage the data once they have been collected. Today, I am going to address myself to the first issue—the design of the questionnaire.

Generally speaking, the optimal design would be one in which the recall of the respondent is maximized and the processing of the data is minimized. The question is—Can both of these conditions be met in one questionnaire?

In an attempt to answer the question of how we can maximize the respondent's recall, let me give you some background information. Basically, there are two kinds of information we can collect that fall into the category "work history." The first is merely a summary of the labor force information for a particular recall period, i.e., number of weeks worked in the past 12 months. The second and more important is a detailed account of a respondent's jobs and employers during a particular period of time. The Census Bureau, from whose experience I will draw upon for most of my data, has had experience in collecting both kinds of work histories. In most instances, the format is fairly standard in the work we have done. Obviously, modifications are made to fit particular needs: in most cases a combination of the two kinds of work histories are collected. We first obtain information about the respondent's current labor force status and his current or most recent job. Then we ask a series of specific questions to obtain a summary of activity during a specified time period—usually a calendar year. Examples include weeks worked, weeks on layoff or looking for a job and weeks when he was neither working nor looking for work. The next series of questions would ask about the longest job the respondent held during the recall period, obtaining occupation, industry, class of worker, starting and stopping dates, etc., for that job. This kind of questioning, although providing an aggregate picture of work history of the population, still leaves us with an incomplete work history for the recall period, since we know nothing about any jobs except the current or most recent one and the longest one.

Obviously, in order to obtain a more complete work history covering a person's working life, we have to inquire about other jobs. The question now is what jobs are important? As you can see, that would be dependent upon several

71

things. An influential factor may be the degree of completeness in which you are interested; another important factor may be the kind of analysis that will be used. Presumably most people are interested in work histories beginning at the point when the respondent stopped attending school, in other words, when he completed his formal education. Probably we would want to know about some major jobs. For these reasons, the most commonly collected "other" jobs, in addition to the current or most recent one, are the first full-time job since leaving school, the longest job since leaving school, and the longest job ever held. As you can see, we now have considerably more information about the respondent.

All the specific jobs I have just mentioned are the usual ones that are recorded in constructing a partial lifetime work history for a respondent. The Census Bureau has inquired about some or all of these jobs on such surveys as the Current Population Survey, the Urban Employment Survey and the Census Employment Survey. I indicated earlier that the degree of completeness required is very important in deciding what jobs to ask about and also what questions to ask about each particular job. For example, in studying labor force behavior of older women in connection with the National Longitudinal Surveys, we asked about such jobs as the longest job between school and marriage, the longest job between marriage and the birth of the first child, the longest job since the birth of the first child and the longest job since marriage. In each case, we obtained the industry, longest occupational assignment on that job, class of worker, starting and stopping dates and reason for leaving that job. In this case, the focal point was marriage and children; each job held during each of these periods is obviously important in collecting a complete and meaningful history from this group of respondents.[1]

With regard to completeness and the work history of another cohort, we collected a somewhat different kind of information from the young men. In this case, we asked about the first full time job since leaving school and the longest job held since leaving school. Instead of asking about the longest occupational assignment on each job, we asked about the starting occupational assignment and the ending occupational assignment. For this cohort, the focus of this survey is the process of leaving school and entering the labor force followed by occupational change.

I have mentioned the National Longitudinal Surveys and some of the questions we have asked in connection with them. For those who are unfamiliar with these surveys, the National Longitudinal Surveys are made up of four cohorts of approximately 5,000 respondents each—men 45-59, women 30-44, young men 14-24 and young women 14-24. There is an initial interview and up to five follow-up interviews of each respondent. One of the purposes of these surveys is to study labor force behavior and factors which affect that behavior. To do this effectively, it is necessary to obtain complete work histories of each respondent. In the initial interview, we obtained a fairly complete work history by asking the

---

[1] The complete questionnaire can be found in Parnes et al., (1970 C).

usual battery of questions I have already talked about, with some modifications based on the particular interest with relation to the cohort. Generally, in the first several follow-up interviews, we asked about at least one of the jobs they held since the last interview about 12 months ago. Specifically, we obtain information about their current or most recent job held since the last interview and then about the longest intervening job they held between last year's job and this year's job. As you can see, this is not satisfactory since we have obtained only partial information about jobs held during the reference period.

In an attempt to obtain a complete work history for a definite recall period, we planned a series of questions to be tested in the summer of 1969. We designed the questions to account for every week during an 18-month period. The purpose was twofold: to obtain good summary labor force experience information and also to obtain occupational assignment information in great detail. Since we were particularly concerned about the recall of nonworking weeks, our sample was drawn from persons who had reported some nonworking weeks during 1968 in the February 1969 Work Experience Supplement to the Current Population Survey (CPS).

The test questionnaire was designed to ask the standard CPS battery about activities "last week." Then we obtained information about prior time periods in a reverse chronological sequence, leading the respondent back to January 1, 1968. We asked the specific starting date and ending date of each occupational assignment as well as each nonworking period during the reference period. The test differed from the CPS Work Experience Supplement in both format and approach. The CPS supplement asks one household respondent about other household members—how many weeks each worked during 1968 and how many weeks each was on layoff from a job or looking for work. These are direct questions such as "In 1968, how many weeks did . . . work either full time or part time (not counting work around the house)?" The test, on the other hand, questioned only designated respondents about their own activities. More important, instead of asking only one question to obtain the number of weeks worked and number of weeks unemployed and out of the labor force, we asked a series of questions to determine exactly when each occupational assignment began (month, day and year) and ended (month, day and year). Each nonworking period was determined in the same manner. The summary labor force experience information was compiled from these starting and ending dates.[2]

A comparison of the test questionnaires and the CPS supplement showed discrepancies in reporting of number of weeks unemployed during 1968. A total of 78 designated respondents were interviewed on this test. Of these, 54 respondents, 69.2%, reported the same amount of unemployment on both the test questionnaire and the CPS supplement. About two-thirds of the remaining 24 respondents reported no unemployment on the CPS, but the work history series

[2]Copies of the complete questionnaires are available from the author, Bureau of the Census, U.S. Department of Commerce, Washington, D.C., 20233.

showed that they actually did have some periods of unemployment during that time. The others who reported different amounts of unemployment showed a reverse situation—no unemployment reported on the test, but some reported on the CPS supplement. Tables 5-1 and 5-2 summarize comparisons of the unemployment data.

We are particularly interested in why these discrepancies occurred. One important factor which may account for the differences may be the method of questioning. On the test questionnaire, the respondent had to account, separately, for each working and nonworking period, rather than give the total number of weeks worked and total number of weeks not worked for the entire year. This in-depth type of questioning and accounting very likely caused these respondents to report their activities more accurately than they had done earlier.

A comparison of the reporting of number of weeks worked during 1968 for those 24 cases who had unemployment discrepancies shows that only 4 reported the same number of weeks worked on both the test and the CPS supplement while 20 reported different number of weeks worked. Again, it is reasonable to assume that the in-depth type of questioning was a significant factor.

Another factor to explain the differences in reporting may be the person who

Table 5-1
Summary of Weeks of Unemployment Reported on Test Questionnaire

	No. of Cases	% of Cases	% of Cases
Total	78	100.0	
Same amount reported	54	69.2	100.0
No weeks on both	48	61.5	88.9
Some weeks on both	6	7.7	11.1
Different amounts reported	24	30.8	100.0
No weeks on CPS, some weeks on test	16	20.5	66.7
Some weeks on CPS, no weeks on test	8	10.3	33.3

Table 5-2
Comparison of Unemployment Reported on Test and CPS

Weeks Reported on Test	Total		0		Weeks reported on CPS 1-4		5-10		11-14	15-26		27+
	N	%	N	%	N	%	N	%		N	%	
Total	78	100.0	64	100.0	6	100.0	4	100.0	–	4	100.0	–
0	56	71.8	48	75.0	5	83.3	2	50.0	–	1	25.0	–
1-4	11	14.1	10	15.6	1	16.7	–	–	–	–	–	–
5-10	7	9.0	5	7.8	–	–	2	50.0	–	–	–	–
11-14	–	–	–	–	–	–	–	–	–	–	–	–
15-26	4	5.1	1	1.6	–	–	–	–	–	3	75.0	–
27+	–	–	–	–	–	–	–	–	–	–	–	–

actually answers the questions. On the CPS supplement, one household member answers for all other members, while on the test the respondent answered only for himself. In eight cases (one-third of those who reported different amounts of unemployment), the CPS household respondent was also the designated test respondent. In the remaining two-thirds of the cases, the CPS respondent and the test respondent were not the same.

With some minor modifications, the series of questions used in the test I have just described was incorporated in the questionnaire for the 1970 Survey of Young Women. We felt that the respondents could cope with the questions and we would obtain accurate and complete work history information. Unfortunately, no data from this survey are available yet, so a detailed analysis of their effectiveness has not been made.

The questions we had tested and subsequently included on the young women's questionnaire were asked in a strictly reverse chronological order, beginning with the date on which the respondent was being interviewed and going back to a particular reference date. We felt we were not ready to attempt a more unstructured approach until we had done some more testing.

The work history questions on the first test were based on the theory that a respondent is able to remember more easily and accurately if he is led backwards in time by the interviewer through a series of questions asking "For whom did you work *before* you worked for . . .?" or "Was there a period of not working *prior* to (date)?" However, we discovered that some jobs were omitted from the work history because the respondent forgot about them or because the questionnaire skip patterns did not allow for the job to be recorded.

Realizing that with this method of obtaining work histories some jobs would be missed, a second test questionnaire was designed to allow for maximum flexibility in respondents recalling jobs and interviewers recording them. In order to obtain the most complete work histories, the new series of questions asked the respondent to remember all of his employer's names first and then allowed for the interviewer to ask further about each employer rather than asking the respondent whom he worked for before . . . and *before* that, etc.

In the summer of 1970, we tested these questions. This time we did not attempt to force the respondent to report jobs and kind of work in a specified order. After reporting their current labor force status, the respondents were asked the names of all their employers and dates of employment since January 1, 1969, followed by a series of probing questions designed to reveal any employers they had overlooked. Next, the respondents were asked to identify any time periods since January 1, 1969, during which they had not worked. Periods of not working when the respondent was on paid sick leave or paid vacation were not included here. Again, probing questions were asked to assist the respondent in recalling any nonworking periods he had overlooked. At this point, a complete work history should have been recorded. As a guarantee that all weeks of the reference period had been accounted for, the interviewer was instructed to review the recorded entries against a calendar and assure herself that the respondent had reported something (either working or not working) for each week. If the respondent had missed some weeks, the interviewer was to inquire specifically about those missing weeks.[3]

Of the 120 persons interviewed, 30 worked for the same employer and 11 were not in the labor force during the entire reference period. The remaining 79 sample persons either worked for more than one employer, experienced changes in their labor force status or both.

Forty-three respondents worked for more than one employer during the survey period. While 39 reported all of their employers during the initial inquiry, two remembered additional employers when asked the probe questions and two failed to report all of their employers until asked about their activities during specific weeks.

Forty-seven persons had both periods of working and not working. Thirty-six remembered all the nonworking periods initially, four more were reminded by the probes and seven remembered only when asked what they were doing during the weeks they had not accounted for.

Four questionnaires were returned with incomplete work history information.

An analysis of the questionnaires showed that:

1. 101 of the 120 respondents (84.2%) reported a complete work history with no need for probing;
2. 6 of the 120 respondents (5.0%) required probing to complete their work history;
3. 9 of the 120 respondents (7.5%) completed their work history only after being asked about their activities during specific weeks; and
4. 4 of the 120 respondents (3.3%) didn't report a complete work history. In these cases, the interviewer failed to follow instructions and did not ask about the missing weeks.

While the test indicates that most of the probe questions were not necessary, the instruction directing the interviewer to review the recorded information and to ask about missing time periods appears to be an effective means for obtaining complete work histories. Only in those cases where the interviewer failed to follow these instructions correctly did we fail to obtain all of the desired information.

This test seems to indicate that respondents recalled the names of all their employers during a given time period and that by using a calendar to help them remember the dates of employment and then dates of nonemployment, they were able to give complete work history information. In addition, this test seems to show that the series of probing questions were unnecessary. The interviewers'

---

[3]Copies of the questionnaire are available from the author.

natural inclination to ask "anything else?", the placement of the one general probe question after the respondent had given the names of those employers he remembered, and the checking of all dates recorded against a calendar at the end of the interview (to be certain no weeks remained unaccounted for) seem sufficient to obtain complete information.

At the present time, we are using the structured method of leading the respondent back in reverse chronological order to obtain our work history information on the National Longitudinal Surveys. However, we have modified the series slightly each time we use it to correct some of the difficulties that became apparent after it had been used extensively. These modifications were made to cover situations that arose as the series was being administered.

We do intend to revise the unstructured series of questions, test them again and try to come up with a workable series of unstructured questions. The major drawback to incorporating the unstructured series into a questionnaire is in the processing area and we have not satisfactorily resolved that yet.

Another approach to collecting work history data was used by the Social Accounts Research Group at Johns Hopkins University under the direction of Peter Rossi, James Coleman and Zahava Blum. In this project, life history information was collected, not specifically work history data. In the life history section of the questionnaire, columns were assigned to each of the variables and rows to each year covered by the survey (1943-1968). The month was defined as the smallest unit of time in eliciting information for various aspects of the respondent's life. This time unit allows changes to take place at the beginning of each month. In principle, if a respondent held twelve one-month jobs in a given year, all twelve would be recorded, each one in a different month. To ensure accuracy in the questionnaire, interviewers were provided with self-adhesive age-strips which they attached to the questionnaire after determining the calendar year in which the respondent was 14. The respondent then had the flexibility of recalling events in terms of either calendar dates or his age, and the interviewer had no difficulty entering it in the appropriate row [see Blum, et al.].

The foregoing suggests that an unstructured interview situation is advantageous in obtaining work history information. In this kind of an interview, we allow the respondent free recall and do not force him into what we, the questioners, consider to be significant recall periods. Obviously, what may be significant for us may be unimportant to the respondent. This free recall allows the respondent to list his employers in any order; this order could be different for each respondent, depending upon which employer he considers the most or least important. A general probe question and checking the weeks reported against a calendar would ensure the interviewer that the respondent has accounted for all weeks within the given reference period. As previously mentioned, the major drawback to this method is getting the information into a structured, chronological order once it has been collected. That is the point to which we should now address ourselves; until we solve that problem satisfactorily, work history data probably will be collected in an orderly, chronological (reverse or otherwise) fashion which can be processed relatively easily.

Methods of Collecting Work
History Information: Comment

Gilbert Nestel

My reservations, about Ms. Argana's paper are motivated more by what she elects to avoid than by what she in fact chooses to discuss.

I think we would agree that our knowledge of how labor markets function would be significantly improved if we also had available more complete information on the market experiences of various age-sex cohort groups. We all accept this statement in its broad contours even though I would argue that it is a vacuous one. What market information are we referring to? What are the monetary and opportunity costs of collecting this data, coding the responses, and then tabulating the findings? Can one define a relevant reference period to measure the behavior and how sensitive are the results to changes in this time domain? And finally, but by no means one of secondary importance, what hypotheses are we going to test with this data? As economists we pay considerable lip-service to concepts of scarcity, benefits, costs, rates of return, constraints, and allocation, yet as designers of research projects, we typically avoid making the necessary calculations before choosing. The cardinal rule seems to be that the more information we collect about the individual, the better the design of the study and the greater the likelihood of explaining his behavior. We then rationalize our position with the argument that what we observe as behavior is the consequence of series of complex interactions between the individual and his environment and that this cannot be studied as a response to a limited number of stimuli. I submit that our failure to sharpen our hypotheses and to recognize the high degree of association among variables has led us to extend the length of questionnaires well into their regions of diminishing returns. Thus as questionnaires become more detailed, the likelihood of response errors and nonreporting biases begin to increase. These costs may turn out to outweigh any additional insights we may derive from the more elaborate instrument.

This is precisely the place where Ms. Argana's paper begins. She accepts our dictum that detailed work histories are useful in explaining current and subsequent labor market behavior. What concerns her is how to efficiently (she uses the word optimally) collect this information. The criteria she chooses to use in evaluating alternatives are twofold: the design should lead to minimum response error and minimum costs of data processing.

Two different questionnaires are considered. In the first, the interviewer asks the respondent to recall his (her) labor market experiences (work history) during each of the weeks within an 18 month period. This information is collected in a reverse chronological sequence, that is, the respondent is first asked to report his experiences during the week of the interview and then backwards in time by one-week intervals until the beginning week of the reference period is reached. The sample consists of 78 respondents who reported some nonworking weeks during 1968 when interviewed in the February 1969 Work Experience Supplement of the Current Population Survey.

The second design relaxes the formal structure of the previous interview procedure. The respondent is initially asked to recall the names of all employers within the reference period and then the interviewer is given the responsibility to probe through a series of questions and the use of a calendar about each of these employers as well as about the periods when the respondent did not work. In all, 120 people were interviewed but only 79 of these worked for more than one employer, changed their employment status within the period, or had both of these experiences.

In each design, the number of weeks unemployed (employed) is compared against the aggregate estimate reported in the CPS survey. The results of these findings are mixed. On the one hand, the data obtained from the more structured questionnaire are more easily coded and processed. On the other hand, the work histories collected from the less structured design involve less probing and appear to be more accurate. In the end, a value judgment is needed to choose between the two alternatives.

As I mentioned earlier, I have several reservations about the methodology employed in this study. First, it is not clear to me what are the criteria for selecting the two samples. The respondents in the first design represent a random subsample of people interviewed in the CPS survey who reported some nonworking experience. In the second design, the criteria for selection are not given nor are we told that the sample consists of the same people interviewed in the earlier period. There is an obvious gain in efficiency to be derived from restricting the composition of the sample in the two periods (panel study). In so doing, we control for a source of variation that is introduced by the selection process.

Second, it would have been helpful if tables were presented showing some of the demographic and economic characteristics of respondents who reported accurately or inaccurately and those who did or did not require additional probing. For example, do the differences in response errors decline with increases in the educational attainment of the respondent? Or do the number of job changes affect the likelihood of a response error?

Third, it is not at all clear that the recall period in the second design is also constrained to an 18-month period. And if it is, then how sensitive are the findings to a smaller or more extended time interval? Other research efforts published by the Census Bureau suggest that the length of the recall period is a more important determinant of response errors than which member in the household reports the information. Is there anything resembling an optimal recall period for a wide class of variables? This is clearly a subject where additional research is needed.

Finally, the small sample sizes in the two studies weakens some of the findings. How stable are the differences as we increase the number of respondents?

These reservations are not meant to negate the findings of this study but rather to suggest that the conclusions presented are at best only tentative ones. This is in the true tradition of statistical inference theory. Data can be used to reject a hypothesis but when they are supportive of it, this is not tantamount to arguing that the conjecture has been verified.

I applaud the efforts of Ms. Argana and others at the Census Bureau for initiating and continuing their research efforts on nonresponse errors. It is high time we redirect our efforts to sources of variation in data other than sampling error. The rates of return from such a redirection may be substantially higher.

6

The Value of Attitude and Opinion Measures in Manpower Evaluation Research

Harold L. Sheppard

This paper is addressed to the issue of the role of so-called noneconomic variables, particularly social-psychological variables in the status and behavior of participants in the labor market. I hope what I have to say has more than some superficial bearing on the problems of evaluating concrete and specific manpower projects with which all of us are concerned. To begin with, I want to present a perspective—a conceptual framework, if you will—that I like to think can contribute to what I call a manpower social science.

The Need for a Manpower Social Science

For many of us trained in economics and who have wanted to be considered as broad gauged, some of the variables outside the panoply of those we were taught to call economic variables we have accepted at best as *dependent* variables, never as belonging to a laundry list of *independent* variables. Maynard Keynes was aware, for example, that *intentions* and *expectations* were probably involved in what we commonly call economic decisions, but he dismissed them largely because he didn't know how to deal with them and solved that problem for himself intellectually by saying they were too unpredictable anyway. George Katona, one of the few social scientists in this country who has tried to incorporate such social psychological variables—independent variables—as expectations into propositions and predictions regarding the economic sphere, has argued persuasively that the alleged unpredictability of such variables does not justify the blindness of economists to them when indulging in economic analyses. In real-life situations, policy-makers and administrators cannot be helped by Keynes' *assumption* (which he considered a conclusion) that changes in money supply or income, price changes, etc., are the sole conditions for making useful theoretical propositions.

Katona insists that knowledge of so-called objective circumstances is not enough of a basis to gain an understanding of how and why people behave differently (which is one of the general problematics of evaluation research). "People's attitudes, motives and frames of reference shape their perception of the environment and their behavior. In order to understand economic behavior, subjective variables must also be studied." [p. 220].

83

In other words, economic phenomena cannot be dealt with by utilizing economic variables alone, unless one broadens his definition of "economic" to include the actor's expectations, motives, etc., that pertain to such economic phenomena as job status, income, market decisions, mobility, and related items. Perhaps because of the great conceptual chasms that separate campus departments from one another (even though they may be parted physically by only a few feet or yards), statements such as those by Katona of 20 years ago still seem to have little effect on administrators and economists engaged in manpower evaluation research.

Specific Measures

Now, for some examples of how selected social-psychological measures have been used, and should continue to be used, in manpower research. These examples come out of my own research experience, but they are not intended to prove the superiority of the specific types of measures used in that experience over other measures. In citing these examples, I am not attempting to defend one particular set of measures, or social-psychological theory. The purpose of citing them is primarily to illustrate the value of *adding* to our manpower research tools some untraditional ones that might sharpen our analytical and prescriptive powers. At times, these untraditional tools may indeed be more relevant substitutes than the usual tried-and-true (and true but tired) variables.

The first set of examples are taken from the research by Harvey Belitsky and myself on the job-seeking behavior of unemployed workers, in Erie, Pennsylvania, during 1964. The study is relevant here, in my opinion, because it sheds light on at least two major facets of manpower evaluation research:

1. the impact of characteristics of individuals on their job or training career chances; and
2. the role of institutions in such career chances.

To begin with, the study revealed that jobseekers differ from one another— for example, in (a) whether they bothered to look for new jobs in the first place; (b) how soon they began the job search, if at all; (c) number of techniques used to find new jobs; and (d) whether they had ever tried to get a job really different from their usual occupations. Each of these, plus other job-seeking patterns turned out to be related to degree of success in finding reemployment. In other words, there were differences in job-seeking patterns, and these differences were related to reemployment success.

The next research-analysis question is, what other variables helped to explain the differences in these job-seeking patterns? We found that such traditionally, time-worn variables as age, skill-level and/or amount of education were not consistently useful. One of the major purposes of the overall inquiry was to explore the hypothesis that social-psychological variables might also be involved, and perhaps be more useful, under certain conditions, than the routine variables mentioned above. We were thus treating these social-psychological variables as possible independent variables in the labor market behavior of workers. The traditional use, if at all, of social psychology has been to see what effect labor market experience has on the subjective side of workers' lives. For example, whether or not unemployment and length of unemployment affects degree of optimism, alienation, political attitudes, etc.

In the job-hunt study, we used a number of attitudinal, motivational, and opinion measures. They included such measures as achievement motivation, achievement values, and job-interview anxiety.

Achievement motivation (as developed by David McClelland, John Atkinson, George Litwin, and others) essentially refers to the individual's willingness and tendency to persist and excel in situations involving the possibility of success or failure. It is ascertained or measured not by the usual method of asking a person to agree or disagree with a series of statements but rather by asking him to tell his own story about some illustrated situations, and by then analyzing the content of his replies in terms of how those replies are characterized by references to striving, achieving, taking advantage of opportunities, etc. I want to quote McClelland and his colleague David Winter directly on this point, because it is critical for evaluation researchers.

. . . when one uses such a measure, he is not talking about some vague psychological quality; rather the quality has been quantitatively measured in a variety of contexts and has been carefully interpreted in terms of a general theory of human motivation. . . . One aspect of it as a measure needs special emphasis for social scientists who are used to getting measures of attitudes and values by asking people. The *n* Ach score is an "operant," not a "respondent" measure. That is, it records *how often* a person spontaneously thinks about improving things, not how interested he says he is in improvement in response to another's question . . . a person may say that he is very interested in achievement, but a careful sampling of his thoughts over a period of time will show that he thinks about achieving very seldom. [p. 10] .

I think this type of motivational measurement could be a valuable tool in our desperate attempts, for example, to find explanations for the success versus failures in manpower programs, whether we are talking about individuals who have varying degrees of responses to training efforts, or who stay or don't stay in jobs after placement. According to the reasoning of people like McClelland, the answers of trainees and workers to questions asking *directly* about why they left or stayed, learned a lot or a little may not be as reliable as knowledge—prior to entry into training or job placement—about their achievement motivation level.

Achievement values, however, are ascertained by asking the individual whether he agrees or disagrees with a series of statements that attempt to get at degree of activism (as opposed to passivism), orientation toward the future or instead toward the present, and individualism as elements in the economic or occupational success of individuals. Examples of such statements are used in the *Job Hunt* study,[1] and adapted from Bernard Rosen's research over many years.[2]

Without giving all the details of our findings, which can be read in *The Job Hunt*, let me indicate one example of the relationship of a joint use of achievement motivation and achievement values. The rate of job-finding success among those workers who were high in both achievement motivation and values was found to be significantly higher than the rate for all other workers. This finding holds, regardless of age or skill level.

Job-interview anxiety was a concept developed for this particular study on the assumption that workers approach the act of job-seeking with varying degrees of fears and expectations. Unemployment and the need for a new job bring a number of psychological dynamics into play. With the help of Lawrence Littig, a psychologist now at Howard University, we adapted a scale from the research literature having to do with test anxiety among students, in order to tap the fears workers may have when facing the prospect of being interviewed for a job.[3]

---

[1] The questions used in the *Job Hunt* study were as follows:

1. "The wise person lives for today and lets tomorrow take care of itself."
2. "When a person is born, the success he will have is in the cards, so he may as well accept it."
3. "It is best to have a job as part of an organization all working together, even if you don't get individual credit."
4. "Don't expect too much out of life and be content with what comes your way."
5. "Planning only makes a person unhappy since your plans hardly ever work out anyway."

[2] See, for example, his "Race, Ethnicity, and the Achievement Syndrome."

[3] Examples were:

"I would like you to tell me something about the way you feel when you know you will be interviewed for a job. At that time, do you feel: Very sure of yourself? A little unsure of yourself? Very unsure of yourself?"

"Before being interviewed for a job, some people are aware of an 'uneasy feeling.' How about yourself? At that time are you: 'Very much aware of it? Quite aware of it? A little bit aware of it? Not aware of it at all?' "

"Before being interviewed for a job, would you say that your heart beats: No faster than usual? Somewhat faster than usual? Much faster than usual? Very much faster than usual?"

"Before being interviewed for a job, do you worry: Very much? A fair amount? Just a bit? Not at all?"

"Before being interviewed for a job, do you perspire: Very much? A fair amount? Just a bit? Not at all?"

"Before being interviewed for a job, how nervous would you say you usually feel? Very nervous? Fairly nervous? A bit nervous? Not nervous at all?"

"Before being interviewed for a job, how moist do the palms of your hands become? Are they: Very moist? Fairly moist? Just a bit moist? Not moist at all?"

"After being interviewed for a job, how much do you worry about the results? Not at all? Just a bit? A fair amount? A great deal?"

One fascinating and critical finding was that the more dependents a worker had, the greater was his job-interview anxiety. Workers with five or more dependents had far greater anxiety scores than all other workers. It seems to me that the extent to which program and project staffs can move to alleviate such anxiety (for example, through competent counseling, role-playing, etc.) may serve to bring about greater effectiveness of some of our manpower efforts. For agencies and personnel preoccupied with the problems of young job-seekers, it should be of interest that among young workers with *low* anxiety, more than three-fifths waited less than one week after being laid off to start their job hunt. But among those with *high* anxiety, only 20% started that soon ($p<.0001$).

As for the relationship between anxiety and reemployment success, we found that there was such a relationship but only among the older workers in our sample (those 39 and older).

In these days when agencies such as the Employment Service (ES) are being critically scrutinized, I also think it relevant to report here that among those workers who did find new jobs, these factors played a role in affecting which *particular* job-finding technique was used successfully in their job search. For example, among workers with *both* high motivation and high values, *none* of them obtained their new jobs through the Employment Service (in contrast to one-sixth of all other job-finders).

Workers who did find new jobs through this agency had a far greater percentage with low motivation and high anxiety than workers finding new jobs through other sources and techniques. Furthermore, workers finding their jobs by going directly to the company gate or hiring office had a higher percentage with the extreme opposite social-psychological attributes—high motivation and low anxiety.

We should not overlook the significance of this type of finding. The fact that one-half of the successful job finders getting their new jobs through the ES were low in motivation and high in anxiety (in comparison to less than one-fifth of all others) suggests the important role that must be played by this type of intermediary agency in the job-seeking problems of certain kinds of unemployed workers. Certain workers need such an institution in helping them in the search for jobs. A combination of low achievement motivation and high job-interview anxiety is one set of characteristics of such workers. Incidentally, when asked to name the best way to find a job, those naming the Employment Service were significantly higher in job-interview anxiety than those citing other techniques and sources.

In more recent research [Sheppard (1971b), pp. 71-80] in 1970, dealing only with white male, unionized blue-collar workers, achievement values as a measure was also used to ascertain its relationship to a number of other manpower-related issues. For example, adult workers (40 and older) who have thought frequently about making a radical change in type of occupation and who indicated they would take advantage of a training program for a better job were characterized by higher achievement values. Given the emerging interest in upgrading programs and mid-career development among the already employed (but discontented) mainstream American workers, this type of information can be useful.

One of the analyses made of the data obtained through this more recent project dealt directly with this topic. We carried out a comparison of workers (all 40 or older) designated as candidates for second careers with noncandidates. The first major point to be made is that as far as such economic factors as hourly wages and total family income are concerned, there were no differences between the candidates and the noncandidates. Such economic variables, in other words, provided us with no understanding of the issue (i.e., who would be most likely to take advantage of upgrading and/or mid-career training opportunities). Even when asked to rate the adequacy of their take-home pay to meet their family's usual bills and expenses, candidates and noncandidates did not differ.

In what ways *did* they differ, then? The critical areas were in the social-psychological realm. As already stated, achievement values differentiated the candidates from the noncandidates for second careers. The candidates were much higher in such values than the noncandidates. Furthermore, a variety of questions directly and indirectly measuring job satisfaction revealed that the candidates were by far much more dissatisfied with their current jobs. Workers' judgments as to how much promotion opportunities their current jobs provided also revealed that noncandidates, by a ratio of more than three to one, compared to the candidates, felt that their jobs had above average chances for promotion. A measure designed to tap how much *discrepancy* between aspirations and achievement the workers had experienced (regarding, for example, how well their current jobs measured up to their original expectations; and whether or not they were ahead or behind, compared to where they were ten years ago) revealed that the candidates for second careers had the greatest proportion with a high discrepancy.[4]

Another measure that I think relates to an issue that will become more and more important in the world of work—and perhaps among the underlying bases for the alleged rise of the blues among workers (not just in America, incidentally, but elsewhere in modern, industrial nations)—is the degree of autonomy that workers feel they have in carrying out their tasks. The candidates for second

---

[4]The three items used in designing this discrepancy index were as follows:

1. How well would you say your job measures up to the kind you wanted when you first took it? Is it very much like the kind of job you wanted? Somewhat like the job you wanted? Or not very much like the kind you wanted?
2. Compared with what you had hoped for when you finished school, are you better off than you hoped for at that time? Not as well off? Or just about as well off as you had hoped for?
3. Compared with where you were 10 years ago, are you further ahead in the things you've wanted out of life? Behind? Or just about the *same* as where you were 10 years ago?

careers were characterized by a much higher proportion saying they had low job autonomy, when compared with the other workers.[5]

These differences between the candidates and the noncandidates for second careers should be of more than academic interest to us. I do not think it a coincidence that these men, desiring an occupational change, reporting lower chances for promotion, reporting little job task autonomy, with high achievement values, and registering a high discrepancy between their aspirations and achievements, etc., happen *also* to be prejudiced by a two to one ratio, compared to the noncandidates, as measured by their opinion that unions and/or management are doing too much in getting good training or good jobs for minority groups like blacks and Puerto Ricans. In this connection, it should not be surprising, either, that a higher percentage of these second-career candidates reported that they had voted for George Wallace in 1968.

Finally, let me make clear that for many aspects, attitudinal and opinion factors can help us pinpoint more precisely—when combined with the traditional variables used by manpower researchers and evaluators—the conditions under which various programs succeed or fail. In some instances, by themselves they may be the *only* relevant variables that help to explain differences in program outputs.

But I do not mean to imply that economic considerations are to be neglected. For one thing, employment security and wage adequacy are obviously indispensable conditions for successful trainee and employee behavior. But they should be viewed as the necessary but not the sufficient conditions when it comes to certain issues. Just one example from my current research on white male union members: It is no surprise that among the workers with some unemployment (during the 20 months prior to being interviewed in the summer of 1970) and who also earn below-average wages (in this case, under $3.50 per hour), their degree of alienation (measured, for example, by such agree-disagree items as "These days a person doesn't really know who he can count on") has absolutely no relationship to how much autonomy, variety or challenge the

---

[5]Two questions were used in my recent studies [Sheppard (1971a, 1971b)] to measure autonomy.

(1) Which statement best describes the kind of job you have:
   — I have no freedom at all to do my work as I want.
   — I have little freedom to do my work as I want.
   — I am fairly free to do my work as I want.
   — I am completely free to do my work as I want.
(2) Which one of the following items best describes how much of their potential ideas and skills are being used on the job by the people working on the same general kind of job as yours?
   — Almost none of what they can offer.
   — About one-fourth of what they can offer.
   — About half of what they can offer.
   — About three-fourths of what they can offer.
   — Almost all of what they can offer.

worker's job tasks provide. Regardless of their task levels, they are all highly alienated. But if we move to that more fortunate group (fortunate in the *economic* sense) with zero weeks unemployment and earning over $3.50 per hour, we find that the nature of their job tasks *does* make a difference when it comes to such vital matters as alienation, aspiration-achievement discrepancy, desire to change to different jobs (even at wages equal to their current ones), etc. Without recognition of certain noneconomic facets about the phenomenon of employment, it can be confusing to researchers and policy-makers alike to find that certain workers with little or no unemployment experiences and with relatively high wages are nevertheless dissatisfied, as measured by any number of survey items [Sheppard (1971a)].

Jumping to a more speculative level of discussion, the many problems—unexpected and sometimes disappointing problems—confronting manpower program managers today, in dealing, for example, with young workers and with the hard-core unemployed, may stem in part from their failure (and ours) to wire into their programs a more conscious recognition of these seemingly intangible, but nevertheless real, solid phenomena pertaining to expectations, and other social-psychological dimensions—many of which can be ascertained and can be measured empirically.

Conclusions

I have presented here only a few examples of the kinds of attitudinal and opinion items that could or should be used in manpower research and evaluation, and which could contribute to the improvement of our analytical insights and program designs, and perhaps even to more effective public policy thinking and programming. I am not an advocate of any one particular set of social-psychological measures or sectarian theories when I say this. I am only pleading for a more truly integrated approach to the tremendous challenges our country faces in the manpower programs in the decades that lie before us, an approach that I prefer to call a manpower social science.

The Value of Attitude and
Opinion Measures in
Manpower Evaluation
Research: Comment

Ralph S. Walker

The first section of Dr. Sheppard's paper contains a rationale for greater use of noneconomic variables in doing evaluation research on the status of behavior of participants in the labor market. It is hard to refute any of Dr. Sheppard's arguments in this section. It has been apparent to those of us in the evaluation game for some time that evaluation based on economic and outcome data can only partially measure the results and identify the problems of manpower strategies.

The call for renunciation of overspecialized discipline rings true. Manpower evaluation is often dominated by economists. The vision of the world held by any specialist is necessarily colored by the discipline in which he has been nurtured. Not only is there a great deal of overspecialization in professional circles, but there is also sometimes openly expressed denigration of the other man's specialties. That this kind of contempt is based on lack of understanding is, of course, a truism.

Evaluation is a complex business, with many facets. This should be self-evident. Yet time after time, we have heard the whole process of manpower program discussed only in terms of economic impact on participants.

It is true that the planning and policies of the manpower programs have for the most part been based on economic concepts, and to a considerable extent, the evaluation of actual programs which has been done by us and by academicians has had this kind of orientation. In our contracted studies, we have rather gingerly included some psychological, social, and life-style questions in our surveys. However, the emphasis has been basically on economic outcomes. Our questionnaires have been devised with this emphasis, and psychological and sociological questions have been inserted as subordinate parts.

Part of the conscious subordination of attitude and opinion measures in manpower evaluation studies is due to the difficulties of administering and interpreting questions on such matters. We have had several instances where the rather mild questions which our evaluators have asked have generated strong opposition, not only among the recipients, but from local, state and regional office officials. All of the usual complaints about prying into people's personal lives and asking questions which have no relevance to the task at hand are quite familiar to us. Since we are a government department, such complaints have to be taken very seriously.

Dr. Sheppard does not address himself to the conditions under which such evaluation is feasible and the circumstances which make the results of such eval-

91

uative research reliable and useable. It is relatively easy to ask attitudinal questions, opposition notwithstanding, and relatively easy to secure answers of one sort or another. However in mass surveys when interviewers use prestructured questionnaires, a legitimate doubt can be raised concerning the validity of the answers to attitudinal questions. Particularly is this true when an attempt is made to secure information retroactively about changes in opinion, attitude or life-style. The recipient's perception of what his situation was several months ago is inevitably colored by his present situation. Also it is colored very greatly by the degree to which he has rapport with the interviewer and the extent to which he has been conditioned to answer frankly.

Experienced, competent practitioners, of course, may attempt to structure the questions so that the interviewee betrays his real attitudes without realizing that he is doing so. These methods have been the subject of an enormous amount of research and validation in psychology and sociology departments. The questions quoted by Dr. Sheppard in his paper are illustrative.

Once the answers are secured, however, there is the matter of interpretation. This is where professionals are likely to disagree. It is absolutely necessary in any kind of major evaluative research to make certain that the professionals who are doing it are competent and do not have fixed opinions which they are trying to substantiate.

Also, in evaluation of a particular program, there is often an urge to label an attitudinal response as "favorable" or "unfavorable," as "good" or "bad." Obviously, this can be quite controversial. Suppose, for example, a longitudinal survey of attitude shows that decreased militancy by ethnic minorities results from participation in a manpower program. Would you classify this as a favorable or unfavorable result? Would your response depend partly on your own color?

It is much easier to interpret economic findings and relate these findings to noneconomists who manage programs in the overall sense because findings concerning savings, health, period of unemployment, promotions, past work history and the like can be understood and accepted by everyone. Findings concerning attitudes and motivations are hard to translate into actual practice and policies.

It is possible that the kind of mass statistical survey which we ordinarily think of as being essential for the evaluation of manpower programs is not at all suitable for the kind of evaluative research which Dr. Sheppard is talking about. Perhaps this is best done by training professionals acting as interviewers with small groups. Unfortunately, over many years, our minds may have become so attuned to thinking in terms of valid statistical samples that we may be inclined to look upon such research as academic exercises.

For this reason, Dr. Sheppard's paper is a valuable contribution toward a more balanced evaluation program.

**Part Four:
Measuring the Non-Economic
Impacts of Manpower
Programs**

7

Measures of the Impact on Health

Stanislav V. Kasl

If one examines the substance of the papers presented in this volume and the range of their coverage, one is mildly surprised to find the variable of health among them.[1] This surprise undoubtedly stems from the fact that the current delineation of the area of impact of manpower programs is fairly narrow and excludes most social-psychological and health variables. However, if we are to build a true manpower social science (to apply the phrase which Harold Sheppard uses in his paper), then we must consider the potential usefulness of some of these variables which have been heretofore ignored. My purpose here is to contribute to the broadening of the conceptual and the methodological basis of future manpower evaluation studies by examining some of the health variables which may be included among the impact criteria. My perspective is a social-psychological and sociological one, not a biological one. You could call it medical social psychology or social epidemiology.

My task, basically, is to answer the question: If we want to measure health variables in a study of impact of manpower programs, what aspects of health can we measure and how do we go about measuring them? Thus, the emphasis is on measures of health and measurement procedures, and the current limitations of such techniques. It is true that this approach implies the belief that some of the measures discussed below will prove useful in assessing the impact of manpower programs, but I will refrain from arguing this explicitly. This is simply because health variables have not been included in past studies of impact and thus there is no accumulated empirical evidence which would support such an argument.[2]

The Orientation of This Paper

In his discussion of the meaning of the Gross National Product (GNP) as an indicator, Boulding [1970] suggests, not altogether with tongue in cheek, that the

[1] This research has been supported by grants from the Health Services and Mental Health Administration (5-R01-CD-00102, 5-R01-HS-00010, K3-MH-16709, K5-MH-16709) and by NIH Traineeship Grant (PHS-5-T01-GM-00005-15). The author wishes to extend his appreciation to all those involved in this project, including all the members of the Changing Jobs Project and especially the respondents and the United Auto Workers (U.A.W.) without whom this research would not have been possible.

[2] Although the title suggests that we are looking at health as an outcome variable, there is no reason whatever why any particular health measure discussed below cannot be used as an input variable, i.e., as an initial characteristic of the individual which influences the nature and the degree of impact of a manpower program.

95

GNP should really be called Gross National Cost. He adds: "I have been arguing for years . . . that the real measure of economic welfare is not income at all. It is the state or condition of the person, or of the society." In this day of great concern with developing social indicators, it can be well imagined that some social scientists will become intrigued by the idea of developing one global index of the well-being of a nation and of its citizens. However, a single index, no matter how great its marquee value, is doomed to become another misleading indicator, especially if one were to try to operationalize some vague concept such as the World Health Organization [1958] definition of health: "Health is a state of complete physical, mental, and social well-being and not merely the absence of disease and illness."

The difficulties of conceptualizing and measuring health, both physical and psycho-social, have obviously received a good deal of attention already, including specific methodological criticisms.[3] Our problem here is how to deal with this complex issue of measurement of health without being superficial or failing to build upon this previous work, while at the same time addressing ourselves to the specific needs of manpower evaluation. I propose to use the following approach: 1) To state explicitly the set of assumptions which underlie the choice of measures which are outlined below. We need to make sure that it is clear what the intended uses of these suggested measures are so that we can avoid exaggerated claims of versatility or validity for them. 2) To anchor the discussion of these measures to our experiences with a recently completed study of the health effects of job loss [Cobb, et al. (1966)]. In this way, our recommendations will be grounded in the empirical data which have been collected in a field setting which is very similar to that in which the impact of future manpower programs might be assessed.

Assumptions about Health Measures
Suitable for Studying Impact of
Manpower Programs

I make the following assumptions about the measures of health which are desired here: 1) In their totality, they should reflect the physical, psychological and social aspects of health. 2) They should be appropriate to a particular data collection procedure, i.e., an interview involving a trained interviewer and a respondent reporting on himself, or a proxy respondent. Thus, such measures will be suitable to large sample surveys.[4] 3) They should show sufficient fluctuation

---

[3] See Bickner, Dohrewend and Dohrewend, Jahoda, Mechanic (1968), Scott, Sells, Sullivan and World Health Organization (1957). For works including specific methodological criticism, see Cannell, et al., Elinson and Trussell, Haberman, Kosa, et al., and Sanders (1962).

[4] This stipulation obviously leaves out certain sources of data: clinical examinations conducted by physicians, instruments such as EKG or X-ray machines, blood and urine samples permitting various biochemical determinations, and the record files of hospitals and private physicians.

with time so that they are potentially sensitive to the kinds of life experiences and environmental stresses to which the target population will probably be exposed.[5]

Given the above assumptions about our measures, we can only hope to develop diverse indicators of morbidity, of impairment and disability and well-being. But, in general, we cannot also hope to use our instruments for differential diagnosis, or to develop additional health measures which presuppose diagnostic information. Thus, for example, Hinkle has proposed a measure of health status which is based on estimating the cumulative increase in risk of death as a consequence of having experienced various kinds of illnesses over a certain period of time. In this procedure, the seriousness of an illness episode is estimated from case fatality rates for untreated cases and the ratings are summed over all illness episodes. However, since this procedure assumes diagnostic information, we cannot hope to develop such an index on the basis of the limited data which will be collected, even though this appears to be a promising impact criterion.

It is true that there exist interview-based diagnostic and screening instruments, such as those for rheumatoid arthritis, peptic ulcer, and stroke, which can be administered by trained nonmedical personnel.[6] However, a decision whether or not to include them in the general data collection of a particular study of a manpower program would have to depend on special considerations, such as a high expected incidence of new cases in that population, or a particular interest in exacerbations and remissions in old cases of the disease where the prevalence in the population is known to be high. For example, it may well be that the ulcer index should be included in studies of health consequences of shift work [e.g., Mott, et al.].

Suggested Measures of Health:
A General Statement

There are several areas in which I feel measurement is necessary. A broad reading of the literature on measurement of physical, psychological, and social health and well-being suggests the following areas as important.

Impairment-disability-functional effectiveness. The basic idea here is the view of health and illness as states of the person which are defined in terms of their relevance to the capacity of the person to perform institutionalized roles. This emphasis is generally labelled as the sociological viewpoint and is identified with

---

[5]Thus, for example, the Cornell Medical Index would appear to be an inappropriate instrument because it is basically a standardized health history which picks up the lifetime prevalance of a certain set of symptoms.

[6]See Cobb, et al. (1969), Dunn and Cobb, and Shekelle, et al.

such men as Parsons and Sanders (1964). In actual measurement, one is concerned with quantifying the extent to which the person was unable to perform usual duties and activities, especially those connected with the primary social roles which the person is expected to fulfill. Inasmuch as no complete enumeration of these activities for each role has been attempted, one generally falls back upon such indexes as number of days absent from work, loss of time from school, days spent in bed or days during which certain duties were neglected. More detailed measures of social role performance are available in such studies as that of Freeman and Simmons, where an attempt was made to determine the extent to which the individual is performing the activities expected of him by significant others. Perhaps the most completely worked out measures are those in the area of activities of daily living (ADL), which reflect primarily the extent to which the individual is able to take care of himself.[7]

It must be noted that the indexes of impairment and disability are by no means a direct reflection of the health of the person, as it might be assessed by objective instruments, laboratory tests, and clinical signs. Rather, they are best viewed as measures of sick role behavior, i.e., the person's perception and evaluation of his state of health, and his decision how to behave about it.[8]

We may also observe in passing that the sociological approach to health as the capacity to perform institutionalized roles runs into certain difficulties when we are dealing with segments of the population, such as the aged, for whom there are no clear roles and expectations in our society. A particularly good examination of this problem is presented by Rosow in his article on the difficulty of measuring adjustment in the normal aged. There is no good solution to this problem short of determining, specifically for the elderly respondent, the activities and duties which are expected of him, or which he expects of himself. The difficulty is actually part of a larger problem of articulating the institutionalized roles and expectations for any segment of the population. Thus, for example, as the leisure role grows in clarity and importance, impairment in one's ability to carry out leisure activities will become as much an indicator of ill health as impairment in one's work role.

Symptoms of pain and discomfort. Another aspect of health which is traditionally assessed is the presence of symptoms of pain and discomfort, of subjective reports of not feeling well. There are many symptom checklists which are available, including those suitable for large-scale surveys.[9] Specific instruments, however, differ in many ways, including (1) the range of content (e.g., acute minor illnesses or chronic conditions); (2) the time period covered; (3) the

[7]See Katz, et al., Lawton and Brody, and Watson and Fulton.

[8]The dynamics of sick role behavior have been examined elsewhere [Kasl and Cobb, 1966] and will not be discussed further here, even though it is obviously an important issue.

[9]See Gurin, et al., Hochstim, Organic and Goldstein, Shanas and Srole, et al.

formulation of questions, and (4) the choice of precoded alternatives. These, and others, are details of methodology to which I can only allude here, but which differentiate the measures in many small ways, some of which could be quite important.

However, we do need to touch on some larger issues. One is that symptom checklists are not measures of impairment. For example, the Langner scale used in the Midtown Manhattan study is referred to as an index of impairment and individuals scoring above a certain arbitrary cut-off are referred to as being severely impaired. In point of fact, we know nothing about the degree of impairment of such individuals, only about their symptoms. There are several community follow-up studies of discharged mental hospital patients which indicate a low correspondence between symptomatology and psycho-social functioning.[10] Symptoms can reflect impairment, provided that the format of the items is altered: we need to ask not only "How often do you have . . .?" but also "How often does . . . keep you from . . .?"

Another point which needs emphasis is that symptom checklists are indexes which are obviously sensitive to individual differences in perceiving and evaluating symptoms, the tendency to communicate or complain about them, and the readiness to act upon them. What may also be involved are biological differences in pain thresholds, and psychosocial and cultural differences in tolerance for pain or discomfort and in alertness to proprioceptive feedback. This whole area is partly subsumed under the label of illness behavior and recent work has greatly advanced our understanding of this phenomenon.[11]

A comment is also in order about the use of a single item, global rating of one's health (e.g., "Overall, how would you rate your health? Excellent, good, . . ."). This measure does not appear to be an indication of either the degree of impairment or of symptoms-discomfort, though it is empirically related to both. It is probably best interpreted as a brief index of morale, especially among elderly respondents. A number of studies have shown that the index correlates poorly with physicians' assessments, and that with increasing age, the proportion of elderly who consider their health as good remains the same while the physicians' ratings of their health as good decreases considerably.[12] The health optimists are higher on personal happiness, are more active socially, describe themselves as young, and are less likely to worry about health matters.

Health—and treatment—related activities. Subsumed here are indicators which reflect either the treatment and medical care received by the respondent, or his

---

[10] See Brown, Freeman and Simmons and Marks, et al.

[11] See Kasl and Cobb (1966), Kroog, Mandler, et al., Mechanic (1968, 1969), Sternbach and Tursky, Zborowski, and Zola (1964, 1966).

[12] See Friedman and Martin, Heyman and Jeffers, Maddox (1962), Stahl, Suchman and Streib, and van Zonneveld.

efforts to return to good health or to maintain it. Traditionally, this would include the following: visits to doctors and paramedical personnel and treatment received, days spent in hospital and treatments received there, and medicines taken, both under prescription and as part of self-medication. An effort should be made to distinguish between health behavior ("any activity, undertaken by a person believing himself to be healthy, for the purpose of preventing disease or detecting it in an asymptomatic stage") and illness behavior ("any activity, undertaken by a person who feels ill, to define the stage of his health and to discover a suitable remedy"). Under certain circumstances, it may also be desirable to measure the adequacy of compliance with medical regimens and the utilization of various sources of follow-up medical care, if one is dealing with a population in which there is a high proportion of individuals with chronic disease or disability which requires continuing care (see Davis and Eichhorn).

Recent studies and reviews have told us a good deal about the dynamics of going to doctors and utilizing medical services.[13] It is clearly an area of behavior which must be assessed in any study of effects on health. However, with our better knowledge, it is no longer possible to assume that such activities as going to a doctor can be unambiguously placed on a (hypothetical, biological) dimension of severity of illness.

Positive and negative affect and mood. It is generally acknowledged that an assessment of mood and affect should be included in an overall measurement of a person's health and well-being, and a number of scales are available to us, such as the adjective checklist of Zuckerman and Lubin and the Clyde Mood Scale, utilizing a card-sort approach. The primary content areas of mood and affect with which one should deal are anxiety-tension-worry, depression and its components (especially hopelessness-helplessness because of its possible influence on development of illness), anger-irritation-resentment, self-esteem, and happiness.[14] A semantic differential approach in which the respondent rates himself and his affects and moods might be a particularly suitable measurement procedure (see Osgood, et al.).

This is not the place to discuss the details and intricacies of psychological measurement. Excellent textbooks and reference volumes are available for this purpose. However, several general comments are in order. One is that we want to eschew the symptom checklist approach to measurement of affect. Instead of asking about such symptoms as "heart beating fast" or "clammy, sweaty hands," we should ask for ratings of affect directly. Otherwise, these measures will overlap too much with our symptom checklist described above. Moreover, symptom-

---

[13] See Anderson, Avnet, Kasl and Cobb (1966), Koos, Mechanic (1968, 1969), Rosenstock, Roth and Stoeckle, et al.

[14] See Hunt, et al., Schmale, Buss, Coopersmith, and Bradburn and Caplowitz, respectively, for each of these areas.

based measures of affect do not necessarily measure the same underlying concept when used across samples which vary considerably on levels of physical health.

A second relevant comment here is that positive and negative affect and mood should be measured separately. It has been our experience, as well as that of others, that positive and negative items, no matter how logically or linguistically opposite in meaning they appear to be, tend to form scales which are relatively independent of each other.[15] Moreover, it is our impression that the construct validity and usefulness of the scale based on the negative items is the better of the two. Thus, I would be opposed to the suggestion that one should construct summary scales which represent the balance of positive over negative mood or affect. It is not clear to me what is involved in this curious phenomenon, but it is likely that response sets of acquiescence and social desirability are playing a role (see Block).

Finally, I wish to point out that the affect and mood scales tend to be surprisingly stable over time. This is perhaps because individuals have a stable image of themselves; in addition, stable response sets, such as defensiveness, may also be involved. The matter can be helped somewhat if we pay attention to the instructions which accompany our measures. A request to the respondent to describe how he feels today should produce more fluctuations in the measure than if we ask how he usually feels these days. It may be wise to ask for a description of mood and affect during the past week even though we really wish to know about the last three months. Another solution to the problem (provided we have collected longitudinal data and are in the process of constructing scales) is to include in a scale those items which show covariation over time rather than those which simply yield high cross-sectional correlations [Cobb, et al. (1970)].

Morale and life satisfaction. A number of life satisfaction measures are available and three of the briefer ones may be recommended here.[16] In addition, there have been several national or large sample surveys which have asked questions which have dealt with this general area.[17] The measures of alienation—anomie perhaps also belong into this general category (see Seaman).

There is some reason to believe, however, that the above scales may not be the most suitable ones for our purposes. For one, they have too much of a life review orientation and thus they may prove too stable and insensitive to changes produced by manpower programs. For another, such satisfaction measures do not adequately consider individual differences in goals and aspirations or the changes in these with increasing age. Thus, for example, the higher job satisfaction found among older workers by Riley and Foner appears to be primarily

---

[15] See Bradburn and Caplowitz, Gurin, et al., Kasl and Cobb (1966), and Schlingensiepen and Kasl.

[16] See Kutner, et al., Neugarten, et al., and Wood, et al.

[17] Included are Bradburn and Caplowitz, Cantril, Gurin, et al., and Srole, et al.

due to coming to terms with one's job aspirations and work goals. A most telling conclusion comes to us from a study by Bortner and Hultsch which analyzed correlates of life satisfaction on a national sample of adults. "Self-ratings reflecting opportunities to select goals and access to means for achieving goals were most predictive of life satisfaction." Similarly, Bickner has emphasized the point that health is a relativistic concept and that conceptualization and measurement must take into consideration the respondent's goals and responsibilities.

In our study of health effects of job loss, we have dealt with this issue by creating a self-anchoring scale. Basically, the man is presented with a set of dimensions such as feeling secure about the future, feelings of getting ahead in the world, getting a chance to use his best skills, learning new skills, sense of respect from others, sense of social support, and so on. For each of these dimensions, the respondent rates how things are right now and how he would like them to be. The discrepancy between these pairs of ratings has proven to be a sensitive indicator of satisfaction.[18]

Daily and leisure activities and social contacts. There is ample evidence that leisure activities and social interaction are closely related to life satisfaction, morale, self-evaluation, and self-assessed health.[19] These activities clearly have a close tie-in with the remainder of the person's life. Moreover, changes in social involvement are accompanied by corresponding changes in life satisfaction and morale, and greater continuity of activity patterns across periods of stress is associated with better morale.[20]

The following content areas should be measured: allocation of time to various activities of leisure and of daily living, and satisfaction with these; nature and frequency of contact with immediate family, friends, relatives, and club members, and the satisfaction derived from these; participation in civic and church affairs, "useful" activities, voting behavior; sleeping, eating, and exercise patterns; time spent napping and doing nothing. The most suitable measurement approach here appears to be the time budget technique (see Robinson).

Other suggestions and comments. The above listing completes my recommendations regarding the measurement of health (broadly defined) in a survey interview setting. My concern was with health as the outcome variable in future

[18]This section has omitted a specific discussion of job satisfaction measures. The literature on these is enormous but easily accessible. See, for example, the useful compilation by Robinson, et al. It is likely that each manpower program will need a special-purpose job satisfaction measure—if any—and no good purpose would be served here by a generalized discussion of such indexes.

[19]See: Havinghurst, Havinghurst and Feigenbaum, Kutner, et al., Maddox (1962), Riley and Foner, Shanas, Shanas, et al., Tobin and Neugarten, and Wilensky.

[20]See Britton, Havens, Maddox (1963), and Palmore.

studies of manpower programs. At this point, I want to add some brief suggestions regarding additional measures which might prove useful.

The programmatic, metatheoretical orientation which underlies the study of health effects of job loss represents a field-theoretical approach in which several categories of variables, other than the outcome variables, are thought to be important.[21] These include (1) variables describing the objective environment, both physical and social, and the changes in it; (2) variables describing the subjective environment (how the person perceives and evaluates his physical and social environment and the changes in it); and (3) enduring characteristics of the person, which can condition (modify) any of the following links: between the objective or subjective environment and mediating processes and reactions (proximal outcome variables); between objective or subjective environment and health (distal outcome variable); and between proximal and distal outcome variables. It is, of course, impossible to make concrete suggestions about the kinds of variables which ought to be measured in each of the above categories without knowing the details of a particular study of a manpower program, but it is felt that this listing is at least a useful reminder of the kinds of variables which could be important. Moreover, I shall try to illustrate below the role of each of these kinds of variables in the job loss study.

In a recent article entitled "Reforms as Experiments," Campbell puts forth a strong argument in favor of setting up experimental or the best quasiexperimental designs for testing the consequences of social ameliorative efforts. Along the way, he discusses the problem of social desirability in self-report measures (the phenomenon of grateful testimonials) collected on recipients of the treatment. Social desirability effects should be particularly strong when (1) the evaluative meaning of the response measure is obvious; (2) the recipient is identified by name with his answer; (3) the recipient gives the answer directly to the agent of reform; (4) the agent continues to be influential in the recipient's life in the future; (5) the answers deal with feelings and evaluations rather than verifiable facts; and (6) the recipient participating in the evaluation is self-selected or agent-selected from among all recipients.

Some of these sources of the social desirability effect can be overcome with better designs, but much of the problem remains in many self-report instruments. The issue is a complex one and the solution of using unobtrusive measures is seldom available to us.[22] Perhaps the best short-term solution is to include in our study a measure such as the Crowne-Marlowe index of the need for approval and then see to what extent the measure accounts for responses on the various self-report indexes.

---

[21] See Cobb et al. (1963) and French and Kahn.

[22] See Block, Norman and Webb, et al.

A Brief Description of the Study of
Health Effects of Job Loss: The
Design and Some Selected Findings[2][3]

The study is a longitudinal investigation of the health effects of job loss and the ensuing unemployment and/or job change. We were able to identify two plants which were going to shut down permanently and where all the employees would lose their jobs. In this way, we could accumulate a cohort of men whom we could then follow at regular intervals of up to two years as these men went through the states of anticipation of job loss, plant closing down and employment termination, unemployment (for most of them), probationary reemployment, and stable reemployment.

Our target population were all male blue-collar workers at these two plants who were married, in the age range of 35-60, and who had worked at the company at least 3 years. Of the men eligible for study, 79% agreed to participate.

The men are seen in their homes by public health nurses. The first nurse visit takes place some 6 weeks before scheduled plant closing; the men are still on their old jobs but they know about the impending shutdown. It is not unreasonable to call this the Anticipation Stage. At the next visit, some 6 weeks after plant closing, the men are either unemployed, or they have found a new job but are still in the probationary period of employment. With later visits (15 weeks, 38 weeks and one year after the closing), more and more men have found new jobs and stabilized their employment situation. Some men, however, experience additional job loss, or get laid off, or go through a voluntary job change. The last visit takes place some 2 years after loss of original job.

During the course of each visit to the man's home, the nurse collects blood and urine specimens, takes blood pressure, pulse rate, height and weight, and uses a structured interview schedule to collect diverse social-psychological and health data. These include his current employment situation, his economic circumstances, his subjective evaluation of his job and financial situation, questionnaire measures of mental health and affective reactions, and physical health data.

The design of the study also calls for the use of controls who are continuously employed men in comparable jobs. They are followed for the same length of time and exactly the same assessment procedures are used.

The men who lost their jobs came from 2 companies. Company A was a paint manufacturing plant located in a large metropolitan area. The men were largely machine operators, assistants in laboratory, and clerks in shipping department; the work was relatively light for most of them. Company B was located in a rural community of some 3,000 people. It manufactured display fixtures used by wholesale and retail concerns, and the men were machine operators, assembly line workers, and a few tool and die workers. The major difference between the 2 companies is the urban versus rural location of the plants.

---

[23] For a more complete description of the study see Cobb, et al. (1966).

The controls came from 4 different companies and were quite comparable to the cases on major demographic characteristics, type of work they did, and the rural versus urban distinction.

The men experienced an average of about 15 weeks of unemployment during the two years following the closing of the plants. In Company A, the experience during the first year was less severe: 25% of the men experienced no unemployment and another 50% had less than 2 months of unemployment. In Company B, the men had a more difficult time finding a job: even some 3-4 months after plant closing, one-third of the men were without a job. By the end of the first year, the men in Company B had experienced an average of 12 weeks of unemployment in contrast to 7 weeks for Company A.

Let us now turn to some of the relevant findings. We shall be primarily interested in changes over time and in the sensitivity of our measures to reflect the major changes in the men's lives: anticipation, job loss, unemployment, probationary reemployment, and stable reemployment. The data on the controls are primarily used to determine seasonal fluctuations and to establish certain baseline measures. All of the results discussed below are seasonally adjusted (when necessary). The reader is referred to other reports of the study for more detail.[24]

Each round of contacts with the cases consists of two nurse visits two weeks apart. During this time, the men keep a health diary with a daily record of their health. One of the measures derived from this health diary is days complaint: a count of the number of days out of 14 on which the respondent checked off that he did not "feel as well as usual." This measure showed the following significant fluctuations. (1) During Phase 1, Anticipation, the men show elevated levels (i.e., higher than controls). (2) The men show a drop from Anticipation to Phase 2, show a rise again between Phases 2 and 3 and then finally come down during the stabilization period of Phases 4 and 5. (3) In an overall comparison of Phases 1, 2 and 3 with 4 and 5, the days complaint are, for the latter phases, lower in 82% of all the cases.

Additional analyses revealed that the differential objective employment experience of the cases had only a slight effect on the pattern of these changes. For example, those men who go from anticipation to employment on a new job during Phase 2 show a somewhat larger drop than those who go on to unemployment at Phase 2, but the difference was not significant.

In contrast, a subjective rating of the severity of the job loss experience did show an association with the magnitude of these changes. One year after plant closing, the men were asked: "How long do you think it took you before things got pretty much back to normal?" Those men who indicated a slow return to normal were those who showed a significantly smaller drop from Phases 1, 2 and 3 to 4 and 5 than those who indicated a faster return to normal. It is also interesting to note that men who scored poorly on a general measure of adjustment,

---

[24] See Cobb, et al. (1966, 1970), Cobb and Kasl (1971), Kasl and Cobb (1970, 1971), and Kasl, et al.

ego strength, showed a significantly smaller drop between Phases 1, 2 and 3, and 4 and 5 than those whose adjustment was good.

Another measure which was coded from the health diary was number of illnesses. The coding here is primarily based on the contiguity of days of not feeling as well as usual and the clustering of symptoms which are described during a probe. This measure is similar to days complaint, of course. It has a lower mean, the variance of scores is lower, and the probe for symptoms makes it a more focused measure than the more general days complaint. The analysis of the data on number of illnesses replicated all of the patterns of changes with phases described above for days complaint. We also found the association with the subjective rating of the severity of the job loss experience and with the ego strength measure.

The next measure, also based on the health diary, is number of days of illness disability. It is a count of the number of days out of 14 when the man didn't carry on usual activities due to illness. It meant that he was in the hospital, home in bed, or at least stayed in the house even though not in bed. It reflects not how the man felt but what he did or didn't do about it. This measure showed the same pattern of fluctuations as days complaint, but they were smaller, less reliable, and not so consistent across the 2 companies. Another way to look at this measure is to treat it as percent of days complaint which are also days illness disability. Among the controls, the overall value is about 26%. Among the cases in Company A, the value is very low during the anticipation stage and the early stressful phases and approaches the value of the controls only in Phases 4 and 5. The cases in Company B show a different pattern, in particular a high value during anticipation.

Several conclusions about the days illness disability measure appear reasonable. First, it appears less reliably sensitive to the objective stresses in the men's lives. Moreover, it shows different patterns of fluctuations in the two companies. From other data, we have good evidence that the men in the rural plant had a much better sense of social support from spouses and friends as they went through the stressful times than did the men in the urban plant. Perhaps this difference in the social setting influences the behavior of exempting oneself from carrying on usual activities. Finally, we have also been able to show that the index, percent days complaints which are also days illness disability, is related to the level of depression: more depressed men are more likely to exempt themselves from carrying on usual activities. In short, the measure, days illness disability, indicates what a man does about his perceived state of health and as such is sensitive not only to the stresses of the situation in which he finds himself but also to the social environment in which he lives and to such affective state variables as depression.

We have looked at other measures which indicate the activity a person may undertake as a result of his perceptions of his health. One measure, still based on the health diary, is days saw doctor, i.e., the number of days out of 14 on which the respondent saw a doctor. This measure has too many zero scores to enable one to perform an adequate analysis of the data. Within these limits, however, this measure showed fluctuations with time like those described above for days illness disability. Another measure, also based on the health diary, was days used drugs. This measure did not show very striking fluctuations over time—perhaps partly because there are strong individual differences in the habit of taking drugs, such as aspirin, tranquilizers, or laxatives. However, what fluctuation there was suggested a pattern of higher drug use during Phases 2 and 3. It will be recalled that only Phase 3 is high on days complaint and days illness disability.

The kinds of data which we collected from the health diary were also obtained elsewhere during the interview, but the period of time about which we asked was "during the last 3 months." The measures based on this longer period of time appear much less sensitive and useful than those based on the two-week health diary.

We have also discovered that the traditional symptom checklist approach—an index consisting of such symptoms as dizzy spells, heart beating hard, shortness of breath without cause—also is relatively insensitive and useless in picking up and reflecting what is happening in the men's lives.

Our indexes of the men's mood and affective states show a relatively poor overall sensitivity to the changes in the objective experience. More definite relationships, however, are detectible when one takes into consideration the subjective evaluation of the job loss experience and such stable personality traits as ego strength. We also have good indication from our data that fluctuations in mood and affect are correlated with changes in our physiological variables, and that classifying individuals according to types of reactions (guilt and depression versus anger and resentment) will also prove very useful in understanding the overall changes in health and physiological variables. But for sheer sensitivity to the changes in the employment experiences, some direct measures of perceived stress (such as a life graph technique of describing fluctuations in well-being) are much better than the affect and mood scales.

Our broad life satisfaction measure, in which the respondent indicates where things are right now and how he would like them to be, has proven to be a particularly sensitive indicator. It has, for example, clearly shown us the big difference in the fluctuations in sense of social support from spouse and friends, which exists between the urban and rural companies. We have also seen that on those components of this measure which deal with the perceptions of the future and optimism about it, that even one and two years later, the men are showing high dissatisfaction, even as the physiological indicators have all come down. It is as if in this domain, there had been a permanently damaging effect of the job loss experience.

Obviously, much remains to be done before we can have a clear picture of the overall effects of this important social stress. In particular, we wish to be able to partition these overall effects into several components: (1) those due to experiences shared by all cases (e.g., anticipation and plant closing); (2) those due to differences in the two companies (e.g., the urban-rural contrast); (3) those due to variations in the objective stress experience (e.g., number of weeks unemployed or number of job changes); (4) those due to individual variations in subjective evaluation of the stressful events; and (5) those due to stable characteristics of the person, either demographic variables (e.g., age, race, job skills) or personality traits (e.g., general adjustment, flexibility-rigidity).

Measures of the Impact on
Health: Comment

Thomas N. Chirikos

Professor Kasl is to be commended for his able survey of a vast and steadily growing body of literature on health status measures as well as for the summary of his research on the health effects of job loss. As such, this paper is a useful contribution to persons engaged in manpower program evaluation, because many will be able to use it as a guide into a new, and to the novice, a potentially threatening field. Having spent time wading through this literature myself, I find it difficult to quarrel with Professor Kasl's coverage, taxonomy, or critique of specific health status measures. I do feel, however, that a principal point of the paper was not sufficiently emphasized, and in the brief space allotted, I should like to underscore this point and suggest a few of its implications.

Simply put, I fear that Professor Kasl has not adequately stressed how difficult it is to measure health status over time, nor has he emphasized the general limitations of many, if not all, of the suggested measures which might indicate some reasonable notion of health status in outcome or impact terms. The need for such emphasis does not, of course, stem from some form of editorial imperative. Rather, it relates to a problem that may not be fully appreciated outside of the health field, but one that is clearly and critically linked to the discussion of manpower evaluation. The problem is that the entire health policy and programming area itself has been, and continues to be, plagued by the absence of readily available or measurable evaluation criteria. Indeed, many of the suggested measures in Professor Kasl's paper have been proposed with this specific purpose in mind. The fact is, however, that we are still some considerable distance from being able to specify (even crudely) the outcome or impact of traditional health service programs, (i.e., public health programs, physician and hospital services, etc.) on health status. Needless to say, such a judgment of the state-of-the-art in a situation where health presumably is directly related to program activity does not augur well for the evaluation of second-order effects as is the case between health and manpower programs.

I do not wish to imply that the difficulties of relating health outcomes to social programs are insuperable, or that manpower program evaluations should preclude *a priori* any assessment of these effects. Indeed, only through these kinds of applied research efforts will new or improved concepts and measurement techniques emerge. But a realistic appraisal of the current state-of-the-art suggests that the value (at the margin) of such policy information to decision-makers is not likely to be great and may, in fact, be exceeded by the cost of obtaining it. If one assumes that the principal purpose of evaluation studies is to provide information inputs into the decision-making process, then there ought to be a reasonable expectation that the results of analyzing any given set of direct or indirect effects may make a difference in policy terms. My concern is that our conceptual and technical capacity for assessing health effects in broad terms is so limited at the present time, that there is no reasonable expectation that the results will make any difference.

Given these difficulties, it may be more appropriate to limit the evaluation of health effects in certain ways. One possibility would be to explore the relationship between health status and income in greater depth. There is, of course, ample evidence that health (at least, as traditionally measured by mortality and morbidity rates) and income are positively related; in fact, there recently have been suggestions that income and related variables such as educational attainment may profitably be used as proxies for health status measures at the community level [Yett, et al.]. No one is quite sure, however, which way the causality runs in this relationship nor do we understand the full range of behavioral differences between high- and low-income families which affect their health. Since one of the avowed goals of manpower programs is to promote the employment and hence the incomes of program participants, it would seem appropriate to evaluate the health effects of raising incomes, particularly in terms of behavior that may be conducive to better health. I have in mind here, for instance, the effects of income on specific variables as nutrition and diet, housing, and the access to adequate medical care. Clearly, such an approach will furnish partial information at best, but since it focuses upon a key variable of manpower programs, it may well yield more to the policy-maker than a broader gauged assessment.

Another possibility would be to limit the evaluation of health effects to a consideration of health status as an input into manpower programs rather than as an output or outcome. This shift in focus stems from the possibility that some manpower programs (e.g., the WIN Program) will be forced to grapple with the relationship between health status and employability. If manpower programs build in such services, it would seem essential to evaluate the nature of the health-employability relationship as well as the effectiveness of alternative programs in dealing with the problem. While the nature of this type of evaluation is clearly of a different order than evaluations discussed previously, it is surely an important task and one that would be of mutual benefit to those in both the manpower and health fields.

8

Measures of the Impact on Education

Gerald G. Somers and Ernst W. Stromsdorfer

The primary objectives of most United States programs in the manpower field are to further employment opportunities and income. In the past decade, these policies have focused on the poor and disadvantaged, with an emphasis on youth. The principal benefits proposed for youth—and, therefore, the basic measures of success—have been in their labor market performance following completion of a manpower program. In spite of the emphasis on youth, the direct impact of manpower policies on education has been accorded a secondary role; and any educational benefits which might accrue from enrollment in a manpower program have been appraised primarily for their contribution to subsequent employment and income.

The major manpower measure with an explicit educational objective is the in-school and summer Neighborhood Youth Corps (NYC). Whereas the out-of-school NYC is geared more toward improving employability than encouraging a return to school, the in-school and summer programs have the "overriding objective . . . to keep boys and girls in school until they graduate from high school, by providing them with supplementary income" [U.S. Department of Labor (1970), p. 9]. The effects of NYC participation are measured in terms of prevention of dropouts or in terms of the years of high school completed. Although success or failure of the program might also be evaluated through changes in grades, attitudes toward further education, interpersonal school relationships or delinquent behavior, some of these outcomes do not readily lend themselves to statistical measures. Thus, the impact on continued school attendance has been the principal basis for evaluative research.

The system of vocational education in the United States predates the enactment of current manpower programs and it is not customarily classed among such programs. One reason for this is its administrative location in the Department of Health, Education and Welfare rather than in the Department of Labor. However, the principal thrust of vocational education, as well as the use of the vocational system for institutional training in a number of manpower programs, leaves no doubt that vocational education shares the goals of manpower policies in enhancing labor market opportunities. In many countries, vocational education is administered jointly with employment policies.

At the same time, vocational education, as envisaged in the federal enactments of 1963 and 1968, has important educational objectives. Vocational and technical programs at the high school, posthigh school and junior college levels provide flexibility and educational options. While preparing students for employ-

111

ment at various junctures in which they might enter the labor market, the vocational curricula may retain a potential dropout in the educational process, thereby enhancing the possibilities of further education if circumstances and preferences should so dictate.

The extent to which students continue their education after graduation from a vocational program may be construed as one measure of the educational effects of enrollment in vocational training. As in the case of the NYC program, the effects of such additional education on future employment and earnings represent a measure of the total impact of the manpower aspects of vocational education. It is this interaction of manpower policies and educational policies that calls for the most sophisticated evaluative measures.

A third area in which manpower policies and educational policies converge is in the basic education programs—compensatory reading and writing instruction for those with severe educational handicaps which limit their employment opportunities. Basic education programs have been included in the Manpower Development and Training Act, the Economic Opportunity Act, the Vocational Education Act and a number of other federal, state and community programs [Greenleigh Associates (1968a)].

In measuring the impact of basic education programs, the evaluator with a manpower bent wants to know whether manpower training enhances the value of the compensatory education, and vice versa. To what extent does basic education improve the labor market performance when separated from or coupled with manpower policies?

Thus, this paper is concerned with measures of the effects of the interaction of manpower policies and education in the Neighborhood Youth Corps, the Vocational Education Acts and the basic education programs. In each case, there are important employment objectives and educational objectives. Rather than focus only on the impact of the manpower programs on education, we have interpreted our mandate more broadly to discuss evaluative measures of the interaction of manpower and educational policies in achieving both educational and labor market goals.

In each case, the discussion draws heavily on research which has recently been conducted at the University of Wisconsin.

The Neighborhood Youth Corps[1]

The In-School and Summer NYC has the following complex of manpower and educational objectives:

1. to increase the probability of high school graduation;
2. to increase the efficiency of learning while in high school;

---

[1] Based primarily on Somers and Stromsdorfer. The study design, selection of samples and other aspects of methodology are specified in Chapters 2 and 3.

3. to increase the option value of return to high school,[2] and
4. to increase the student's future earnings by improvements in his labor market efficiency, through such factors as improved labor market discipline, skills learned on the job, or through additional education.

It is notable that the principal premise by which these goals are to be achieved is that students from low-income families will be induced to continue their high school education if the opportunity costs of continued attendance are reduced by giving them jobs.

There were four measures of educational impact used in our national follow-up survey of NYC participants and control groups: 1) probability of high school graduation; 2) number of years of high school completed; 3) probability of college attendance; and 4) probability of postsecondary education other than college. Multiple regression models were used to measure the net impact of the NYC program on these indexes of educational benefit. In addition to NYC participation, the regression models control for the effects of age, income per capita per family, urban-rural place of residence during school, number of times the respondent dropped out of high school, father's education, ethnic origin, sex, and a discriminant function (designed to reduce bias due to differences between the experimental and control groups).[3]

Using this analysis, the NYC program taken as a whole has a zero effect on the probability of high school graduation and years of high school completed. When subgroups are studied separately, only black females and American Indians experience a positive effect on their probability of graduation from high school. The positive effect for blacks is due solely to the experience of black females.[4] These results are found in regression models which express NYC participation in dummy variable form. Use of a dummy variable formulation means that every NYC participant has the same weight in the analysis regardless of whether he was in the program a long or a short period of time.

When NYC participation is expressed as a continuous variable in terms of number of months in the program, the NYC program is seen to have a small positive effect. Namely, one additional month in the NYC tends to add one extra day in school attendance.

However, the NYC program has a positive and relatively large effect on the probability of college attendance or other postsecondary education for those NYC participants who graduate from high school. Since our labor market analysis shows significant earnings benefits for NYC graduates, this suggests that the

---

[2] See Weisbrod (1964), Appendix C for a discussion of the option value of education.

[3] See Somers and Stromsdorfer, pp. 133-142, for a discussion of the discriminant function and its estimation.

[4] This finding for black females conflicts with that of Robin in his study of black NYC participants in Cincinnati.

higher earnings due to participation in the NYC may have been partly responsible for enrollment in further education.

The regression analysis also permits us to measure the relationship between income and continued education—a basic assumption of the NYC program. It appears that the premise upon which the NYC program is based may be an incorrect one. There is a gross positive relationship between income per capita per family and graduation from high school. However, when the total sample is broken down into various sociodemographic subgroups and income per capita per family is considered in conjunction with other sociodemographic variables, in almost every case the effect of the income variable on high school graduation is zero or negative. Thus, for those persons still in high school, the family income variable may not be the most important variable affecting dropout behavior. It may be the case that approaches other than raising family income may be needed to change the propensity of students to drop out. In fact, small amounts of work and earnings may simply whet the student's appetite for full-time work.

However, once a person has graduated from high school, earnings per NYC participant do appear to be an influence on one's likelihood of going on to college or some other form of postsecondary education.

Finally, as noted above, other measures of educational impact, such as grade point average and classroom attitudes could also be utilized, but this was not done in our study. Nor did we carry out detailed analysis of the effects of further education on future employment and earnings, since the average follow-up period of about 18 months was too short to do so.

The measures used indicate that direct economic benefits of the NYC program are more important than the direct educational benefit of continued high school attendance for the sample as a whole and for major sociodemographic subgroups. This finding is generally confirmed by other research utilizing measures of the in-school NYC impact on continued education in high school [U.S. Department of Labor (1970), pp. 9, 10].

Vocational Education[5]

National samples of graduates of vocational programs in high schools, posthigh vocational schools and junior colleges were surveyed in 1969, three years after their graduation. Comparisons were made with a control sample of graduates of academic programs drawn from the same schools or localities. Although the principal focus was on analyses of labor market experience during the three-year follow-up period, efforts were also made to measure the factors influencing the decision to take additional education after graduation from various vocational technical programs. Additional education, in turn, was entered as one of the independent variables in regression equations designed to explain differences in

---

[5] Based on Somers (1971). Sampling and methodology are discussed in Chapter 2.

wages on the first job and on the last job in the three-year period. As in the case of the NYC follow-up survey, other measures of the quantity and quality of additional education might have been utilized, but the survey data and research resources limited these possibilities.

The principal contribution of the research is to pinpoint the differences in postgraduate experience after vocational programs in high school, posthigh vocational school and junior college. Based on cross-tabulations, it appears that relatively few graduates of postsecondary vocational schools (6%) and junior college vocational programs (13%) go directly to full-time or part-time education immediately after their vocational graduation. As might be expected, a larger proportion of high school vocational graduates (29%) than posthigh school graduates take additional schooling after graduation and a larger proportion of graduates of high school academic programs than vocational programs (53%) move directly into full-time or part-time education.

However, many of those who went on to full-time education directly after their vocational graduation spent a substantial proportion of the three-year survey period in full-time employment as well: junior college vocational graduates—75%; posthigh vocational graduates—46%; high school vocational graduates—51%; and high school academic graduates—44%.

When regression results are examined, the probability of some additional education after graduation from a vocational program is significantly greater for those who graduate from junior college, as compared with high school vocational graduates, and it is significantly less for those who graduate from a postsecondary vocational school. These results differ from the simple cross-tabulations with the introduction of such intervening explanatory variables as geographic region, vocational program area, relatedness of first and last job to training field, the socioeconomic status of the first job (SES), father's education, sex, age, marital status, race, the rural-urban (size)—suburban setting of the school, and the student's grade point average in the vocational school. Although a number of the remaining partial regression coefficients have the expected sign (interpreted as probabilities of taking additional education), only sex, marital status and grade point average are statistically significant.

It should be noted, however, that the independent variables, taken as a whole, explain only about one-third of the variance in probability of taking additional education. Moreover, the impact of school level is such that when separate regressions are run for junior college, postsecondary and high school graduates, even the significance of sex, marital status and grade point average is removed, although their signs generally remain the same as in the regression for the total sample.

The variable, "additional education" was entered along with the other variables included above to explain differences in the vocational graduate's wage rate on his job at the time of interview. The results indicate that additional education after vocational graduation adds significantly (approximately 30 cents per hour) to the wage of high school graduates. But relative to vocational high school graduates, additional education makes no positive contribution to the wage of post-high and junior college vocational program graduates on the job held three years after their vocational graduation.[6] Of course, a longer period of follow-up might produce different results.

One might tentatively conclude, however, that a substantial number of graduates of high school vocational programs take additional education and that this adds significantly to their wage income within three years after their high school graduation. Relatively few posthigh vocational graduates take additional education, and, for those who do there is no enhancement of wage rates within three years. Although the graduates of junior college vocational programs are even more likely to take additional education than high school vocational graduates, their wage rate three years after junior college is no higher than that of their counterparts who went directly into the labor market after junior college.

Basic Education[7]

Efforts to measure the benefits of basic education programs have been almost entirely in terms of improvement in the reading achievement or other educational achievement levels of the trainees. This research, utilizing before-and-after achievement tests, has almost always shown some improvement in achievement levels attributable to the compensatory education. However, the test measures have seldom shown great leaps forward in reading and other literacy tests; and in the absence of measures of labor market impact, the question remains as to the manpower impact of basic education, i.e., its effects on employment and earnings.

Only a few studies have attempted to examine the labor market performance of basic education enrollees, and with varying degrees of rigor in the research design, the results have been conflicting. The Milwaukee follow-up evaluation permitted Myron Roomkin to adopt a more analytical approach in one case study.

Roomkin reports the results of regressing posteducation average hourly earnings (E) on eleven specified regressors for 69 male and 100 female observations separately. The model is found to explain 33% of the variance in $\overline{E}$ for male participants in the study, and approximately 20% of the variance in $\overline{E}$ for females. The multiple correlation coefficients (R^2) for the analyses are statistically significant at the .10 and .05 levels for the male and female equations, respectively.

Concentrating on the earnings effect of basic education, the analysis shows

[6] For a similar result, see Corazzini.

[7] Based primarily on Roomkin, Greenleigh Associates (1966), Greenleigh Associates (1968b), and Anderson and Niemi.

that males experience an increased wage rate of 52 cents per hour and females gain five cents per hour. Unfortunately, these coefficients are not significantly different from zero at the .05 level of significance.

Roomkin's analysis also shows that vocational training, when taken in addition to basic education, but not coordinated with it, adds to female earnings but not to male earnings. A possible explanation is seen in the fact that achievement tests show that male graduates of basic education programs who enter vocational training are the less able students. To some extent, vocational training may be utilized for further compensation by those who gain little from basic education, but even this is not enough to improve their earnings.

Roomkin concludes that his findings agree with those of other studies of compensatory education or efforts to induce dropouts to return to school.[8] The economic returns on such an investment are usually very small. Short-term basic education programs, unless closely integrated with other manpower skill training, preferably on-the-job, are not likely to raise achievement levels or employer desires sufficiently to improve the enrollees' economic welfare.

Conclusions

The measures discussed above relate to the interaction of manpower policies and educational attainment primarily in terms of marketplace criteria. Generally, they show that short-term manpower policies are not very effective in inducing further education that will enhance future earnings, and short-term basic education is not very effective in achieving the goals of manpower policy aimed at improving employment and earnings.

More research and more sophisticated measures may well reach contrary conclusions. More detailed analysis by larger samples of sociodemographic subgroups may give more positive results, as in the case of black females. Noneconomic measures may also point in more favorable directions. However, it may also be that the approach adopted in many of the manpower educational policies for the disadvantaged should be changed. The relationship between work experience, income maintenance, vocational training and basic education is complex; and programs that hope to advance labor market performance by concentrating on any one of these approaches, with the hope that they will somehow merge effectively with the others, may not succeed. A more carefully planned and rigorously designed integration of manpower and educational policies may be needed to further the employment and earnings of the disadvantaged.

Our measures of the labor market value of postsecondary vocational education are conflicting. There appears to be a significant return for high school graduates who go on, but our three-year time period of analysis was too short to assess any wage benefits for junior college vocational graduates who transfer to a

---

[8] See Weisbrod (1965), Ribich, pp. 34-60, and Hansen, Weisbrod and Scanlon.

four-year college or university. Few graduates of postsecondary vocational schools take additional education, and this appears to be a rational decision. There is some evidence that this form of vocational education is not as efficient in cost-benefit terms as vocational courses at the other two school levels; and there is no wage advantage in taking additional postsecondary vocational education compared to high school and junior college vocational graduates.[9]

The measures discussed in this paper have all of the advantages and disadvantages of the analysis of investments in human capital. They permit some precision and provide some worthwhile inputs for a broader evaluation. But it must be recognized that they do not include noneconomic satisfactions, attitudes and other welfare considerations. Moreover, as noted in the preceding paragraphs, the measures do not fully cope with the heterogeneous and complex character of investments in human capital. The multiple outputs of manpower programs such as the returns to work experience, manpower training and education cannot be simply aggregated. The combined return is crucially determined by the timing of each of these investments and the procedures and supportive services by which they are combined.

However, these are limitations of the present state of the analysis of human capital, and advances in the measurement of the impact of manpower—education programs are linked to advances in the theoretical underpinnings.

---

[9] Although details of the cost-benefit analysis and returns to human capital investment have not been included here, these results, presented in the larger reports, generally confirm the findings of the above analyses.

Measures of the Impact on
Education : Comment

Howard Rosen

Professors Somers and Stromsdorfer attempted to measure the effectiveness of the Neighborhood Youth Corps (NYC) in keeping participants in school until they graduate, the success of vocational education in getting students to continue their education after graduation, and basic education's ability to improve labor market performance when separated or coupled with manpower programs.

The major criticism that can be directed toward the Somers-Stromsdorfer paper raises an interesting philosophical point in the evaluation of social programs. Can we measure the effectiveness of programs if the participants in the program may not agree on the objective or even be unaware of the purpose of the program? Congress may have stipulated the objectives, the administrators implementing the program may be agreed on the objectives, but the participants may not be in agreement with what we are trying to achieve. One may ask why should the participants in a NYC program finish school if they see no need for a diploma and believe that they will not be considered for a job which may require this type of credential?

This suggests that if people are in a contest, all the participants should agree on the measurements to be used in determining who won and they should also agree what winning means. Without this kind of understanding, we really do not know what we have evaluated.[1]

The Somers and Stromsdorfer paper also raises some interesting questions about approaches to evaluative research. One approach suggests that effectiveness can be measured by simply comparing two variables—for example, the ability of a program to keep a youngster in school as compared with economic benefits. This approach as noted by the authors of this paper, omits variables such as grade point averages, classroom attitudes, and the effects of further education on future employment and earnings. Thus, there may have been other variables not measured which were more significant in affecting the results than the variables that were measured.

---

[1] Somers and Stromsdorfer could have also moved evaluative research ahead if they had avoided cloaking their research with professional jargon or theory. To say, ". . . the principal premise by which these goals (NYC) are to be achieved is that students from low-income families will be induced to continue their high school education if the *opportunity costs* of continued attendance are reduced by giving them jobs." is a simplistic mis-use of perfectly good economic principles to a situation to which they are not applicable. One can talk about General Motors' opportunity costs or a middle-income white youngster's opportunity costs but the application of this principle to the NYC youngsters is highly questionable. The alternative opportunities available to the NYC youngsters were not explored by Somers and Stromsdorfer. It does appear that they may have applied their own economic and social standards to a group of youngsters whose job outlook, income, job opportunities, social life and patterns of behavior were far removed from their own.

The second approach suggests that measurements of effectiveness of programs such as NYC should not and cannot be conducted without taking into account socioeconomic variables such as attitudes of participants, family structure, size of family, participation in welfare programs, employment experience, life patterns, physical surroundings of schools, quality and kind of teaching, aspirations and expectation of participants, attitudes of teachers, reaction of peers and parents toward education and the value system of the ghetto.

Somers and Stromsdorfer could have made a more significant contribution to the literature of evaluative research if they would have provided their readers with some basic information about the participants in the programs they studied. For example, one may ask whether the authors had an obligation to note that one-third of the NYC participants were living in female-headed households, almost 40% of the youngsters were in families with eight or more persons, one-third came from families living on public assistance and 40% of the young people had never had a paying job before their NYC experience.

In turning to the authors' evaluation of vocational education, one is immediately struck by their failure to examine the meshing of vocational curricula with colleges, universities, junior colleges or technical institutes. Somers and Stromsdorfer discovered that relatively few graduates of postsecondary vocational schools and junior college vocational programs go on to full-time or part-time education. Before generalizing about their findings, they should explore whether graduates of postsecondary vocational schools can move directly into a college curriculum and get full credit for their previous education. There may be obstacles to transference which may explain why more of the graduates of vocational curricula do not go on for advanced education.

One other piece of information which could be useful is whether their graduates aspired to advanced education or wanted to move into occupations requiring additional education. Again, this is another case of determining whose values are we studying? Is it right for us to assess programs unless we know the total pattern in which the participants and the world in which they live are understood?

In their exploration of basic education, the authors concluded that economic returns of an investment in compensatory education are usually very small. They make the point that unless this short-term education is closely integrated with other manpower training, it is not likely to raise achievement levels or the enrollees' economic welfare. Somers and Stromsdorfer need to emphasize that the need for compensatory education may be related to and caused by a complex set of problems. The inability to read or write may have been caused by psychological, physical and social problems which will not disappear even if, as a result of a compensatory course, we are able to raise reading and writing achievement levels.

Basic education is just one of the deficiencies found in the clientele of manpower programs. Even when the education is integrated with other manpower training, the people we are trying to help carry with them habits, reactions and attitudes which may offset increases in achievement. On the other hand, we too often put the blame on the participants in the programs of not doing more with their newly acquired education and training. We need to direct more of our attention to the institutions which failed to educate and train them in the first place. We also need to further examine the set of obstacles that are placed before them when they apply for jobs. These obstacles include irrelevant tests, the prejudice of employers and closed labor markets.

To summarize my reaction to the Somers-Stromsdorfer paper:

1. We need to know considerably more about the values of the people we are studying.
2. We need to make sure that there is agreement about the objectives that we are trying to achieve in manpower programs.
3. We need to be more sophisticated in our evaluation by recognizing the limitations of short-term intervention of counseling, education and training on life-long experiences and habits. Even the effects of these short-term interventions cannot be understood or measured until we make greater use of long-term evaluation studies of those exposed to manpower programs.

Above all, there is a great need to acknowledge that we are still novices in conducting evaluations of manpower programs. We must be the first to explain the strength and weakness of our evaluations to harried administrators who so desperately need sound advice in making decisions.

9

Measures of the Impact on Crime

John J. McDonnell

The past decade has been marked by steadily increasing crime rates; growing concern over the problems facing the correctional systems of the country; and, a realization that the existing criminal justice system is unable to respond to the current demands being placed on it, let alone those forecast for the decade ahead. It has generally been agreed that without major changes in this system, these problems are destined to become even more severe. It seems clear that changes must be made and, in fact, some changes are already being introduced. One area in which changes are being made, with moderately encouraging results, is the use of manpower programs as a strategy in offender rehabilitation.

There is abundant evidence and theory supporting these endeavors, based on the following propositions:

1. postrelease success, in terms of reduced criminal activity, is critically related to the employment skills and potentials of offenders;
2. employment skills and potentials are improved through manpower programs; and
3. therefore, offenders who receive manpower program services are less likely to be involved in criminal activity once they are released.

It is on these foundations that manpower programs have been developed to reduce criminal activity among released offenders.

For the past two and one half years, Abt Associates has conducted an evaluation of vocational training provided in correctional institutions under the Manpower Development and Training Act (MDTA) Section 251.[1] This was a large-scale evaluation which included an analysis of the program's impact as well as other matters. In this discussion, we will draw on the experience gained in that study to point out some areas of special concern and to suggest some recommended approaches to measuring certain aspects of this impact. It is hoped that these suggestions will be useful to others concerned with such impact evaluations, and will permit a better understanding of some critical factors, thereby leading to improved measurement of impact and analysis of the factors which influence it.

[1]See McDonnell, et al.; this evaluation was conducted for the Office of Policy, Evaluation and Research, Manpower Administration, U.S. Department of Labor.

Level of Investigation

The impact of manpower programs on crime is lacking in specificity. Since we are interested in measurement, we must define more precisely what is to be measured. In my opinion, there are two approaches which may be taken to measuring this impact. One is analogous to the macro analytic, or national aggregations approach to economics; the other is analogous to the micro analytic, or individual participant approach to economics.

Following the macro approach, one could consider crime in the aggregate and focus on such summary statistics as the FBI's Uniform Crime Reports. This report presents crime rates for most of the large metropolitan areas of the country. Changes in these aggregate statistics over time could then be examined in light of changes in the levels and types of manpower programs operating in the area during that time. Such an approach to measuring impact has innumerable difficulties, among them: changes in criminal activity indexes reflect not only real changes in criminal activity, but also variations due to the changing importance placed on reporting such activity; redefinition of criminal activity; and, steadily changing populations in the area. For such reasons, we do not encourage the use of a macro approach to measuring the impact of manpower programs on crime.

Instead, we recommend that impact measurement be made at the micro level, focusing on the individuals who have received manpower program services that may reduce their inclination toward criminal activity.

The next question is: what individuals should be considered? In theory, all those receiving manpower program services could be considered since they, like everyone else, have some law-breaking tendencies which may be nothing more than occasionally exceeding a speed limit while driving. However, until further advances have been made in measuring an individual's criminal tendencies, it would be difficult to detect any changes in these tendencies which could occur after receiving manpower program services. For these reasons, it seems more appropriate to concentrate on those individuals who have exhibited rather clearly defined criminal tendencies, namely those who have been convicted of crimes. Throughout this discussion, we will be considering only these individuals, although the general approach is also applicable to those who have been arrested.

We should also recognize, however, that manpower programs for these individuals have other impacts as well. To the extent that these programs tend to reduce the overall crime levels, they clearly have an impact on society in general, and especially on the entire criminal justice system, including police, courts, prisons and parole sectors. Unfortunately, discussion of impact in these areas is beyond the scope of this paper.

Having defined a microapproach to the measurement of impact, and having identified the individuals to be measured, we can now address some important questions which must be answered before any measurements can be made. The remainder of this discussion is devoted to the consideration of these questions, along with recommended answers and techniques for relating the manpower program services to the individual's criminal activity.

Definition of Variables

Throughout this discussion, we will be concerned with conventional crime, as distinguished from organized crime, business crimes and other kinds of crime that involve different kinds of activities and consequences, and that are unlikely to be influenced by conventional manpower programs. Conventional crime, according to Korn and McCorkle, refers to acts of law-breaking which are known to, and acted upon by the police; all other acts which violate laws are not criminal. Such criminal acts can be conveniently classified into two categories:

economic, i.e., crimes against property, including burglary, larceny, robbery, paper crimes and auto theft; and

non-economic, i.e., all other crimes, including assault, drugs, alcohol, homicide, manslaughter, sex crimes, and miscellaneous crimes and misdemeanors.

Now let us consider the measure of impact. Traditionally, recidivism has been used as the measure of a program's impact on an individual's tendencies toward criminal activity. On this subject, Conrad has said that:

programs are designed to do two things: to offset the damage done by the artificial experience of confinement, and to change the offender into a person no more likely to commit an offense than any other normal citizen. To test these programs, statistical tables of recidivism of increasing sophistication are developed. A good program will be reflected somehow in lower recidivism; an ineffective program will not [p. 171].

Thus, recidivism seems to be the most appropriate measure of impact.[2] This may seem like a very simple and straightforward measure, yet it has its own complexities.

First of all, it is necessary to distinguish among the various levels and stages in criminal cases. Nathan Mandel has suggested the following typology:

---

[2] Conrad goes on to say, however: "We do not propose that recidivism should be abandoned as a measurement. But we do question whether the messages conveyed by tables of recidivism can be clearly understood in their present forms. The efficacy of correctional service is only one among many forces impinging upon the offender after his release. It may play no part in his success; it may play a limited part, or it may have a crucial influence. It is necessary to establish expectations for different kinds of offender"[p. 298]. This is sound advice and later in this discussion, we will suggest an alternative approach to analyzing recidivism data which takes account of these concerns.

I Convicted for commission of felony
II Returned to custody as violator of parole
   —for commission of an alleged felonious offense (not convicted)
   —for commission of a misdemeanor (convicted or not)
   —technical parole rules only
III Convicted
   —and sentenced for one or more misdemeanors (other than traffic), but not a parole violator
   —of one or more traffic violations resulting in fines of $100. or more, or jail or workhouse sentences of thirty days or more, or both
IV Charged or fingerprinted or "wanted"
   —for a felony even though no record of conviction is available
   —for one or more misdemeanors (other than traffic) even though no record of conviction is available.

In measuring impact of manpower programs on crime, it is necessary to decide when an individual should be considered a recidivist. Glaser has stated that the basis for evaluation of prison programs should be long-run postrelease felony information, i.e., just the first category. However, if we accept the literal meaning for recidivism, i.e., return, then it would include the first two categories. Moreover, if we expand our concern to the pretrial intervention program which the Department of Labor is currently sponsoring, an entirely different set of entries would be appropriate. In our opinion, the evaluator should include whatever recidivism categories he considers most appropriate for the program being evaluated.

Having established recidivism as the dependent variable in measuring the impact of manpower programs on crime, we can now consider the independent variables. These are generally divided into participant, program and environmental characteristics. This is standard practice in every good impact evaluation, and there is no need to belabor the point here. In general, the evaluator must define the relevant variables in each of these groups, taking account of the hypotheses to be tested, the results of previous studies in this and related areas, and the feasibility of objectively measuring or categorizing observations of these variables.

For environmental characteristics, this will include appropriate institutional and organizational variables and indicators of gross economic levels likely to influence the program's impact on its participants. Program variables should be related to the quality and availability of services provided by each component of the program, as well as the quantity of these services provided to each participant. Special concern should be given to participant characteristics, recognizing that the individuals served by such programs have some characteristics that distinguish them from the usual recipients of manpower program services. Therefore, in addition to collecting information on the traditional socioeconomic variables, consideration must also be given to the criminal characteristics of these individuals. For example, a program focusing on convicts might include such variables as age at time of first conviction; total number of convictions and/or revocations of parole; offense for which committed; most frequent offense (for those with multiple convictions); time served on present commitment; employment experience prior to commitment; work, training and educational activities while committed. A review of reports on evaluations conducted in related areas will provide a far more extensive list of variables, but these are sufficient to illustrate the point.

Control Group

No impact evaluation is complete without a control group, and having just considered the characteristics of the trainees, it is now appropriate to turn to control group considerations.

It is generally agreed that random selection of trainees and controls from the population of eligibles is most desirable from a methodological point of view. In practice, however, it may be quite difficult to adhere to this approach in evaluating the impact of manpower programs on crime. Based on the programs with which we have been involved, this has not created a serious problem because the programs have tended to be small in comparison to the target populations. In these cases, in our opinion, satisfactory control groups can be established from the program overflow—those who would have been enrolled in the program if it were large enough to accommodate them. A control group could be randomly selected from the overflow, when it is clear that the selection does not involve some "creaming" process. However, this is often difficult to confirm, so that controls will often need to be selected on the basis of a stratified sample. When this is necessary, the stratification variables should be selected on the basis of the variables most likely to influence post release success.

At this point, it must be recognized that a manpower program's success in reducing its participants' inclinations toward criminal activity should not be considered in isolation. Its success in this area will be closely linked to its success in other areas, especially employment success. There is considerable evidence to support the position that a manpower program's impact on the criminal activities of its participants will be highly correlated with their success in obtaining and retaining satisfying employment. For these reasons, we recommend that stratification variables be selected taking account of both criminal and employment factors. Specifically, we suggest that age, race, education and type of offense be used in stratifying, and that the number of categories for each of these variables should be determined based on the total number of controls to be included in the study.

These variables are suggested based on findings of our recently completed evaluation. It showed that recidivism and employment impact were closely associated with trainee characteristics. With respect to their criminal history, trainees with noneconomic offenses had lower recidivism rates than those with economic offenses. This is consistent with Glaser's finding that "the most recidivistic category consists of economic offenses not involving violence (larceny, burglary, auto theft and forgery), and the most recidivistic single type of felony is auto theft" [p. 44].

Beyond the special barriers related to a criminal record, postrelease success was strongly influenced by the same personal characteristics that play a major role in labor market success among the general population. Generally, trainees who were twenty-five years old and over did better than younger ones; whites did better than nonwhites; and, those who had finished high school did better than those who had not. The link between recidivism and employment success was quite obvious when examining racial differentials. There was strong evidence of labor market discrimination in favor of whites even after accounting for the other critical variables.

Follow-Up

Follow-up is considered an essential part of all manpower programs and impact evaluations. From the individual's perspective, it should provide and coordinate post program supportive services. From the evaluator's perspective, it must provide the impact information essential to the evaluation of the program. In manpower programs intended to have an impact on criminal activities, follow-up takes on special significance. The individual's postprogram success cannot easily be determined without it, and his success is often critically dependent on the follow-up services received.

It is paradoxical and frustrating, therefore, that following-up on many of these individuals is so difficult. Of course, if the individual is on parole, then follow-up can and should be coordinated with parole activities. However, many of the individuals served by these programs are not on parole, and even those who are often complete parole before final impact information can be obtained on them. In the papers in this volume on "finding and interviewing the hard to locate," some useful approaches were suggested for coping with these problems. However, for the exoffender population, a few more suggestions seem appropriate. First, formally distinguish between the provision of follow-up services and the collection of follow-up information. It is the responsibility of the program to provide the services, and the responsibility of the evaluation to collect the information. Although the services should be provided to all program participants, it is seldom necessary to collect the information on all participants. Therefore, the evaluation should consider a sample of participants, sufficient in size to satisfy the statistical requirements of the study, following the same procedures used in determining the size of the control group.

Once the members of these groups have been designated, it is critical that they be personally involved in the study. Otherwise, it may be extremely difficult to obtain postprogram performance information on them. However, even when this is done, there is likely to be a substantial percentage of the program's participants and controls who cannot be found.

When this situation arises, it is extremely important to do two things. First, compare the characteristics of the respondents with the characteristics of the total participant and control samples to determine the representativeness of the two groups. For this purpose, the characteristics already suggested (age, race, education and type of offense) should be emphasized, although others may be added. Second, select a random sample of the nonrespondent participants and controls and determine their recidivism status, in order to assess the nature and extent of any bias which may exist in the respondent data. This is certainly not an easy task, but there are sources of such information on the nonrespondents. For example, in dealing with offender populations, it is possible to obtain such information at the national level through the F.B.I. and the Federal Bureau of Prisons; and at the state and local levels through the state's Department of Corrections, and its jail system. Admittedly, this involves considerable effort especially if you are involved in a nationwide evaluation where it is difficult to establish the essential linkages with the sources of such information. It is for this reason that we believe evaluations of manpower programs intended to have an impact on criminal activity should concentrate in a few areas where arrangements can more readily be made for obtaining access to such information.

The frequency at which postprogram performance information is collected is also an important factor. Ultimately, it is determined by the goals of the study and the resources available to achieve those goals. Often impact evaluations range from 0 to 5 years after the individual leaves the program, with the first year considered to provide short-term measures of success which may or may not be correlated with long-term impact. However, in our opinion, it is critical that recidivism data be collected at regular intervals throughout the first year on all those who have received program services regardless of whether they successfully completed the program or terminated before completion. It is during this period that the individual is likely to place greatest reliance on the manpower program services he has received. The degree to which these services were deficient is likely to be closely associated with the probability of his reincarceration. For these reasons, we strongly recommend that follow-up information be collected at monthly intervals during the first year after leaving the program. If this is not feasible, then this information should be collected at least on a quarterly basis. In succeeding years, we believe that collection on a semiannual or annual basis would be appropriate.

It is clear this would result in the accumulation of a large volume of postprogram performance information. We have recommended this to facilitate the use of a model of recidivism which has a sound theoretical foundation and distinguishes the influence of participant characteristics from the influence of other characteristics, as will be discussed in the following section.

Data Analysis

The impact of a manpower program is the resultant of many variables, which we have grouped into three categories: participant, program and environment. All of these variables interact to produce the observed impact. The goal of data analysis must be to determine the nature and degree of this interaction. Standard practice dictates that multivariate analysis techniques be employed to relate the dependent variable, recidivism, to the full array of independent variables. The methods of regression and correlation are essential to this task. However, it is appropriate to suggest the use of a model in analyzing the impact of manpower programs on crime.

Since the turn of the century, the Poisson process has been applied as a model for a wide variety of behavioral phenomena. For example, this process has been used to show that individuals have different "proneness" to accidents, depending on personal characteristics. In their simplest forms, these models have assumed that the probability of an accident occurring in a given time period is unaffected by the number of preceding accidents, and of the interval elapsed since the last accident. Expanding on this approach, other research has shown that the individual's accident proneness may change from one time period to another. It has been suggested, therefore, that the proneness of a person in a period may be decomposed into two factors. One is a personal factor called his "pronity" to that kind of occurrence; and the other is a period factor, standing for the conditions prevailing during the time period being considered. Such a modified Poisson model of recidivism can be used to investigate variations due to individual, program, and environmental characteristics. The Criminalistic Institute in Denmark has conducted some work in this area. It is our opinion that the application of such models to analyzing the impact of manpower programs on crime could be quite valuable.

Conclusions

Our recently completed evaluation of inmate training programs has shown that in overall comparison to the control group members, the program participants had significantly lower recidivism rates during the first six months following release. Although the difference was small, approximately four percent, its importance is magnified when viewed in light of the large numbers of exoffenders steadily flowing out of the nation's prison systems. Because of the implications for both reducing human misery and facilitating improved operation of correctional facilities, these differences should not be ignored.

The finding that the trainees had lower recidivism rates tends to support the use of manpower programs in offender rehabilitation. Past research and evaluation studies have indicated that a strong direct relationship exists between unemployment and adult property crimes.[3] The theory implies that the predilection towards law-abiding behavior or criminality occurs in proportion to variations in economic stress: the more severe the economic stress, the greater the likelihood of crime. Theoretically, by reducing such stress one should also reduce economically motivated crime.

The emphasis in the inmate training program has been on assisting the individual through job training to achieve vocational skills sufficient to ensure steady and satisfying postrelease employment, thereby reducing economic stress and the likelihood of further crime. But the application of manpower programs to offender rehabilitation is a relatively new area. Inmate training programs have been operating for only a few years. Other manpower programs are now being designed and implemented "to change the offender into a person no more likely to commit an offense than any normal citizen." Someday, these programs will also need to be evaluated to determine what kinds of programs are appropriate for what kinds of offenders. In the words of the Gluecks in their preface:

Only through a careful examination of the product of our penological mills could we ever learn of their value. The grist of these mills consists of thousands upon thousands of young men and women (largely the former) who are annually poured into them by a society that has never been very clear as to just what it expects the mills of justice to grind out, and how the task is to be accomplished . . . Inspections of those mills are valuable, but insufficient. More necessary is a careful, periodic analysis of their grist; and still more important is a thoroughgoing, honest evaluation of their product.

---

[3] See Aller, Mandell, et al., and Pownall.

Measures of the Impact on Crime: Comment

Belton M. Fleisher

There are two points of particular importance in McDonnell's paper upon which I would like to comment. These deal with the groups to be studied and the model within the context of which the impact of manpower programs is to be measured.

The optimal groups to be studied are discussed in the section dealing with the level of investigation. I believe that McDonnell correctly views the difficulties involved in dealing with the measurement of impact at the macro level. This is because available data on statistics of crime are obtainable for geographic areas so wide (e.g., census tracts or cities) that it would be difficult if not impossible to identify the role and importance of manpower programs within them. However, I should point out that the geographic areas pertinent to such macro studies cannot be entirely ignored, because environmental variables, such as labor market unemployment and other factors generally thought to impinge on criminal activity, are usually available only in forms defined over such regions. Thus, even though McDonnell's suggested micro analysis has the advantage of pinpointing the impact of the manpower programs to be investigated with respect to the individuals studied, it would still be impossible to avoid the troublesome problem of locating the individual subjects within appropriate geographical areas for purposes of defining and measuring whatever environmental characteristics are thought to influence their behavior. This problem of correctly locating the subjects of the study becomes very important when questions are raised having to do with the interaction between program effectiveness on the one hand and labor market conditions, the location of firms hiring trained workers, and the economic and demographic characteristics of the neighborhoods inhabited by members of the sample, on the other.

Since the problem of measuring environmental characteristics cannot be avoided under any circumstances, it seems to me that it would raise no further difficulties to expand the scope of possible sources of groups to be studied at what McDonnell refers to as the micro level to include any group of people (adults or youths) enrolled in manpower training programs, regardless of their previous criminal records. Granted, it should prove fruitful to study the recidivism of previously convicted criminals as it is affected by manpower programs designed especially for them, but should it not also be illuminating to study the criminal behavior of other participants in manpower training programs as well? Presumably, in most training programs, it would be possible to identify individuals with respect to the populations from which they come in such a way as to estimate the effect of training on the probability of subsequent criminal involve-

133

ment without raising problems of measurement and identification that are un-avoidable in studying the effect of such programs on persons with known prior criminal behavior. Furthermore, even in programs not specifically oriented toward persons who have been convicted of previous crimes, it should be possible to identify individuals who happen to have records of conviction; thus the *differential* impact of training programs on the two groups of individuals could be studied.

The question of an appropriate model discussed, somewhat too briefly in my opinion, in McDonnell's paper, is correctly viewed as of crucial importance. Only by properly identifying the variables influencing criminal behavior and placing them in the context of an appropriate model can the influence of any factor on this kind of behavior be isolated and measured. From this point of view, McDonnell's reference to the high correlation between the effectiveness of training programs with respect to improving the participants' labor market success and to reducing the incidence of recidivism is most suggestive of appropriate paths to follow in search of a useful model. It would appear necessary to be able to answer the question whether the effect of a training program on labor market success is a *causal* factor in reducing criminal behavior or, rather, simply another measure of the impact of such a program on the individual. This is an important distinction; it bears on the following question: Do individuals differ in obvious or obscure personal characteristics which result in differing responses to identical conditions imposed by training programs and their environments such that some manifest a reduction in criminal activity and an increase in labor market success while others do not, or do individuals differ in environmental circumstances which affect the impact of training programs on their labor market success and, as a consequence, on their subsequent entry or return to criminal activity? The answer to this question will have to deal with such issues as the relationship between racial discrimination, labor market success, and crime as well as with the importance of associating training programs with labor market conditions of relatively easy access to subsequent employment opportunities. Raising this question brings us back to the starting point of McDonnell's paper: cogent evaluations of the impact of manpower training programs on crime should provide evidence bearing on the theory of the effect of training—that the effect does operate *through* the impact of training on employment opportunities—and on possible causes of differences in such effects. Whether such differences are attributable to personal characteristics (including race and discrimination, and psychological attributes) or whether to differences in labor market conditions and the industrial-occupational structure of the labor markets receiving the output of training programs is of the utmost importance to the understanding and improvement of the effectiveness of manpower programs on criminal behavior.

10 Measures of the Impact on the Community

Garth Mangum and R. Thayne Robson

The manpower programs of the 1960s—programs designed to enhance the employability and earnings of various disadvantaged groups in the society—have multiplied into an interdependent but amorphous complex in the cities and states throughout the land. With funds severely limited relative to the serious employment handicaps, eradication of which is the objective of all the programs, evaluation is needed to ascertain that the scarce dollars are spent as efficiently as possible. The important question is not "Which manpower program has been most cost-effective in achieving its objectives?" It is "What combination of manpower services can make the greatest contribution, within given budgets, to alleviating the employment problems of the disadvantaged?" Efficient delivery of those services then becomes the task at hand.

But manpower programs and services do more than contribute or fail to contribute to the employment and earnings of enrollees. They both absorb and create experienced staff personnel with consequences for other public and private efforts using similar personnel. Participation in the programs inevitably affects the attitudes and services of public agencies serving the poor, both existing and new. If one is to know the real worth of the manpower programs, he must measure the total net impact on the community.

However, communities affect programs as well as vice versa. Each program was introduced into an existing economic, political and social environment which strongly influenced the nature of the programs and in part predetermined their relative success or failure. Problems and circumstances also differ among communities and may require a different set of programs, services, or policies. Hence, the evaluation study must answer two questions: 1) "What was the total net impact of the whole complex of programs in each community?" In other words, "In what way do communities differ today from what their condition would have been had there never been any manpower programs?" 2) "In what ways have the differing economic, political and social environments required differing policies or influenced the relative success or failure of the programs?"

To measure impact requires not only a before-and-after comparison—"how were things before the manpower programs and how are they now?"—but sufficient laboratory control to abstract from changes which would have occurred in the absence of the programs. It is necessary not just to identify the program's goals and see if they were achieved and at reasonable cost, but to find what else

135

happened, positive or negative, which, though perhaps unforeseen or unintended, is still part of the impact.

Of course, it is as unreasonable to expect identification of every impact as it is to attempt to draw a map which is a complete though microscopic representation of all the features of reality. The manpower programs—those employment-related public programs introduced under the authority of the Manpower Development and Training Act, the Economic Opportunity Act, and the 1967 Amendments to the Social Security Act—were all concerned for the employment and earnings of certain target groups. The critical impact, therefore, is on the lives of the enrollees and their families. As a result of program participation, will they experience more stable, more satisfying and better paid employment in the future? Even if so, will the improvement be sufficient to justify the cost?

However, there are, in general, two approaches to achieving that goal, depending upon the obstacles to satisfactory employment and earnings. If the problem is the individual's lack of skill, experience, education, motivation, or habits, the answer is most likely to be found in programs which change him. However, if the obstacle is in the structure and functioning of the labor market, that must be changed. Some of those changes may require programs, as for instance, relocation, transportation or housing, to bridge a geographical gap between people and jobs. However, for other obstacles such as institutionalized discrimination or culturally biased placement tests, drawing attention to their existence and generating sympathy for the victims may be the first step to their elimination. Such identification may be a useful by-product of program operation.

Each program brought into communities the spending impact of program budgets and the personal and political impact of attractive jobs. The expenditures may have provided an economic stimulus. The jobs may have provided patronage in the traditional manner, becoming the base for new political relationships. The jobs could also offer ladders for upward mobility to the underprivileged.

In each community at the beginning of manpower programs, there were certain institutions important to the effective functioning of that community's labor market. There were, of course, employing institutions, private and public, and unions representing the employees therein. There were the public schools providing the basic education and skills essential to functioning in the labor market, as well as in life as a whole. There were various assisting agencies such as the public employment service, vocational rehabilitation agencies and others. With the advent of the manpower programs, the experience, the objectives, and the target groups with which each of these agencies worked changed, sometimes traumatically. What was the impact on preexisting community institutions? Were they improved in their functioning or impeded in their operations?

In addition, certain new institutions emerged, designed to fill holes left by existing agencies, to perform new services or to substitute for those thought not to be working effectively. Some of these were general institutions now present in almost every community of any size, others were specialized and particular to the community, either meeting some particular need or serving a particular target group in that area. Assessment of the impact of the manpower programs on the community must consider its impact on those preexisting institutions and the impact on the community of those new institutions created specifically to administer manpower programs.

The program enrollees, though largely disadvantaged, were part of the human resources available to the community. Labor shortages might be alleviated, job vacancies filled, workers made more productive, the labor force upgraded or the labor market's functioning improved. But a variety of programs were involved, furnishing different combinations of service to people of different characteristics and problems in labor markets of diverse structure and under a wide range of economic circumstances. If program results were favorable or unfavorable, eliminating or improving deficient programs required answering which services in what combinations for which enrollees under what conditions worked or did not work.

Employment and Earnings Impact

This introduction serves to indicate the broad spectrum of manpower program impacts on the community. It is likely that efforts to determine which of the possible impacts is most important could engender considerable disagreement. We have already indicated our judgment that the ultimate objective of manpower programs is to improve the employment and earnings experience of those who enroll. Just how much the employment and earnings measures must improve for a program to be justified is subject to some debate. If one follows the economists' dictum that the enrollee must be made better off without any nonenrollee being made worse off, the earnings increase must add enough to the gross national product to repay the cost with interest. However, manpower programs have been justified primarily as a means of giving disadvantaged workers some compensatory advantages in job competition. As long as income redistribution is a specific objective or allowable means a less rigorous test is allowed. That is, was the enrollee from the appropriate target group and were his gains from the program participation greater than those which could have been obtained by simply giving him the money. Follow-up data can be collected which provide partial but highly valuable measures of the before-and-after experience of enrollees in manpower programs. These data provide the single most important measure of program impact.[1]

---

[1] The collection of follow-up data on program enrollees can also provide limited insights into the changes in enrollee attitudes that occur concurrently with program participation. These impacts are important and whether the direction of change is considered good or bad will depend on one's values. Positive attitudes of the enrollee toward himself and the society around him can be one of the important measurable impacts of manpower programs.

Macroeconomic Impact

One exceedingly direct impact of the manpower program upon the community in which they occur is the number of staff jobs and the dollars expended for materials, services, and salaries in the operation of the program. Manpower programs do create jobs and have been the means for identifying able individuals among target groups, testing them in the crucible of administration and program experience, moving them up through the ranks and out into other programs or other public or private employment. This impact, while exceedingly important, is not easily measurable at least in the upward mobile. This impact is both macro and micro, but it would not occur without the considerable levels of program activity added on to both community based and traditional organizations.

Impact on Community Institutions

There are few quantitative ways of measuring the institutional changes which have occurred as a result of the manpower programs. Change is more often a qualitative than a quantitative phenomenon. Where there are quantitative measures of change, it is exceedingly difficult to isolate those changes which occurred because of the presence of any single influence. Yet change can be assessed qualitatively by comparing systems at varying points in time and identifying significant differences. Judgment is then necessary to assign credit or blame to causes and contributing factors.

The primary institutions of the labor market are the employing establishments and the households from which the employees are drawn, but a number of secondary institutions support and impact upon the primary relationship. The schools, public and private; the public employment service; employers, public and private; unions; and basic political structures are all institutions amenable to change as a direct result of manpower programs. It is far more difficult to identify and measure changes in established institutions than it is to point to newly created institutions as a measure of manpower program impact. The new institutions, such as community-based organizations, skill centers, CEP, CAMPS, and NAB-JOBS are easier to measure in quantitative terms as manpower program additions to the institutions in each community. But the qualitative significance is the more important impact of these institutions, whether they are considered temporary or permanent.

Just how much pay-off will come from greatly expanded efforts to measure the reorientation of established agencies, the changes in community attitudes, and the changes in employers' recruitment, selection, hiring, and promotion practices remains to be seen. There is enough work in this area to keep all available social science researchers busy for the foreseeable future. Program evaluators should at least entertain the thought that changes in the institutions could be more important in the longer run than the impact upon present and past enrollees.

Labor Market Impact

Since the goal of manpower programs is steadier and more satisfying employment and higher earnings for their enrollees, these programs are certain, if successful, to have an impact on the local labor markets. Among the possible impacts are 1) increased labor force participation, and therefore, a larger labor supply; 2) improved skills among those in the labor force, the importance of the latter depending upon the meshing between the skills supplied and those in demand; and 3) a reduction in labor market frictions because of the increased exposure to and familiarity with its institutions as a result of program enrollment.

Those program enrollees who find themselves more steadily employed after enrollment may have filled jobs which would have been taken by others or they may reduce unemployment, either by filling otherwise vacant jobs or by reducing the frictional period between job opening and placement. There appears at the moment to be no adequate means of measurement of labor market impact. Even if a job vacancy series were available for all occupations and industries in each labor market, the present magnitude of program enrollment is probably too small in relation to the total size of the labor force, employment, and unemployment to have a measurable impact. The best measure of labor market impact probably is a comparison between the occupations for which training has been provided and the occupations in demand in the labor market. The danger here is that occupations characterized by high turnover and therefore frequent vacancies and hirings are confused with changing total demand in an occupation.

Impact of Mix of Services and Universe
of Need

Assuming that the net impact of program services upon enrollees can be measured through good follow-up data, it still remains to determine the impact of particular mixes of service upon the enrollees and vice versa. Presumably good follow-up data would provide insights into the value of particular combinations of service if there were measurable differences between enrollees in terms of the services or programs in which particular groups had been enrolled. Before serious measurements of the contribution of particular services or mixes of services can be made, greater efforts must be made to identify the alternatives in more discreet terms so that the tools of measurement can be applied. No one has yet categorized the cafeteria of possible services in such a manner that measurement of the value of each individually or in some predetermined mix is possible.

Summary

The total impact of all manpower programs on enrollees, economics, labor markets, and institutions is amenable to measurement in some respect, dependent upon informed judgment in others, and subject primarily to conjecture in a few. To know for certain which is which is the challenge for the evaluators. Careful measurement is certainly to be pursued and will add greatly to our knowledge of manpower program impact. But measurement by its very nature in a highly dynamic and changing environment will never substitute fully for the qualitative judgments of informed experts.

Examining all programs, agencies, and services being provided in a particular community or labor market allows one to judge the appropriateness and relative effectiveness of the various activities. What agency is most committed and competent to achieve the desired objectives, what services best meet the needs of the target groups and what delivery systems appear most effective can become apparent to an extent not possible in a single program evaluation. Manpower program evaluation is still in its infancy. Most of the other social programs have thus far avoided serious evaluation. It is a credit to the Congress and to federal administrators that the art and practice of manpower program evaluation has progressed to the point that this conference could have been held. Our parting sermon is that all good evaluators must be engaged in a constant search for objective criteria and data for judging the performance of manpower programs and the institutions that administer them.

Measures of the Impact on
the Community: Comment

James A. Hefner

It was not until around the middle of the 1960s that manpower programs considered the institutionalized environment as a factor in the employment of the disadvantaged. The attitudes of employers, inadequate cooperation from the educational system, managerial ineptness, and inadequate organizational structure and planning on the part of the manpower agency staffs were major reasons why manpower efforts during the decade were unsuccessful. However, the lack of success was due in part to the experimental nature of the programs and inadequate administration. Although some of the programs may have been based on invalid premises, on the whole, the basic idea of preparing people for employment is an essential part of any human resource development effort.

Indeed, for any human resource development effort to be successful, to be devoid of invalid premises, effective evaluative techniques would be amiss if they did not include the factors above. Mangum and Robson agree with this point, as I understand their paper. However, I think that many of these ideas were not clearly expressed by them.

I agree with Mangum and Robson that manpower programs should be evaluated in terms of their total impact on the community. Although it is unclear to me what they mean by community, such a definition is essential if we are to measure various impacts of manpower programs on the disadvantaged and institutions surrounding them. Whether we mean by community the area where the pretrainee lives, or the nonghetto, or both, may be arrived at objectively or subjectively. In any case, community impacts of manpower programs will not be the same.

Current evaluation of manpower programs is constrained by specific techniques and by manpower objectives. Constraints of the former are administrative monitoring and cost-benefit analysis; the latter constraints involve selecting out objectives and adding weights to them. These constraints do not allow the manpower evaluator to measure the total impact of manpower programs on the community, however defined. Mangum and Robson seem to agree, but endorse the collection of data as the proper technique for evaluating quantifiable parameters in the community.

Effective evaluation of community structures is no easy matter. How does one, for example, evaluate 1) the residual of organization; 2) participatory skills; 3) power utilization; 4) community interest; and 5) pride? Should weights be assigned to each community variable? Who decides these weights? These questions and many more like them are answerable. Yet they require a type of community theory for economists to get at them. Once this barrier is torn down, manpower evaluation becomes inclusive and more accurately depicts the state of the program under consideration.

As a final note, I think that the manpower evaluator should be aware of the competition that goes on among agencies for various slices of the manpower pie. Such competitive conflicts arise from old institutions versus old institutions; old institutions versus new institutions; and new institutions versus new institutions. The evaluator should ask himself "Is there a measure of the impact that these struggles have on manpower programs?" Of course, the effectiveness of the evaluator in handling this question and others like it depends on who he is and judgmental inputs. Unfortunately, too few evaluators have the confidence of the disadvantaged community.

**Part Five:
Finding the Hard-to-Locate**

11 Finding and Interviewing the Hard-to-Locate: The DMI Experience

Hilda N. Barnes

It has been said that, "Every year, if not every day, we have to wager our salvation upon some prophecy based on imperfect knowledge." This holds true even for prophecies based on well-founded survey research. Sampling and response errors that crop up in the most effectively conducted research effort add to the burden.

The researcher dealing with particular subgroups such as the disadvantaged experiences a peculiar set of frustrations. On the one hand, the subgroup may represent a population that is the focus of special legislative programs designed to meet some specified objectives such as to raise that group's level of living; hence, there exists a need for accurate measurement. On the other hand, the very characteristics that define the population under study may create a set of circumstances that makes locating, meeting, and interviewing a projectible sample drawn from the designated population group, difficult in the extreme.

Yet, while finding the hard-to-locate can be a difficult task, it definitely should not be considered an impossible one. From Decision-Making Information's (DMI) experience, successful completion of that task depends upon such mundane elements as good preplanning, an approach of casualness, proper interviewer selection and training, continuous supervision and interviewer counseling. Lastly a reasonable time schedule and an adequate budget also help considerably. A study, thus executed, can produce completed interviews with between 70% and 80% of the respondents in a sample universe. An increase in both dollars and time can substantially increase sample recovery upwards toward 90%.[1]

The DMI experience is based on survey research with segmented population groups over an extended time and a large number of studies. Many of our procedures have been developed and tested over a long period. The DMI experience, as it specifically applies to the evaluation of the impact of manpower programs, is based on two studies. One was a longitudinal study conducted in four cities. The study called for four waves of interviewing, the first at the training site and then

---

[1] Since the criteria stated are not unique, but instead common to most well-executed surveys, the question might be asked, "why then aren't all studies involving the hard-to-locate equally successful?" That would be difficult to answer since there are no uniform standards or approaches universally accepted across all survey research efforts which can be measured with one well-defined scale. The implementation of survey criteria even with similarly defined standards vary tremendously. Therefore, DMI results have to be interpreted in view of DMI methods of operation. In our recent work with finding the hard-to-locate, we have been fairly successful in tracking and in interviewing them.

three follow-up interviews at three month intervals. Sample recovery varied from 80% to 92%. The second experience was in conducting a national study on the Outcomes of MDTA Program Participants. Here we were talking with people who had been out of the programs an average of 18 months. The study was conducted in 40 localities with almost 5,200 respondents being interviewed. The sample recovery rate will be over 80%. The precise figure is still to be calculated.

The Approach to the Respondent

Much of our success we attribute to the conscious effort to encourage DMI interviewers to use a very individual and personal approach when contacting respondents. All contacts were very much on a person to person basis. Interviewers made friends with the respondents. There was nothing official in the inquiries made to find them or in the approach when they were interviewed. In essence, all attempts to arrange for the interview pointed to a hoped-for conversation rather than an investigation. This principle applies in all interviewing, but definitely more so when one attempts to reach specific population segments not readily accessible. Interestingly enough, many of the same methods apply whether one is attempting to locate and interview a manpower program participant living in a ghetto neighborhood or an executive living in a high-income area.

This approach is based on the assumption that most people like giving their opinions and enjoy being interviewed if it is conducted, and the initial contacts are made, in a friendly and nonthreatening fashion. On the other hand, an official approach can be, and we found often construed to be threatening and/or an invasion of privacy. In sum, the single most important ingredient in reaching the hard-to-find is to approach them as individuals with a positive, friendly, and enthusiastic manner. Other principles and criteria, however important, are subservient to the individualistic approach.

The Questionnaire

To achieve the degree of informality necessary for the personal approach while at the same time attempting to measure accurately the respondent's background, work history, perceived training benefits, and basic attitudes with reliability and precision, requires a properly designed field instrument as well as the proper interviewer and interviewing environment.

The questionnaire should be written in a conversational tone, taking into account the specific segment of population for which it was designed. The vocabulary used should definitely be that of the spoken, not the written word. The language of the interview schedule should not be condescending nor should it be so erudite that it confuses the average respondent. The vocabulary used should permit the respondent to meet the interviewer on an equal basis. Attempts to use "ghettoeeze" unless it has universal usage, can hurt interviewing rapport much more than it can help it. Similarly, technical jargon, formal terminology, while common to the survey researcher as well as the manpower evaluator, can and often does have adverse effects in the field interviewing situation. The interview then takes on the appearance of an official inquiry and the critical personal and friendly approach is lost. However, the recording of responses to questions as well as their coding must be precise and must meet all the quality controls and rigid standards set forth for producing measurable information.

To ensure measurable data, it is essential that the field interviewer be given virtually no latitude in the manner in which questions are asked. Even probes for amplification and clarifications of responses should be controlled. Therefore, the entire language of the questionnaire should be in simple basic conversational English and should be selected so that the interviewer can comfortably use the exact words as written without individual interpretation. Diversion from the instrument as written can destroy the effectiveness of the measure. Worse still, many deviations in handling specific questions can diffuse or obscure what could be important and meaningful findings. The survey instrument should be physically well designed for easy recording of the responses. This is essential in the interviewing phase as it permits the interviewer to concentrate on talking to and observing the respondent rather than forcing him to hunt for the proper place to record an answer.

Interviewee Selection

Interviewers should be carefully selected for an assignment in reaching the hard-to-find if optimum results are to be achieved. The essential criteria for selection of interviewers would include the following:

1. Proven experience on similar assignments.
2. A sense of responsibility and perseverance.
3. The ability to have and/or to develop a sense of involvement in the importance of the study while maintaining a sense of neutrality and objectivity in tracking respondents and conducting the interviews.
4. A willingness and a flexibility to work in the ghetto areas. The interviewer should be prepared to work evenings and weekends as needed.
5. The ability to identify with respondents without either being overwhelmingly sympathetic, condescending, or disdainful.
6. A high degree of resourcefulness in tracking respondents, which goes beyond using the obvious means of locating people and the willingness to follow all leads in finding respondents. In short, we like our interviewers to have St. Bernard instincts as well as bull dog tenacity.

7. The ability to approach the assignment with enthusiasm and to consider its completion a challenge and an achievement.

8. The ability and willingness to spend long hours beyond the normal interviewing day to follow up leads on finding people, to make phone calls and to write personal letters and notes to respondents.

9. Some foreign language facility in neighborhoods where respondents have limited English.

10. The basic interviewer skill necessary to follow sample and questionnaire instructions with precision and care while maintaining a conversational manner in talking with each respondent.

Much has been said of the use of indigenous interviewers in studies involving ghetto populations. Being indigenous to the target population may prove helpful in many instances; however, indigenity alone should be of secondary importance. The first and foremost considerations in selecting interviewers are set forth above. If interviewers are indigenous to the group and/or to the area being studied and meet all other requirements, one would have the best of all worlds. However, selecting interviewers who meet the indigenous criterion alone can in fact be detrimental to the study.

While the survey interviewer should meld or blend into the respondent's environment to establish good rapport, he does not necessarily have to be part of that atmosphere. The survey interview should not be confused with a jury trial where one is supposedly judged by one's peers. The interviewer's only function is to obtain accurate information. The respondent is under no obligation to consent to the interview unless he wants to. It is the mesh of the interviewer's and respondent's personality that makes a good interview possible. In this regard, it has been shown that it is often easier to talk about yourself more openly and honestly to a relative stranger whose personality is outgoing and friendly than it is to talk about yourself to one of your peers.

The selected interviewer must be properly trained for each study and each study phase. Training must cover in great detail the proper handling of each question and each survey procedure. A large-scale national study requires the services of between one and two hundred interviewers. As mentioned above, each of the interviewers must handle the questions in precisely the same way if measurable results are to be generated. The willingness on the part of the interviewers to go the extra mile in reaching and talking with program participants is often based on the need to impart to each interviewer the zeal and the enthusiasm that is generated when he realizes that this survey is "special." Each interviewer has to feel that he or she is searching for "truth," or working for a cause or building a better mouse trap. It takes that level of involvement to search for and make friends with difficult respondents.

The attempt to motivate has been a very important part of DMI's field training, not only at the start of the interviewing, but throughout the entire field period. Periodic rebriefings were held to maintain a high level of interest and enthusiasm. Interviewers were kept abreast of survey progress. Interesting experiences and helpful hints which worked in some areas were passed on to other areas by memos and bulletins. Interviewers were given opportunities to discuss their experiences with field directors and supervisors as well as the project staff. These close ties, while very time and energy consuming, gave interviewers a much greater feeling of survey participation than if they had just gone out to get interviews. The same network of communication makes checking on quality control infinitely easier and in turn produces more complete survey information.

Contacting Respondents

I would now like to turn to a discussion of the difficult task of physically reaching the hard-to-locate respondents. The initial task of the interviewer is to determine where the interviewee lives, works, goes to school, spends his time—in other words, to find out where this person exists. The second task can be more frustrating and difficult than the first; it is to physically locate the respondent so that the actual interview can be conducted.

For the most part, these people are easy to talk with once found. They generally appear forthright in talking about themselves and their employment activities. They are seldom hesitant in talking about their aspirations, but are less willing or unable to verbalize their expectations. Refusal rates are very minimal, seldom exceeding two or three percentage points. These refusal rates are substantially lower than those experienced in the average population study. This low level of refusal may be attributable to the extra efforts put forth in obtaining the interview or may be indicative of the population segment under study. Nevertheless, minimal refusal was consistently encountered and should be construed as an asset in interviewing the hard-to-locate.

In determining the whereabouts of respondents, all the accepted methods were utilized and in some measure proved successful in completing interviews with the less elusive respondents. For the more difficult-to-find respondents, interviewers had to be extremely resourceful and just plain persistent in tracking down each and every lead to reach the respondent and/or determine his whereabouts. Let me briefly review the standard procedures that DMI used and then mention some more unorthodox ones.

Initially, all respondents were sent letters informing them of the study, its purpose, and sponsor. They were told that an interviewer would call on them and were asked to cooperate by agreeing to the interview. Respondents were given the option at this time as to where they wanted to be interviewed. The interviewing time and location was definitely set up for the convenience of the respondent.

After the initial letter, the last known addresses for survey respondents were visited; generally, this was during daylight hours to facilitate locating specific addresses and also to ease the task of making casual inquiries about the respondents who were not at home when the interviewer called. A small segment of the interviews were completed at this stage. The bulk of them were not. After this initial visit, the sample respondents not interviewed were classified into two categories: first those who either resided at the address of record or at a known address, or were institutionalized, were in the armed services, or were deceased and second, all the others. Throughout the course of completing a field study, the dimensions of these two major categories changed. The other group diminishes in size as the whereabouts of respondents are found. Initially, the first group grows in size as more and more respondents are found, but later diminishes slowly through the successful completion of interviews.

Notes paraphrasing the contact letter with the interviewer's name and a phone number were left at respondent's homes, or with neighbors, landlords, friends or relatives at the time of the interviewer's first visit. Respondents were asked to call the interviewer to set up an appointment for the interview at a time and place of their convenience or even to call to say they refused to be interviewed and did not want to be bothered. If a toll call was required, they were told to call collect.

The procedure of leaving notes or writing letters to respondents was repeated numerous times. Interviewers sent handwritten personal notes as well. The phone number generally given to the respondent was that of a local survey coordinator who would set up an appointment and arrange the interview at the convenience of the respondent. In addition, individual interviewers frequently used their home address and telephone numbers where respondents could call in the evening or on weekends.

Giving the respondent the option on where the interview was to be conducted was helpful in persuading the more hesitant respondents to go along with the interview. Actually, most interviews were conducted in the respondent's home, but having other options available made many respondents more comfortable. This was particularly true among some of the foreign-born respondents who were apprehensive about having the interviewers come to their homes. As a result, some interviews were conducted in lunch rooms, coffee shops, schools, meeting rooms, automobiles, etc.

The coffee shop or lunch room was by far the most common place for conducting the interview outside the home. Whenever this occurred, the interviewer paid for the respondent's lunch, dinner, or snack. This proved fairly inexpensive and established a congenial environment for the interview. Only one respondent ordered a steak dinner, much to the shock of the interviewer. Another ordered and downed three martinis, leaving the interviewer in a state of shock. These were, however, definitely isolated incidents.

If the respondent had to spend money for transportation to meet the interviewer, he was reimbursed immediately for that expenditure. The latitude and flexibility given the interviewer and respondent on where the interview could take place was particularly important for maintaining an atmosphere of friendliness and informality throughout the interview session itself.

One of the interviewers was particularly successful in conducting interviews in her car. She drove several of her respondents to work so that they would take time for the interview. Similarly, she picked up their children at school and helped in other ways. In turn, the respondents gave the interviews not because it was demanded or required, but simply because they wanted to.

It was not unusual for respondents to set up appointments for interviews and then fail to cancel them or show up for the interview. In some areas, this happened repeatedly with the same respondents. Interviewers had to be persistent in ignoring the many broken appointments and keep making new ones until the interview was completed. In many of our more successful interviewing areas, it became somewhat of a game between the interviewer and the respondent. Initially, we were somewhat apprehensive about the animosity that could be created by this persistent tracking. This did not materialize. When the respondent was finally found or pinned down, it was with lightheartedness and good humor. From an administrative standpoint, this game of hide and seek between respondent and interviewer did add to field costs and administrative frustration.

Other Tracing Techniques

In addition to personal visits, interviewers used the telephone frequently and effectively to track respondents and set up appointments for interviews. Although we provided telephone numbers which respondents could call, only 15% to 20% of the respondents used this system. However, having a local phone number and name of a specific person whom they could contact seemed important to most respondents.

As many as nine or ten visits were made to complete an interview. These would include tracking efforts to locate a current address, name or telephone number, unproductive visits when appointments were not kept, as well as the normal reasons for unproductive field visits. Tracking the whereabouts of respondents was by far more time-consuming and required more skill, imagination and perseverance than conducting the interview.

In small towns and rural-type areas, there appeared to be less mobility and respondents were somewhat easier to find despite the fact that street addresses were not always available and being able to make contacts by telephone was more difficult. However, the distances between respondents was long. As a result, the rural-type interviews were just as time-consuming as the urban ones, but for different reasons. Finding rural people was easier—they did not seem to disappear as readily. Also, it was easier to find friends, neighbors or relatives who could give us information or pass on messages. However, driving fifty to one hundred miles each way to locate a respondent was not at all unusual.

In the highly urban areas, the mobility was much higher and obtaining information was more diffcult and time-consuming. Interviewers really had to make repeated efforts and make friends with people in the neighborhood to obtain information. In addition to personal visits, letters, notes and telephone calls, a number of other devices were used. Some were productive in some areas and yielded nothing in others.

The local post office was a good initial source of information. In rural areas, they were the single most important source in helping the interviewer locate respondents on the map with only name and rural route numbers. They spent time in giving directions on how to reach the respondent's home and often supplied information on the respondents themselves. In urban areas, the post office was helpful in supplying address changes if they had any on record. This, however, almost proved as a source of last resort, since it was time-consuming and so many respondents did not notify the post office of their moves.

Information from neighbors, friends, local grocery or drug stores was often productive. Even if they knew nothing or little about a respondent, they could and often did supply leads on girl friends, parents, and other relatives, who if tracked down would frequently have information about the respondent. If they were reluctant to give out information, they would generally pass on a note or have the respondent call himself or have someone call for him. Tracking a respondent through these sources would from time to time bring one face to face with the respondent without the interviewer knowing it. Only after the interviewer was able to assure the respondent about the confidential nature of the interview and that he or she really had no official connection with the government and was not a bill collector, did he identify himself as the person being sought.

Local community agencies were often helpful and did supply information about respondents in some areas. Local SES offices were most helpful in many areas in being able to supply current addresses or had some knowledge of when respondents may have left the area. In other areas, they were not as helpful. Former employers or employers of training in the case of OJT were also often good sources of information. In some areas, particularly with male respondents, unions were a good source of supplying current addresses. They also were able to supply us with information on their current jobs and working hours. In addition, they were willing to pass a message or note on to the respondent. Churches, parish houses and religious organizations could occasionally give information on finding the respondent or a friend or relative who in turn could supply a further lead.

Program administrators were helpful in some areas, particularly where respondents were back in other programs. However, this was one of the less productive sources because program administrators often did not have any more current information than what was obtained in selecting the sample.

The use of cross-indexed street address directories, where they existed, were useful in locating telephone numbers, correct addresses and most importantly the names and telephone numbers for neighbors as well as possible family members with the same last name within the neighborhood. Searching the telephone book for people with similar names (only if the names are distinctive) was also a source used to locate respondents. Going to public school records in some areas provided names and addresses of children with similar names who in turn provided a clue to finding respondents.

Landlords and real estate companies were contacted. They rarely were able to supply a new address or much information about a respondent, but did serve as a validation source in ascertaining that in fact the respondent no longer lived at the address of record.

Stopping people, either adults or children, on the street where the respondent had lived and casually asking about him was often productive in supplying information for finding the respondent directly or for making further tracking efforts.

One of the most productive sources for locating people was a respondent who himself had completed an interview. He or she would often know many of the people we were looking for or know friends or relatives, or possible places of employment where the interviewer could make further inquiries. In some areas, respondents actually helped us locate people that were lost to us by every other source of inquiry. They were also able to give us considerable information on respondents no longer in the DMI sample universe, that is, those in jail, those that had completely left the area, those that were institutionalized or those that had died.

There were literally dozens of other devices used in finding individuals, but the ones covered above are the major ones. However, it is important to stress again that although tracking was successful, it was dependent upon the interviewer's approach, the fact that he or she made friends with the respondent and met him on an equal basis.

In all cases after the formal questionnaire was completed, the respondent was given an opportunity to go beyond the questions and air any of his grievances, hopes or thoughts about training programs, or his job opportunities. Few of these comments added any useful information, but they served to clarify some of the responses and left the respondents with the feeling that he had had an opportunity to talk about his side of the picture.

Conclusions

On sum, a successful interview depends on the interaction between the interviewer and the respondent. Much thought and work goes into interviewer selection and training. Respondents are not selected because they are willing to be interviewed or because they verbalize well. However, the respondent's task can be made easier and more productive by adequate preparation and by proper explanation. Individual letters and notes explaining survey purpose at the onset are important and do help immeasurably. This is evidenced by the fact that some respondents upon receiving a letter with a personal signature respond to those letters. Some are eager to be interviewed and want to be sure not to be missed. Others will not be available, but want to relate as much of their background and experience as possible. Others are bitter because they cannot find a job and want to talk about it. Some respondents who do not feel comfortable or able to write English will have wives or children write. The thread throughout this unsolicited correspondence is the fact that these people do respond to a personal approach and can be made to feel that they do have a stake in the program success or failure and that it is closely allied with their own activities.

As a result, it would appear that the role of the respondent would be enhanced if he were made to feel that his contribution to the study was extremely important and not a device to check up on him.

No survey research will yield perfect knowledge. But given a soundly conceived research plan, a workable and nonbiasing interview schedule and high recovery rates of the sample respondents, sound knowledge about these important target population who are hard-to-locate can be acquired.

12

Finding the Hard-to-Locate: The NORC Experience

Celia Homans

During the fall of 1969, the National Opinion Research Center (NORC) began collecting interview data for a longitudinal study of 10,000 participants in four federal manpower programs—MDTA (Institutional), JOBS, Job Corps, and Neighborhood Youth Corps. This study was funded by the Office of Economic Opportunity (OEO) and U.S. Department of Labor (DOL). NORC has worked as a subcontractor to Operations Research, Inc. (ORI) who are responsible for the design and analysis of the survey. The design for the study calls for four waves of interviews with a sample of enrollees in ten cities.[1] This study is the most extensive experience NORC has had with a large population of people who have been in federal manpower programs. It is, therefore, the experience which provides the material for this paper.

The overall response rates have been high for this study; 94.1% for Wave I and 95.4% for Waves II and III combined (to May 17, 1971). The overwhelming majority of cases that are "Not In Response" (NIR)—67% for Wave I and 69% for Waves II-III—are NIR because the respondent could not be located.[2] These figures reflect the most difficult residuals of difficult cases. Hard-core refusals (after repeated attempts) are not usually amenable to conversion efforts. We believe their number here to be near the irreducible minimum. The top priority for NORC in maintaining an adequate completion rate for this population has been, therefore, to expend a high level of effort to interview hard-to-locate respondents. The OEO and DOL have agreed with this priority, and have provided the funds to make it possible.

There are, of course, many reasons why people are hard to locate. The most common reason is that they move. A second reason may be that they wish to remain unlocated, even when they are at the address which the interviewer holds in his hand. A third reason is that some individuals may have no permanent address, and must be located in ways other than discovering a new address. And still a further variation on this theme is those cases where individuals have "semi" addresses; they move around a lot (for financial reasons, or because they

---

[1] Chicago, New York, Atlanta, Cincinnati, Dallas, Detroit, Los Angeles, Norfolk, Philadelphia, and Seattle.

[2] Refusals made up 19% of the NIRS in Wave I and 18% in Waves II and III combined, temporarily unavailable 3% and 2%, respectively, and other reasons 11% in both cases.

155

are fugitives, or because this is, in some young groups, a way of life). For them, this week's address is next week's cold trail. There are, of course, other hard-to-find respondents—those in institutions, in the armed services, or women who marry and change their names. But movers compose the largest group of hard-to-find cases.

At the beginning of this study, there was no direct information which gave us a clear indication as to the mobility of this particular population. However, some CPS data served as an indicator that we could expect a much higher mobility rate in some parts of this sample than that of the general population. Of particular interest is the mobility rate of 44.8% for unemployed females 18-24, and the 39% mobility of unemployed women 25-34. We also made note of the 40% mobility of men who are manual workers, aged 18-24, and the astronomical move rate of 47.6% for men with incomes $3,000-4,999.[3] Using these data, an estimate of 30% per year mobility for this population was assumed at the time we began the study, because of the wide age spread of the study, and the plan for an even distribution of the sample according to even age, sex, race cells, rather than cells proportional to program enrollment.

We have found that this estimate may be approximately correct for the "control" population for this study (a probability sample of persons having characteristics which made them eligible for program participation, but who had not participated in one of the four federal manpower programs in the past year). In the Wave I interview, respondents in the control group, in response to the question, "How long have you lived at your present address?" answered as follows:

Less than 6 months	20.9%
6 −11 months	13.5%
12−35 months	27.5%
36−59 months	14.0%
60 months or more	23.3%
No information	1.1%

The enrollee interviews done at the time of entry into the program indicated that the population of persons in programs might be different from the control sample and from the general population in this respect, since these persons reported they moved at a rate of 45% during the year *prior* to entering the program. We recently drew a sample of enrollees (10%) in the study, and tabulated the mobility rate for these persons between the first and second (exit from program) interview. The average length of time between Wave I and Wave II is four and one-half months. The mobility rate, overall, is 24% with about 80% of this being intracity moves. The same tabulation for the time between Waves II and

---

[3]These and other figures are available in the U.S. Department of Commerce study of mobility between 1968 and 1969.

III (four months) shows a similar pattern. As expected, the percentage of persons moving out of the city is larger between Waves II and III (34%), but the overall mobility rate is the same between the Waves. These figures indicate that the mobility rate of this population of enrollees in manpower programs may be as high as 60% to 75% annually.

The primary assumption which NORC makes about hard-to-locate respondents is that there is no such thing as magic; that there are no easy ways to solve the problem of hard-to-locate respondents; that there is no one method which provides consistent success. It is a matter of increments, of being careful, of reading well all the information about a person, and making *all* efforts that seem most likely to result in success. A second assumption we make is that every case requires constant scrutiny to be sure that cases which will be problems are quickly identified, and given special treatment as soon as possible. In general, these manpower cases follow a procedure which we think permits maximum effectiveness of time and money. There are routine steps prior to fielding a case; there is a stringent monitoring of cases while they are in the field; and there is a quick change of procedures for cases as soon as they are identified as difficult-to-locate.

Following is the kind of progressive effort that is routine practice for each of the ten NORC offices involved in this manpower survey.

Precautions and Prefield Efforts

Beginning with Wave I, interviewers have routinely collected information about respondents as they complete the interview. This information is transferred by the interviewer to a locating information page. The information on this page is the sum of the best thinking we could do to try to have information that would lead to a respondent on a succeeding wave, if he were hard to locate (Exhibit 12-1). If we were planning for this kind of survey again, we would collect and add to each respondent's file his Social Security number. We would delete the union designation; it has been virtually useless. And we would add a section for the interviewer to enter a physical description of each respondent—weight, height, coloring, and distinguishing physical marks. The reason for this last item is to aid in describing the respondent to persons who may know him, and to aid in identifying respondents who deny their own identity. Information from the locating information page is given to the interviewer who is assigned the case for the next wave.

On the whole, the most useful information we have collected has been names and addresses of relatives. Very few people completely lose touch with their families. The ones who do are by far the most difficult of the hard cases. But time and repeated effort with the family of a respondent will usually lead to his whereabouts, eventually. However, since the time requirements for interviews do not permit endless patience, it is often necessary to take a different route to the respondent.

NATIONAL OPINION RESEARCH CENTER EXHIBIT A
University of Chicago   NORC
              4501
Locating Information Page   10/69

Respondent's Name _____ Case No. _____

Sex _____ Race _____ Age _____

Interviewer Instructions: This sheet must be filled out for each respondent on each wave on waves II-IV. Report only changes of information previously recorded (change of address, change of employer, etc.), and/or additional information. Wherever there is no change, check appropriate box.

1)	2) Person most likely to know where R is:

Correction of
R's name (if any) _____
Change of address
Street: _____
City _____ State _____
      Home
Zip Code _____ Phone _____
	Relation-
	Name _____ ship _____
	Address _____
	City _____ State _____
	         Check Here
	Phone _____ No change ... ☐

3) Relative-Reference #1	4) Relative-Reference #2

Relation-
Name _____ ship _____
Address _____
City _____ State _____
       Check here
Phone _____ No change ... ☐
	Relation-
	Name _____ ship _____
	Address _____
	City _____ State _____
	       Check here
	Phone _____ No change ... ☐

5) Friend-Reference #1	6) Friend-Reference #2

Relation-
Name _____ ship _____
Address _____
City _____ State _____
       Check here
Phone _____ No change ... ☐
	Relation-
	Name _____ ship _____
	Address _____
	City _____ State _____
	       Check here
	Phone _____ No change ... ☐

7)	8) Place other than home where respondent can be found (hangout)

Employer _____
Address _____
City _____ State _____
Phone _____
Supervisor _____
       Check here
Phone ____ Ext. ___ No change ... ☐
	Name of place _____
	Kind of place _____
	Address _____
	City _____ State _____
	       Check here
	Phone _____ No change ... ☐
	Respondent's
	Nickname _____

9) Household sample groups only Segment _____ Line _____	10) Office use only date R due to complete program Day of Month __ Month __ Year _____	11) Wave II: Union name and card # _____ _____	12) Date this infor- mation obtained _____ Wave # _____

Interviewer's Name _____ Interviewer's No. _____

Exhibit 12-1

There are two prefield checks NORC has routinely used with respondents. 1) Several weeks before an interview is due, we write to the respondent. The wording of these notes or cards depends upon a number of things. During the Christmas season, we sent Christmas cards to all respondents. We have sent thank you letters from OEO. And NORC has sent its own letter of thanks, always with the notation "Address correction requested." Partly, these notes and letters are to help reinforce the legitimacy of the interview, and to help the respondent remember the interview experience. Partly, they are to give us the first clue as to which respondents have moved. Respondents whose letters are returned are immediately flagged, and office staff begins to try to locate the new address for a respondent before the case is sent into the field. 2) In cases where the letter has been delivered (does not return), we make a routine call from the office even closer to the assignment date to determine further that the respondent is still living at the address he last gave us. If not, again, search procedures are begun even before the case enters the field. We make these efforts to attempt to ensure that a case is "clean," easy to complete, and without undue complications before it is assigned to the interviewer in the field. Even so, a considerable number of cases turn out to be hard to locate in the field.

Interviewer Field Efforts

The routinely trained interviewer is instructed to make calls which 1) determine for sure that the respondent has moved; and 2) gather and record as much information as possible within the geographic area of the old address. This includes conversations with persons in the neighborhood who were given as references—with neighbors, with stores, bars, postmen, children on the block—all the routine neighborhood sources.

The NORC approach has been that any interviewer may be asked to do this kind of basic local investigation upon finding that the respondent may have changed addresses, but that the effort done by the average field interviewer should be minimal, well defined, and take only a brief period of time. The major effort in finding hard-to-locate respondents is done by persons who have personal qualities that are useful in completing difficult cases, and by persons who have special training in techniques that are not necessarily appropriate for the interviewer in the field.

We do not allow interviewers to check with any sources at a citywide level, or with any agencies where we have already set up routine locating channels. If the interviewer gets a substantial lead in the neighborhood as to the respondent's whereabouts *and* the lead indicates that he is still in the neighborhood, she may pursue this lead. If the respondent is in another area, the case will be reassigned to an interviewer who lives closer; or, if it appears to be a very difficult case, it will be reassigned to a specially skilled tracer.

Tracing

Tracers for this survey come in two varieties in most NORC offices:

1) Telephone tracers. In New York, Chicago, and Los Angeles, one staff member does only telephone tracing. In other cities, this is the responsibility of supervisors and part-time staff. A case that is returned from the field because it is difficult to locate is not immediately assigned to another interviewer. It is usually assigned to the telephone tracer. The most common procedure for this tracer would be to continue a check of the personal references and then begin to check likely community sources. There are obvious advantages to centralizing this effort. It limits the number of contacts we make with any one source, agency, or informant when we are tracing through community sources. The person who makes the inquiries has the advantage of repeated conversation with the same people—a working relationship can be established which enables him to collect information about people in a routine fashion with little loss of time, and without repeated explanations, clearances, etc.

In addition, several respondents can be checked at one time with one call to a contact within an agency. The kinds and numbers of such contacts vary with the size of a city, and with the skill with which the office has been able to establish working relationships with various agencies, government groups, etc. The list is not surprising and contains the usual predictable contacts: jails, police, courts, probation offices, welfare offices, training programs, Armed Services World Wide Locators, schools, Urban Renewal Authorities, Public Housing Authorities, food stamp programs, surplus food programs, hospitals, morgues, and finally newspapers. Tracers are experienced in making sensible decisions as to the places most likely to yield leads to a given respondent. For example, a young woman, 18 or over, is routinely checked with welfare; under 18 with the schools.

There are other kinds of telephone tracing that we routinely do as well. These are further long distance checks on the respondent's references. Diligent use of the services provided by Ma Bell in making long distance calls can produce colonies of relatives or friends in rural areas. Some recent migrants to the city return to the rural South. We have traced some respondents from Cincinnati to Georgia and back again in the process of completing one interview, all by phone.

Respondents who do move long distances from the city in which they lived when we first interviewed them present a particular set of problems. In cases where a telephone interview is possible or desirable, the problem is just one of the proper time, a telephone, and a willing respondent. Willing respondents, convinced of the importance of the interview, will often be available at prearranged times, and will find telephones that can be used to complete interviews, even if one is not available in their residence. Respondents who cannot be reached by phone, or who are unwilling to consent to the interview over the phone, need a different kind of effort. NORC has manpower offices in ten cities, and part-time interviewers in approximately 100 other Primary Sampling Units (PSU's) throughout the country. These part-time interviewers have been a great help in locating and interviewing respondents who move into areas near them. More than 100 interviews have been completed by PSU interviewers—and many more than that have been done by distant manpower offices for each other.

PSU interviewers have also been a great aid in completing interviews with respondents in the military. Their routine interviewing often involves interviewing on military bases in a PSU, and these interviewers already have base contacts that make the completion of military interviews easy. Locating respondents in the military is also routine, through the Armed Services World Wide Locators.

2) Personal tracing. The second kind of tracer needed to work with samples of this kind—indeed, with any sample of the urban poor—is the expert detective who has the ability to find the unfindable, to ferret out that isolated bit of information and promote it into a real, live respondent. He is the person to whom a case is assigned when every live lead is exhausted. NORC manpower offices have these individuals in every city. They seem to have some characteristics in common: 1) greater physical stamina than the average person; 2) personal charisma; 3) a very high self-confidence; and 4) fingertip sensitivity to what they see and hear. In this kind of search for people, we have had no experiences where it is not mandatory that such a tracer have knowledge of the community in which he is working; we take as a given that he must share racial and/or ethnic qualities of the area in which he works. (We take this as a given for all urban interviewing.) Most of the cases which we assign to this tracer are of two kinds: 1) cases where the respondent has literally disappeared, and where all the leads to his whereabouts are exhausted; and 2) cases where we have some indication that a respondent is around, but has not been reached by the best approaches of the standard field interviewer.

The first category of cases are those that are normally pursued by contacting people other than the respondent, usually without the respondent's knowledge of the hunt. Success in finding these people is usually a function of whether the individual we are seeking is known to *anyone*. Since few people live in absolute isolation—chances of success are good. The techniques in such a search are those dictated by the characteristics of the case, but a general statement is that every lead, no matter how slight, is investigated thoroughly.

Completion of the second category of cases usually involves getting messages to a respondent which are convincing enough to encourage his participation in the interview. The technique is largely a function of the tracer's hunches about the person he is seeking. For instance, one of our tracers described a difficult case in this manner.

I finally got this gal to talk to me on the phone because I learned that she works in the same place as a buddy of mine. But she's not about to give me that interview yet, so we don't even talk about it. I guess I've spent maybe two hours talking to her. I never give her a chance to say "no" to the interview. Whenever she brings it up, I won't even listen . . . we talk about all kinds of other things. In fact, without even knowing it, she's answered nearly half that questionnaire. I'll get her, soon. Right now, I know her like the back of my hand.

This is one kind of case that has been repeated in every city.

The second typical case in this category is the person who is hiding or wishes to avoid public discovery. In general, with respondents who have reason to be extremely apprehensive, the best tracers are exquisitely sensitive. An interviewer may carefully take off his overcoat, open his jacket, open his briefcase, and spread his body in such a fashion that the respondent and anyone else can easily see that he is unarmed. In approaching a door, a tracer uses "a friendly knock— rap,—rap, a de rap,—rap, rap"—one that cannot be associated with hostile force. Then he stands well back from the door, so that he can be easily seen through the keyhole. One tracer takes his wife along on cases where suspicison is likely to be high, since, as he says, "My wife is a nice looking gal, but she looks strictly straight. No policemen would be traveling with her; nor a bill collector; nor a welfare worker."

These are extremely personal styles. The actions can be taught; I suspect that the knack cannot be.

The problem of bias is one of concern in these kinds of cases. There is at least one researcher [Shosteck] who feels that "Even when the persistent interviewer succeeds in locating the respondent, the suspicion aroused by 'someone' looking for him can substantially distort the interview." And the problem of social distance (the lack of it) between the interviewer and the respondent is of concern in the case of the girl whom the interviewer has known over some period of time in persuading her to complete the interview.[4]

As evaluation research becomes more elegant, perhaps we can address ourselves systematically to these problems. At this point, our effort is to work closely with individual interviewers who handle these cases, to reinforce their orientation to the task (there is no need to reinforce their zest for the detective game), and to make the general caveat that it is better to collect the data, even with bias, than to live with the alternative—an inadequate completion rate.

Special Hard-To-Find Groups

We have had noticeable numbers of respondents in penal institutions of various kinds, and have found a nearly standard procedure for them. In New York, Los Angeles, and Chicago, one interviewer has a permanent pass to the city jails. This interviewer conducts all jail interviews. Again, our effort has been to create the minimum number of contacts with an institution. We routinely check the jail

---

[4] See Dohrenwend, et al., and Weiss (1968-69) for recent discussions of this problem.

records for all persons who may possibly be incarcerated. There are some clues that immediately alert a supervisor to the possibility that a respondent is in jail. Relatives say "He's away," or "He's working out of town," or "I don't know where he is, but he'll probably be back in a few months." Any response similar to this is automatically a jail check. Any man over 18 who has disappeared is also an automatic jail check. Police records are available, if officials in authority are informed fully with convincing evidence as to the legitimacy of the project. We have conducted interviews for this study at prisons all over the country with very little difficulty—including three at San Quentin.

We don't have any firm figures as yet on Wave IV cases in prison, or in drug rehabilitation centers. The number of such cases *is* increasing. Interviewing a person in a center is often facilitated by the agency which was responsible for entering the person into the center. Again, however, it is not possible to stress too strongly that the person making the contact with agencies of this sort must be thoroughly prepared to provide the kinds of information that will enlist their aid. In this regard, our work has been greatly aided recently by a letter written from OEO to such officials, which we use when it seems appropriate.

Another major characteristic of an urban sample of this kind is the large number of Spanish-speaking respondents from Puerto Rico and Mexico. Some of these people seem to flow back and forth to and from the United States. We have had fair success with Puerto Rican respondents—we have a staff of interviewers scattered in that island. Mexico presents a much more serious problem. A large number of enrollee respondents on the NORC manpower study who have return to Mexico have been virtually lost. Our experience has been that many of the men and women who come to large metropolitan United States cities to work for a few months and then return to Mexico are residents of inaccessible rural areas and have reading skills at such a low level that no questionnaires can be completed by mail. (Mail questionnaires are a last resort that we use with respondents in Vietnam, Germany, and other distant parts of the world.)

Office Management and Hard-to-Locate Respondents

One of the major regular activities in manpower local offices is the continual reevaluation of cases that are in the field. In an office with a large sample, forty or fifty cases may need to be examined and scheduled for new action in a given week. The decision as to "what next?" is usually made by the supervisor in the office. She may decide to give more time and effort to a case that looks quite dim, if she observes that it is located in a program where the number of NIRS is high; or if it is in an age, sex, race cell where NIRS are more numerous. Local offices do regularly observe the NIR rate from these two perspectives—and the individual who represents an especially troublesome cell will get preferential treatment. Decisions as to whether to pursue the case by phone, or by assigning it to a field tracer are also made by the supervisor.

Some time ago, staff in the central NORC office responsible for overall supervision of the study began to notice what we now call (for lack of a more original notion) battle fatigue among supervisors in dealing with hard-to-find cases. A sign of this kind of fatigue was the appearance of NIRS submitted for approval which didn't look hopeless. Then we began to observe that, as we made field trips to local offices, supervisors would pull out batches of tough cases for the visiting supervisor to see. Soon, we began to make this kind of examination of difficult cases a regular part of the central office supervisor's visit. The objective is to freshen the vision of the local supervisor and to establish conversation about these kinds of cases which can continue by long distance telephone. We believe that over an extended period of time, the hard-to-find cases in this kind of survey finally weary the administrator to such an extent that it is difficult to read the information about respondents with intelligence, and to make sensible decisions as to the action which is required. The task in supervision is, then, to add concern, perspective, a sense of support, and a fresh eye to the old, old problems. Tracers are people who do not lose zest for the hunt; supervisors are often another breed, for whom the ultimate sameness and tedium of this kind of work is discouraging.

In summary, NORC's experience with populations in federal manpower programs is that the hard-to-find cases are largely people who move, that the movers that are most difficult to find are those who seem to disappear, that methods used to find the hard-to-locate must be multiple and diverse, and that success in this effort is a function of time and money well spent. In surveys where the data are not badly damaged by cases being in the field longer, and where sufficient money is available to pursue these cases diligently, finding the hard-to-locate is not a barrier to a satisfactory completion rate.

13 Finding the Hard-to-Locate: A Review of Best Practices

Morgan V. Lewis

Usually, the authors of review articles begin with a statement concerning how impossible it was to review all the literature related to their topic and how they had to set some arbitrary restrictions on what they would cover.[1] Our problem was just the opposite. Written descriptions of how to find highly mobile potential respondents from poverty populations are almost as hard to locate as the respondents themselves. We tried to emphasize low-income populations because a review of methods applicable to individuals who leave forwarding addresses, have credit records, pay taxes, etc., has been published by Eckland. These sources are far less useful for poverty groups for even if an address is found in such records the odds are that it is not a current address [Olendzki, and Wilner, et al.]. We found that researchers who study poverty groups do not do research on their own methods. Discussions of research techniques were occasionally available in the original research reports, but no researcher was encountered in this review who was willing to risk his pool of potential respondents to an experimental test of the effectiveness of different techniques.

Our main sources for the studies in this review were the annuals of *Manpower Research Projects* published by the Manpower Administration of the Department of Labor and the ERIC guide *Manpower Research Inventory* published by the Office of Education of the Department of Health, Education and Welfare. We reviewed these publications for the past four years and selected all the studies that sounded as though they might involve hard-to-locate samples. Those studies that were selected were ordered directly from the authors as well as from the National Technical Information Service of the Department of Commerce. The review is thus limited to those we could obtain from these sources. From those we reviewed, only a few presented any discussion of the effectiveness of the techniques they used. Most of these discussions consist of the impressions of the researchers as to what worked and what did not. Such information, of course, is a huge step beyond the rules-of-thumb that most of us operate with, but it is still far short of experimentally tested methods.

In this review, the results obtained by different investigators who used *some-*

---

[1] I wish to thank David N. Hughes of the Franklin County, Ohio, Welfare Department, formerly with the Institute for Research on Human Resources, for his assistance in developing many of the ideas presented in this paper. I also wish to thank John K. Walmer, graduate assistant in the Institute, for his help in reviewing the studies discussed.

165

what similar methods are compared. We stress the word somewhat for we found no two studies in which the same technique was used with similar populations. From these comparisons, we attempt to draw some inferences as to techniques that seem to hold promise for increasing the effectiveness of follow-up techniques. The emphasis of the review is on techniques that can be used to locate a sample that has scattered from its point of definition, such as a follow-up of high school dropouts or former trainees in a MDTA course. Special emphasis is put on highly mobile, low-income respondents who lack the stability of families of higher socioeconomic status.

The studies that provide the background for most of the review are summarized in Table 13-1. The results presented in the column labeled "completion rate" are the function of many interacting variables but they do strongly suggest

Table 13-1
Summary of Follow-Up Results with Hard-to-Locate Samples

Study	Sample	Completion Rate	Follow-Up After	Indigenous Interviewers	Response to Mailings	Payment to Respondents
Baldwin	Former inner-city students	59%	2 to 4 yrs	Unsuccessful	20%	$2.00
Bright	Household follow-up	96%	6 to 7 yrs	Not used	8%	None
Bylund	Former Navaho students	48%	Unknown (estimated 2 yrs)	Not used	25%	None
Gurin	Inner-city job trainees	89%	6 to 12 mos	Successful	<1%	$7.50
Harmeling	Appalachian migrants	61%	1 to 2 yrs	Not used	Not used	None
Kaufman	High School dropouts	59%	30 to 33 mos	Partial Success	37%	$1.00 mailing; last resort, $10
Lewis	Inner-city job trainees	55%	8 to 10 mos	Successful	3%	last resort, $5
Mandell	Inner-city NYC	Unknown	Unknown (estimated 6 mos)	Successful	Not used	$5.00
Miles	Rural youth	72%	Unknown (estimated 6 yrs)	Not used	All mail	$1.00, 2nd mailing
Miller	Appalachian job trainees	67%	6 to 18 mos	Not used	Prewarning	None
Pownall	Released convicts	82%	Unknown (estimated 1 yr)	Not used	Not used	$2.00
Rogers	Former rural students	80%	8 to 18 mos	Not used	Not used	None

that with sufficient investment of resources virtually all persons in a follow-up sample can be located. Bright's results are the most noteworthy. She reports on a follow-up of household interviews that were conducted six to seven years earlier. With persistence, a two-year period of data gathering and the assembling of a new staff "... who came with fresh enthusiasm and new ideas about how persons might be located," information was obtained for 96% of an original sample of 11,324 people. Most research studies cannot devote this length of time but with a more intensive effort and more incentives to respondents than Bright had available, Gurin achieved nearly comparable results. With a similar investment of resources, most follow-ups should be able to achieve completion rates of 80% or better.

The review is organized around the following topics: the use of indigenous interviewers, methods of paying interviewers, use of incentive payments to respondents, and the use of mail requests and questionnaires. Most of the discussion is devoted to the proper utilization and payment of indigenous interviewers, for their performance appears to be the key to successful follow-up of low-income samples.

Use of Indigenous Interviewers

Indigenous interviewers have almost always been used in survey research. The middle-class, white housewife who questions other middle-class, white housewives about their use of washing products is about as indigenous as one can get. When interest focused on extensive data gathering from inner-city neighborhoods, it did not take researchers long to realize that a different type of interviewer was necessary. When researchers began to use residents of these neighborhoods, typically black and of low socioeconomic status, the term "indigenous interviewers" arose to describe them and distinguish them from the more typical white, middle-class, college-educated interviewer.

For the highly mobile individual who lacks traditional roots, follow-up must rely mainly on informal contacts. Almost all of the studies summarized in Table 13-1 reported they used informal sources such as neighbors or storekeepers. Even Miles, who gathered his data by mail, had the addresses he obtained from school files checked by long-time local residents before sending out his questionnaires. To use such contacts, it is usually necessary for the interviewers to be truly indigenous to the area where the interviews are to be conducted or to remain in the area long enough to establish their credibility. It is essential that the interviewer develop some feel for the life style of the individuals to be interviewed. With this feel, he can guide his search much more effectively. In his follow-up of Navaho Indians, for example, Bylund utilized the manager of the trading post on the reservation and the close-knit family ties and friendship patterns which extended over the vast geographic distances of the southwest.

The particular characteristics that indigenous interviewers should have de- pends on the function they are to perform. Men are usually necessary if inter- viewers have to spend any amount of time waiting in bars or pool rooms for a prospect or contact to show up. Our own experiences in Columbus [Lewis, et al.] , as well as those of Gurin and Drotning indicate that it is very difficult to attract qualified black males on a full-time basis. We and Gurin had more success using males on a part-time basis, especially to make late evening and other odd- hour contacts. Our full-time women interviewers would attempt to reach poten- tial respondents during more traditional hours, would verify addresses and where possible would establish a personal relationship with a woman who had a contin- uing contact with the individual being sought. Once a relationship had been established, these women frequently gave our female interviewers helpful advice on where or when it would be possible to conduct an interview. This help often extended to attempting to persuade the respondent to cooperate with the inter- viewer. If the women could not complete the interview during conventional interviewing periods, the men would try for late evening hour contact in the respondent's usual haunts—street corners, bars, etc.

Indigenous interviewers need more supervision than typical interviewers. Baldwin's lack of success with indigenous interviewers, Drotning's comments, and our own experiences all indicate the importance of supervision. If the inter- viewers are truly indigenous to the poverty culture, an investigator should not expect them to adopt the habits and characteristics of middle-class interviewers as soon as they are hired for the project. Much of the supervisor's time must be devoted to maintaining morale and motivation. As should be abundantly clear from this discussion, seeking and interviewing highly mobile respondents is in- herently frustrating and discouraging. A day of knocking on doors and receiving guarded if not outright hostile responses—if one receives any response at all—is not conducive to an enthusiastic attitude toward's one job. An understanding supervisor who permits his interviewers to unload some of their unhappiness can be essential to maintaining their efforts. The supervisor, however, has to be care- ful to strike a careful balance between understanding and indulgence. The super- visor must insist on a defined minimum level of performance or his interviewers will substitute excuses for performance.

Method of Paying Interviewers

Because of the difficulty of this type of follow-up, the value of a per interview basis of payment is the subject of some controversy. A per interview rate has the distinct advantage of allowing an investigator to estimate his interviewing costs quite precisely. It also tends to act as a selection device by retaining the inter- viewers who are able to produce and causing the unproductive to quit. Two in- vestigators, Gurin and Homans, report successful use of a per interview rate.

Gurin reports that for those interviewers who were retained, less than half of all hired, this method of payment provided "as much or more" than the usual hourly rate. Homans, in a personal communication, reported that interviewers of low socioeconomic status ". . . responded to an incentive to make efficient use of time," and that the per interview basis gave an ". . . interviewer, an absolute 'fix,' in advance upon her. . . ."[2]

Researchers are often concerned that per interview payment will lead to cheating—actual faking of interviews—or to sloppy, incomplete interviews. These, however, need not be major deterrents to the use of a per interview rate. In a follow-up study, it is not too difficult to control for cheating. The supervisor typically has some information about the sample that does not have to be disclosed to the interviewers. This could be social security numbers, information on type of training received, the occupations of parents or some similar items that can be obtained from the source that is used to select the sample to be studied. The same data can be requested on the interview schedule and the information the interviewer obtains can be compared with the original source. Careful editing of all completed interviews can also control for sloppy or hasty interviewing that results in missing data.

There are some other considerations, however, that are contrary to the use of a per interview rate. One of the best sources in the follow-up of a group of people who have had some common experience or who are from the same neighborhood, are the respondents who are located and interviewed. They can often furnish nicknames, addresses, hangouts, etc., for individuals who are being sought. By pooling bits of information gathered by all interviewers a good deal can be learned about the people who are most difficult to locate. Such pooling requires a sense of common purpose among the interviewers and a willingness to share information. A per interview rate which rewards individual performance is contrary to the necessary group spirit. A per interview rate can also lead to dissention among interviewers as to who receives what assignments.

It may be possible to devise some type of group incentive that rewards increased production and is not detrimental to cooperation among interviewers. We would recommend that the details of the system be worked out with the interviewers used in a particular study. It might take the form of a group incentive of a fixed amount of money to be divided among the interviewers for every interview above a set quota. Interviewers who surpass the group average might be allocated a larger share of the incentive payment. Whatever form the system takes, it should be developed and agreed to by the interviewers.

Although we have no firm evidence, it was our impression that the interviewers did engage in some voluntary restriction of production in our Columbus study. Without any official statement, a consensus arose between the interviewers and the administrators that for regular referrals (not the hard-to-find) minimum acceptable performance was about one interview per working day. It was

---

[2] In a personal communication dated February 4, 1969.

rare that an interviewer ever turned in more than one per day. It is not hard to understand why the interviewers might have restricted their production. They were literally working themselves out of jobs. The sooner all the follow-ups were completed, the sooner their work was over. They also knew that if they did not approach minimum production standards they also would be out of a job. An income maximizing strategy for them was thus to produce just enough to keep their job and to prolong the interviewing as long as possible. In the face of this strategy, it is doubtful that a group incentive system would prove very powerful.

We did use the incentive of a group raise in hourly pay rate for more production, but this seemed to be effective for only a short time. A better technique may have been to set a firm deadline for the completion of interviews and to have provided an incentive for all interviews obtained before that deadline.

Some other considerations also enter the decision as to a regular hourly rate or per interview payment. One factor concerns the potential pool of interviewers and the ease with which they can be recruited and trained. If a large number of possible interviewers are available, many extra ones can be hired and trained and the per interview rate will select out the more able. If the pool is small, there may not be enough interviewers to do the job if only those who are able to earn an adequate wage keep working. It may be necessary to substitute some efficiency for greater total production. There is also the danger that if many interviewers cannot earn a decent income on a per interview basis, the organization conducting the interviews will become known as exploitive. If the organization acquires a bad reputation in the community, it can make recruitment for new interviewers difficult and also may make some respondents less cooperative.

Use of Incentive Payments

The information on incentive payments like most of the other presented is also uncertain. On the one hand, there is the usual report from researchers of the general cooperation and low percentage of outright refusals. On the other hand, there are reports of the inability to locate respondents and the fact that the highest completion rate (89%) we found for a study of highly mobile youth was achieved using a $7.50 incentive payment [Gurin].

If it does nothing else, the offer of an incentive payment apparently gives the interviewer a talking point. He has something of benefit to offer his potential respondent and he can mention the money offer when asking for possible leads from friends, storekeepers, landlords, etc. Our interviewers in the Columbus study reported that the offer of money was viewed with considerable skepticism by many respondents. They found it hard to believe they would be paid for just answering questions. Frank Friedlander of Case-Western Reserve University has suggested to us that once a source becomes credible in the community, the incentive is more effective and in some cases interviewers are even sought out.

If the word goes out that the interview is an easy way to pick up a quick $5.00, the interviewer may find locating respondents is too easy. Too easy in the sense that some people will impersonate the individuals being sought. A birth-date is a very valuable screening device in this case. If the interviewer has reason to doubt a respondent's identity, a question as to the respondent's birthday can usually weed out an imposter.[3]

Use of Mail Requests and Questionnaires

The evidence on the effectiveness of using the mail to contact respondents is also equivocal. Baldwin used a letter to inform respondents about his study and re-quested that they return a prepaid postcard verifying their address. His letter offered two dollars as an incentive for cooperation. He received a 20% response. Gurin used a letter that requested his respondents contact the research office to arrange for an interview for which they would be paid $7.50. He received less than a 1% response.

The use of the mail to collect data also has had quite varied results. Miles achieved quite good response rates. His first mailing to about 1600 teenage youth yielded a 41% response. A second mailing to the 935 nonrespondents in-cluded a one dollar bill and resulted in responses from 54% of those who did not respond to the first mailing. The two mailings yielded a total 72% response. Walther, however, was much less successful with samples of approximately the same age. With one sample, Walther used two mailings and included a promise of $1.50 incentive payment in the second mailing. He obtained a 45% return. The first mailing yielded a 32% response and an additional 13% responded to the offer of payment. Single mailings with the promise of remuneration yielded 41% and 39% responses in two different cities. Kaufman reports a 37% response to an offer of a one-dollar payment for returning a postcard confirming one's address. This sample consisted of high school dropouts who had taken part in a retraining project.

The apparent effectiveness of enclosing a dollar in a mailing suggests this might be a good way to obtain limited information or perhaps addresses for later personal contacts. The covering letter could ask the respondent to return a post-card verifying his address. If the letter explained that the respondent would be paid for the interview, the good faith money sent in the initial mailing could enhance the credibility of the offer.

A Suggested Procedure

To summarize this review, we would like to outline a series of steps that, in our opinion, would yield the largest response for the lowest investment. These steps,

[3]With regard to the amount of incentive to offer, John McDonnell has indicated that $5.00 was as effective as $10.00 in a follow-up of former convicts in his study.

it should be emphasized, are intended primarily for locating the highly mobile residents of a poverty area, who lack traditional roots, and who cannot be located through usual methods. We would expect that they would be equally effective with any other group, but with less difficult groups such maximum effort may not be necessary.

1. Obtain as much data as possible from the source that is used to define the sample. Samples to be followed up are usually selected from records maintained by schools, training programs, prisons and similar sources. As much identifying data as possible should be abstracted from the institutions records. Birth dates and social security numbers are especially good anchor points. These can be used to verify the identity of respondents and also can be used to validate interviews. Alternative addresses, such as individuals to be contacted in case of emergency, can be very useful.

2. Send a letter to the last known address requesting an interview for which the individual will be paid. Enclose a dollar bill and a prepaid postcard the individual should return to validate his address. The studies reviewed suggest that if the addresses are not too old this mailing should yield at least a 20% to 25% response. At the very least, the undelivered letters will indicate which addresses are no longer current. The dollar bill should increase the credibility of the offer to pay for the interview. In our opinion, it is best to avoid certified mail as this has negative associations such as a court summons or an unpaid bill.

3. Use a combination of full-time and part-time interviewers. Pay the full-time interviewers on an hourly basis plus a bonus and the part-time interviewers at a per interview rate. Use the regular interviewers to make initial inquiries and to establish relationships with possible sources of referral. Use the part-time interviewers to make odd-hour (late evening and weekend) contacts with the individuals the full-time interviewers cannot contact. To counteract any tendency of the hourly paid interviewers to stretch out their work, set a firm deadline at which time all interviewing will stop. Provide the opportunity for the interviewers to make more money before the cut-off date by completing more interviews.

4. Do not have the interviewers attempt to make initial contacts by phone. Even if appointments are made the probability is not too high that they will be kept. The interviewers time is better spent making personal visits. There is also some evidence that refusals are more frequent when requests are by phone [Brunner and Carroll].

5. Pay the respondents five dollars for participating in the interview. While direct refusal to participate in interviews is very rare, refusal by being unavailable is common. The offer of five dollars provides some incentive to make oneself available. The incentive payment is also a positive feature that the interviewer can emphasize when inquiring about the individual and attempting to obtain leads.

6. Ask respondents who are located and interviewed to provide leads to other individuals being sought. Prepare a hard-to-find list and have the interviewers show this to everyone they interview. Update the list weekly removing names obtained and adding new ones. Do not have more than 30 names on any list that is shown to respondents.

Using these steps with a sample that is fairly geographically restricted and where it is possible to obtain personal referrals, completion rates of 80% or higher seem highly possible.

**Part Six:
Sources of Economic Data
in Manpower Evaluation
Studies**

14 The Uses of Internal Revenue Service Data

John L. Fischer[1]

Established in August 1964, the Job Corps is a nationwide program designed to provide, usually in a residential setting, basic education and job training to poor, out-of-school, out-of-work young people. Since its inception, over 300,000 enrollees have passed through the program. As with all the other manpower training programs, ways were sought to obtain information on terminees, by way of follow-up, which would provide leads toward program improvement and evaluation of impact. Various methods were considered, some of which were tried. The Louis Harris polling firm was hired to search out exenrollees for interview. Enormous problems and costs are encountered in this method of follow-up. The Social Security Administration participated with Job Corps in 1967 in an effort to solve the problems. While this has proven to be an excellent source of information at a relatively low cost, this method doesn't solve all problems. So, rather than expect to discover a follow-up method which would be a panacea, Job Corps decided, in late 1968, to develop various methods which would reinforce each other. It was at that time that Job Corps turned to the Internal Revenue Service (IRS).

After several meetings, it was agreed that the two agencies would cooperate in the following ways.

1. Job Corps would supply to IRS a magnetic computer tape which would contain individual records of terminees with the following data elements:
     Social Security number;
     last name (1st five letters); and
     up to an 8-digit numeric code.
2. IRS would, on a reimbursable basis, match the Job Corps tape to its master file, and for every match, write out the 8-digit code field, the gross earnings *and* the total tax paid for the two calendar years then available. A joint return indicator was also included as part of the record. Further, IRS would

---

[1] While the title of this paper is initiated with *The Uses of* . . . , a more appropriate title may have begun *How to Use.* . . . The results of this initial Job Corps probe into the IRS data bank can certainly be discussed and are available upon written request to appropriately interested parties. I elected not to do this since 1) the data are several years old, which leads me to, 2) I probably would have had to smother the presentation with caveats, and 3) it is my considered opinion that your prime interest is in how to extricate IRS data for your needs.

177

sort the resultant file on the 8-digit code and delete any cells of less than three individuals in them. This latter action would provide confidentiality of any given individual's record, inasmuch as no code would contain less than three individuals and their identifying characteristics had been deleted.

On this maiden voyage with IRS, it was decided that while eight digits were allowed in the code (an arbitrary maximum determined by Job Corps to be ample), four digits would be quite sufficient. We were interested in the time period in which enrollees entered or left the program, the type of center the enrollee attended, the age of the individual, and the category of termination. The foregoing provided Job Corps with three periods of enrollee activity to review. Because of the tax years available, calendar 1966 and 1967, the information retrieved from IRS provided preenrollment and postenrollment earnings information. Admittedly, this information, pre and post, were not for the same individuals, but it was the best that could be accomplished on a first-time basis, and additional information could be collected for these "first-cut" individuals in later years simply by resubmitting the same input tape to IRS when their next series of data become available.

Problems with These Data

On the first-cut population, Job Corps submitted approximately 12,000 names to IRS. Of that number, approximately 5,000 records were dropped because either the cell size was less than three, or the individual record found no match. Of the remaining 7,000, approximately 600 records could not be used because they were joint returns. Boiled down from the original 12,000 records, the net returns providing useable records tallied 6,400, or 53%. I prefer to leave it to IRS to comment on that response rate. There is a multitude of reasons for this, one of which causes concern and I will discuss it later. Suffice it to say that by and large, Job Corps was pleased with the response.

One shortcoming of this method is the possible bias from the records which weren't returned because returns couldn't be found. Are the bulk of these records for individuals who were low-earners and therefore declined to file? We can guess, but this is an avenue for further exploration. Another possible bias is that we do not have a military indicator available, i.e., did the total taxable income result from service in the armed forces? While the first situation would cause upward bias in the data, the latter situation would cause downward bias. Do the two situations wash out? We don't honestly know. In subsequent submissions of data to IRS, it is the intention of Job Corps to screen out those individuals who are known to have been placed in school or military. Or, if the military group is large enough, we may decide to submit its as a separate group for matching.

Another disadvantage is that a single figure is given for an entire year's earning and it is impossible, from this source alone, to determine whether the income was spread over the entire year or accumulated in a significantly shorter time span. This is a difficult hurdle and requires more investigation.

Other Considerations

While income tax information is considered sacrosanct, the service is available to *anyone* pursuant to Section 7515 of the Internal Revenue Code (Title 26), whereby there is a provision for IRS to make special statistical studies, compilations, and other services upon written request. IRS will perform this service for any governmental or private agency as long as reimbursement is provided.

The entire cost to Job Corps for this matching service was approximately $7,000. This included designing the computer programs according to the parameters previously discussed, several test shots on the computer, and the final matching process. Had Job Corps elected to submit additional data close on the heels of this initial run, the cost incurred would have been the marginal cost of the matching process.

Finally, IRS requires a minimum of six months lead time to construct a computer capability for selecting information according to your specifications. Don't bother to make a request in the first five months of the calendar year, during their busy time. The request should be signed by the head of the agency, should explain the purpose and the use to be made of the data, and should be addressed to the Assistant Commissioner of Planning and Research, Internal Revenue Service. Programs developed are normally retained by IRS for one year. It was explained that improvements are made each year in the master file, thereby making last year's programs obsolete.

Conclusion

The methodology which Job Corps used is two years old; however, I recently checked with my colleagues in IRS and determined that, in fact, the facts I've related, procedurally, are current. It is generally felt that the power of this method of follow-up lies in the fact that IRS will permit the eight-digit code to accompany the individual's record and that it will be imbedded in the earnings and tax information record which is retrieved. The code can be defined by the user in any manner deemed appropriate. The single elements of the code can be grouped into multidigit codes, such as numeric state codes. Other considerations for Job Corps data are race, educational level upon entry, reason for termination (i.e., program completed, resignation, disciplinary discharge, etc.), length of stay in the program, as well as a host of others. The one precaution is that the more elements built into the code, the higher the probability that cell sizes of less than three will be encountered. The real uses of the IRS information bank are left to your knowledge of your program, and your imagination.

15

The Uses of Manpower Administration Data

Martin Koenig

I believe that some knowledge of the data the Office of Manpower Management Data Systems (OMMDS) has available can make a valuable contribution to your role as program evaluators. What I want to indicate are the types of data available and a number of potential applications. Specifically, I will be describing: 1) the broad purposes met by data; 2) sources of data: enrollee file, project status file, follow-up file; 3) measures of immediate impact; 4) cost as a measure of impact; 5) problems in using cost data; and 6) some long-range solutions.

In the space of this paper I can only touch on these topics, but it should be sufficient to give you a feel for what data resources are available.

Broad Purposes Met by Data

Basically, our data banks exist to serve three broad purposes: national information, program management and program evaluation. National information contains high-level summary data geared to policy-makers rather than program managers. Our "customers" for this type of information would include the Secretary of Labor, the Manpower Administrator, members of Congress and the White House. This type of data may best be characterized as providing highlight information about program activity. It answers, in admittedly abbreviated form, questions of people, places and dollars: How many people in our programs, how many have benefited, and at what cost? Now these, of course, are the very same questions that should be asked by program managers in evaluating their activity. The difference lies in the level of specificity of the data. National information, being summarized, omits details, subtleties, the nuances of data so important to anyone doing probing, in-depth assessment. It is essentially results-oriented, rather than process-oriented, and, as with any other highly synoptic presentation, is subject to oversimplification.

National information is our simplest application of information, normally gotten by extraction and summarization from what is literally a vast quantity of data. It is this store of data which is the basis for our two primary uses—program management and program evaluation.

OMMDS gathers data in support of both efforts, but its emphasis has been on program management. This is because manpower programs are initiated in a

181

short period of time, and undergo rapid, continual change. Long-range goals are not clearly defined or agreed upon. Our priorities are to assist in making programs operational and to provide maximum staff support to immediate, on-going efforts. In addition, hard data suitable to long-term evaluation has only recently become available in some programs. When—and if—our programs become more stable, with clearly defined goals, and the longitudinal scope of our data increases, we will be engaged in more long-term evaluation.[1]

Sources of Data

The OMMDS data banks are centered in an Enrollee Characteristics File, which can be thought of as the input to our program, a Project Status File, equated to program processes and immediate results, and our Follow-Up File, measuring long-term program impact.

Enrollee File. The Enrollee Characteristics File contains basic socioeconomic characteristics on all enrollees in manpower programs, captured at enrollment time and maintained in a national data bank. Associated with each enrollee's record are termination data, gathered when enrollees leave the program for any reason. The termination data would normally include the reasons for termination, the wages and occupations of individuals moving into employment, and (for delivery system programs) the various components individuals have gone through.

We are dealing here with a mass volume file that involves linking two separate input documents—an enrollee form and a termination form—by means of a Social Security number. The data are submitted by local projects which vary considerably in their capability and enthusiasm for accurate data recording. As might be expected, this has resulted in severe problems of data completeness and accuracy. A number of techniques have evolved to cope with these problems, but one should be mentioned here, because it entails use of a technique analytically valuable in its own right. We supplement our individual enrollee and terminee records with a summary of characteristics related to reasons for termination. This summary form, covering enrollments and terminations for an entire project, is submitted on a monthly basis by each project.

---

[1] There is one other factor that affects our ability to collect the detailed, sophisticated data needed for evaluation. It also creates restrictions on the usefulness of the data we do gather. This is the reporting atmosphere in which we function. Over 10,000 individual projects send us data. Often these projects face severe organizational and technical problems which have an adverse effect on the quality and timeliness of what they submit. We attempt to minimize this burden by asking for only an absolute minimum of basic data, rather than trying to collect all the variables that might prove useful to program assessment. It is important to keep these considerations in mind as we discuss our data banks.

Project Status File. Our Project Status data bank yields, on a monthly basis and for every manpower project, the key activities of that project, i.e., how many people enrolled, how many receive different types of services, and what happens to them? How many are placed in jobs, in what jobs, and how many drop out? As a management tool, the answers to these questions give an incomplete story when we look at results in an absolute sense. True performance assessment clearly requires some standard, or benchmark, in the form of project goals, which we also maintain in our data bank. A third variable, the costs of project activities, comes into our bank from two sources. For certain programs, such as JOBS, program costs reach OMMDS directly associated with project activities. For many of our programs, cost data are submitted by projects to the Manpower Administration's financial office, which supplies them to us on tape. We, in turn, integrate them into our Project Status data bank.

This bank actually consists of two major subsystems, one oriented to work and training programs, the other—ESARS (Employment Security Automated Reporting System)—geared to the more traditional Employment Service (ES) activities. The dichotomy reflects the newness of the role of OMMDS as a merger of several separate data systems. Over time, the two subsystems will be more closely integrated, reflecting the growing closeness between ES and other program activities.

Follow-Up File. The final data bank contains follow-up information. Based on an extension of our Enrollee Bank, it makes available an integrated picture of enrollees' socioeconomic backgrounds, the manpower training they received, and their reasons for leaving the program. Most importantly, these factors are combined with enrollees' earnings after one and two years, as reported by the Social Security Administration. A control group of nonenrollees, otherwise matched on most socioeconomic factors, is used to isolate the earnings impact of the program. Several advantages over other follow-up approaches are to be found in this system. First, it avoids the problem of nonresponses, which plagues field follow-up efforts. Second, a more complete and accurate earnings record is available than would be obtained by direct enrollee interviews. Third, the use of a control gives us a potential for what I believe can fairly be considered scientific research.

One drawback of the system is its lack of operational impact. Following-up only at the national level divorces local projects from the responsibility of contacting dropouts for possible readmission, as well as from the knowledge and evaluation of their own performance. Another problem is the composition of the control group; some challenges have been raised about particular factors we use for matching purposes which must be resolved before findings can be used with full confidence.

The potential for applications of follow-up data becomes complicated by a major manpower policy issue—the confidentiality of data about individuals. Right now this presents a sticky legal and administrative issue, and until it is resolved, the release of individual information from this or the enrollee data bank is restricted.

Some Measures of Immediate Impact

Ultimately, all the factors of component mixes, and target populations, and services provided in relation to different groups, must be translated into some standard, quantitative barometer of program success. For certain programs, this means the placement rate. On a short-term basis, our Project Status and Enrollee Files contain placement data giving us placement rates, occupations and wages. In many cases, we also have the enrollees previous employment history and are capable of supplying pretraining and posttraining profiles. Here again, the placement rate as an absolute figure is far less critical than when it is assessed against some performance expectation, either based on a contractual goal, or a standard drawn from the experiences of similar projects.

Programs which are essentially income maintenance in nature lack a true operative goal beyond the subsidization and training provided during the length of the enrollment. For these programs, the statistics of current and cumulative enrollment, obtained from the Project Status File, and the expenditures for training allowances obtained from the financial system would be the critical measure of immediate economic impact. The retention rate and the utilization of available positions become the key determinants of program success.

Turning from income maintenance to delivery system programs, the clearest, most quantifiable measure of success are the placement rate and the placement wage, both currently available. Of course, we recognize the limitations in using a fixed point in time event, such as placement, as an index of total impact: it obscures the dynamics of long-term income improvement, job mobility, security and so forth. We are working toward a greater incorporation of longitudinal data into our system through use of our Social Security Follow-up System. In addition, at the project level, for several major programs, we require local follow-up; although the data collected are not submitted to the national office, they are maintained locally in reasonably standardized format, available for on-site evaluatory purposes. For those programs which have introduced upgrading components, our data banks have been extended to cover preenrollment, during, and postenrollment earnings, which significantly extend the longitudinal coverage.

Costs as a Measure of Impact

The cost of providing program services as well as the cost in relation to results achieved are the added variables that must be taken into account for proper evaluation. For manpower programs, cost information affords two areas of insight: it supplies a management tool essential for intelligent program planning and control, and is, in itself, a significant indicator of the economic impact of our activities.

With rare exceptions, manpower programs provide wages, allowances, or stipends to enrollees. Minimal as these may be, in the aggregate they presumably have a direct economic impact on the community targeted by the programs and in a very direct way, on the income level of the enrollee and his family. Other program costs, summarized for program reporting and analyses purposes, will also have a substantial, even if somewhat less direct impact on the local areas.

For purposes of program management, cost figures become vital for good planning, and as a control measure of actual operations. Actual costs should be compared to planned costs periodically during the life of a project to surface such problems as start-up delays and disproportionate administrative overhead costs in relation to enrollee levels. Comparisons between projects of the unit cost of all enrollees, and unit costs of placements, should provide a good common indication of project efficiency.

Problems in Using Cost Data

Having briefly pointed to the importance of cost data for program assessment, let me now note what is available in the way of OMMDS cost data, and what some of our problems are. At this point, we do have available in our Project Status File, the costs reported by each project normally as part of its monthly invoicing process. For a program such as JOBS, which is funded on the basis of unit costs for each specific occupation, we have costs for placements, by occupation. When coupled with the wage data of terminees, this should allow us to weigh the relative costs of placement in different occupations against the economic gains to be derived. Management officials would then be in a position to make quantitatively based choices on the types of occupations in which to concentrate new funds. By associating cost figures with project goal and activity data, we derive unit costs for enrollees and placements, and can compare actual expenditures during the life of a program to both obligational figures, and where available, quarterly anticipated expenditures. Our knowledge of enrollee characteristics permits us, by proportioning total costs, to assess how much we spend on different target population groups.

What are our problems in gathering and analyzing cost data? Aside from the purely technical and mechanical difficulties experienced in the computer linkage of program activity data with cost data obtained from the financial office, our problems lie mainly in the classification of cost categories, and the level of reporting. Historically, cost information had been treated as bookkeeping entries, charging costs to a great number of line items—heat, light, capital equipment, staff salaries, etc., which could be linked to meaningful program categories only with great difficulty, if at all. Today, we are trying to establish a minimum number of uniform categories that are clearly related to the purposes of the program, such as training costs, supportive service costs, enrollee wages, etc., and which would also be applicable to all programs. The proposed decategorization of manpower programs would facilitate this latter point, as well as making it imperative for comparative purposes. Another difficulty for evaluation has been the variability in the meaning of "costs." For proper evaluation we believe it should mean the expense incurred when some activity is undertaken, regardless of the actual or delayed disbursement of funds, the latter being an approach which many of our projects have previously used. An "incurred cost" definition is now a requirement for all projects and should permit a more valid analysis of the true cost of our activities.

The level of cost reporting still presents great difficulties to us. Do we try to garner costs at the level of specific components, or the overall project, or even at the state level? Imposing cost controls only at the highest possible level, which seems to be the trend in our programs, does afford us the greatest possible flexibility and responsiveness in the transfer of funds among local program units, yet it also has the potential for obscuring management problems and distorting precise evaluation. Our present thinking, and this is still quite tentative, is to provide for only broad formal cost controls for payment and contractual purposes, yet still require of projects that they submit more specific cost figures, perhaps at the component level, for analytical purposes.

Yet another sticky area in the analysis of program costs is the comparison of actual expenses to obligations. Many projects, although funded on a yearly basis, do not contemplate use of all funds during that year. By treating obligated funds, and the enrollee positions they translate into, as immediate benchmarks against which we should measure current costs and enrollments, we tend to exaggerate the degree to which a project is underutilizing its resources. Our solution to this is to attempt to use phased goals. Projects would be measured against the dollars they planned to spend at different stages in their existence, and their enrollment capability would accordingly vary during the year.

Any of the problems I've discussed up to now get compounded when our evaluation extends to comparisons between programs. Here we are faced with an additional order of difficulties, that stemming from the differences between programs, in the fundamental nature of their goals. Stemming from this are differences in program definition, structures, and techniques. The obvious differences between income maintenance programs and delivery systems need no further elaboration. But there are subtle definitional differences between comparable programs which can skew the analysis of results. As an example, Public Service Careers (PSC) is likely to be compared to JOBS for a measure of the relative efficiency of two employment programs. Yet, PSC places greater emphasis on long-term institutional change such as job restructuring, removal of formal credential requirements, etc. The long-term economic impact of these nonclient-oriented services is a real one, and presumably quite appreciable, yet we have no hard, quantitative capability for assessing their value. Obviously, our inability to explicitly measure nonclient services is a potentially distorting factor in cross-program comparison, although this might be redressed in part by on-site evaluation studies of the indirect impact of the program.

One of our best prospects for measuring and comparing the long-term impact of the programs is the Follow-Up System using Social Security earnings data. If, in spite of the difficulties mentioned above, we can arrive at comparable cost figures, then the relative benefits of the program as determined by enrollees' postprogram earnings, may be measured against the cost of each. This introduces a much greater element of rationality to our selection of program mixes than we now possess.

Some Long-Range Solutions

In closing, I should like to point out that the major obstacles we currently face in the refined utilization of our data for program evaluation lie in noncomparable definitions of key data items, and the uneven, often poor quality of the data itself. Noncomparability exists largely because of the highly categorical natures of the programs, which have developed without common sets of standards. Our task here, in line with the move toward decategorization, is to develop a set of comprehensive definitions that will apply to all program elements, yet will not limit the innovative features that some sponsors may build into their programs. The second major problem, data quality, is being addressed through a greater reliance on regional offices to collect, edit, and make first-line interpretations of project data. Moving this activity to the regions, which are in a better position to monitor the data, gives them the means to assess the immediate performance of the programs under their direction. In turn, it frees OMMDS from day-to-day data operations, permitting us to devote our resources to the development of more useful systems and more sophisticated evaluation applications.

16 The Uses of National Longitudinal Survey Data

Herbert S. Parnes and John R. Shea[1]

Conceptually, cost-benefit or cost-effectiveness analysis of manpower programs rests fundamentally on the answer to the following question: In what ways and by what amounts does the labor market experience of the participant during and subsequent to the program differ from what it would have been had he not participated? The answer to this question for participants in a program permits the calculation of at least the readily measurable portions of the individual or social benefits stemming from the program as well as the opportunity costs of the participant's involvement.[2] The question is clearly not an easy one to answer. The ideal research design would involve comparison of the experience of a treatment group and a control group, each composed of individuals randomly selected from among the applicants for a particular program.[3]

Frequently, however, this ideal experimental design is not feasible. This is especially true when the evaluation of a program is to be made retrospectively. In such cases, one wishes a comparison group consisting of persons as nearly like the participants as possible from the standpoint of all characteristics likely to be related to labor market experience or to the efficacy of the program. At the very least, the relevant aspects in which the control group differs from the experimental group must be known. The purpose of this paper is to explore the usefulness of the National Longitudinal Surveys (LGS) as a source of comparison groups for the evaluation of manpower programs. After a brief description of the design and objectives of the LGS, we shall assess the usefulness of the data they yield for the purpose under consideration.

Design and Objectives of LGS

Since 1966, The Ohio State University's Center for Human Resource Research has been conducting longitudinal studies of four segments of the United States

---

[1] The authors wish to thank Michael Borus for useful comments on an earlier draft of this paper.

[2] Of course, valid measurement of social benefits frequently depends on the validity of assumptions concerning "displacement" and other possible effects, see Weisbrod (1966).

[3] See Borus and Tash.

189

civilian population: young and middle-aged men who were 14 to 24 and 45 to 59, respectively, in 1966; women between 30 and 44 years of age in 1967; and young women 14 to 24 years of age in 1968. (For convenience, these groups will hereafter be referred to as the "boys," "men," "women," and "girls," respectively). The study is being conducted in cooperation with the United States Bureau of the Census under contract with the Manpower Administration of the Department of Labor.

For each of these cohorts, the Census Bureau has drawn a probability sample of 5,000 individuals located in 235 local areas of the country. In order to permit statistically reliable estimates for blacks as well as for whites, the sampling ratio for the former is approximately four times as large as for the latter. Thus, within each cohort, the sample consists of roughly 3,500 whites and 1,500 blacks.[4] Each sample of individuals is being interviewed periodically[5] over a five-year period to permit the accumulation of a detailed record of labor market activity as well as of changes in a large variety of characteristics that are hypothesized to be associated with labor market behavior.

In brief, the overall purpose of the studies is to identify the complex of factors that influence various facets of labor market behavior and experience: e.g., labor force participation, unemployment, occupational status and earnings, job satisfaction, and the several varieties of labor mobility. Specific objectives vary among the several cohorts being studied. The process of occupational choice and of early accommodation to the labor market are of special interest in the case of the boys and girls; for the women, we are concerned with the problems related to reentrance to the labor market after children are grown or in school; in the case of the men, the retirement decision receives particular attention.

It should be emphasized that the Longitudinal Surveys were *not* designed to evaluate the effects of particular manpower programs. While information on training outside of regular school is obtained from the respondents in all four cohorts, we have no means of identifying with confidence the specific program under which the training took place. What is more important, the number of individuals in the samples who would have been involved in a specific program at a specific point in time would almost certainly be too small to permit meaningful analysis. Nevertheless, the data do have potential value as a means of developing control groups with whom the participants in manpower programs can be compared in an evaluation of the programs. The remainder of the paper will

---

[4] Actually, this figure also includes a small number of non-Caucasians who are not black. The data permit separate identification of whites, blacks, and all other races combined, although the last-mentioned category includes too few cases for separate analyses. For a more detailed description of sampling, interviewing, and estimating procedures, see Parnes, et al. (1970a).

[5] In the case of the boys and girls, the interviews are conducted annually in October and February, respectively. Following the first two annual interviews, the men have been surveyed biennially. Interviews with the women have also been biennial, except that the last two will be only a year apart.

point up the characteristics of the data that appear to be particularly useful from this point of view.[6] At the same time, their limitations will also be described.

The LGS Samples

There are several characteristics of the LGS samples that bear upon the usefulness of the data for the purpose under consideration. To begin with, the fact that not all segments of the population are covered is an obvious limitation. Moreover, the fact that the sample size in each case is only 5,000 means that the number of persons having characteristics comparable to the clients of specific manpower programs may be fairly small. A very rough indication of potential numbers is provided by the data in Table 16-1, which indicate for individuals with selected characteristics in each of the four cohorts the proportion who experienced some unemployment in the twelve-month or calendar-year period prior to the initial survey.

On the other hand, the character of the samples confers some very real advantages on the data for purposes of developing control groups. Not the least of these is that each sample is a microcosm of the total civilian population within

Table 16-1

Estimated Percentage of Unweighted Sample Cases Who Had One or More Weeks of Unemployment in the Base Period Preceding the First Interview, by Color

Cohort and Group	Whites		Blacks and Other Races	
	Number of Sample Cases	Percent with Some Unemployment	Number of Sample Cases	Percent with Some Unemployment
Men 45-59 (with work experience)	3,539	8.9	1,484	16.6
Women 30-44				
Married, spouse present	2,986	5.3	1,084	11.3
All other	470	11.3	543	12.5
Boys 14-24				
Enrolled in school	1,182	19.0	370	22.3
Not enrolled	1,373	15.9	655	25.4
Girls 14-24 (with work experience and not enrolled in school)	1,583	18.9	611	32.5

[6] As indicated recently by announcement in many of the major journals, data tapes may be obtained at cost through the Chief of the Demographic Surveys Division, Bureau of the Census, U.S. Department of Commerce, Washington, D.C. 20402.

the designated age-sex cohort. Moreover, it can be subdivided according to the characteristics of the labor market (i.e., sampling area) in which the respondents reside—e.g., rural vs. urban, size of community, diversification of industrial structure, level of unemployment, etc. The limited size of each sample is to some extent compensated by the deliberate oversampling of blacks, a group from which the clients of manpower programs come in disproportionately large numbers.[7] Finally, it would seem that the samples of boys and girls should be particularly fruitful sources of control groups for evaluations of the Neighborhood Youth Corps and the Job Corps programs, since virtually all of the clients of these two programs would have been members of the universe represented by these two samples.

The Timing and the Longitudinal Nature of the Surveys

The initial surveys of the men and of the boys were conducted in 1966, and the final ones in 1971. For the women, the corresponding dates are 1967 and 1972; for the girls, 1968 and 1973. This timing clearly constrains the circumstances under which the LGS can generate adequate control groups for evaluating manpower programs. The ideal situation would be one in which the experimental group were in a manpower program during precisely the 12-month period between the first and second surveys of say, the boys. In this case, the 12-month period prior to the first survey would provide benchmark data for the control group comparable to the pretraining experience for the experimental group; the period between the first and second surveys would permit an assessment of the opportunity costs of the training to the trainees; and the period between the second and last surveys would constitute a four-year period during which the apparent consequences of the training could be measured.[8] Such a happy coincidence of dates is, of course, more than can be expected; it is presented simply to illustrate the ideal and, by implication, the problems that are involved by departures therefrom.

Within these constraints, however, the timing of the surveys, as well as the

---

[7]Among whites, the proportion of respondents living in families with poverty-level incomes as of the first survey was 4% in the case of the men, 9% for the women, and 10% for both the boys and the girls. Among blacks, the corresponding percentages were 16, 34, and 49. Families with poverty-level incomes are defined in terms of *H.R. 16311*, the 1970 version of the proposed Family Assistance Plan (FAP). These are the proportions of respondents in families that would have qualified for some payment under FAP had *H.R. 16311* been in effect during the twelve-month or calendar-year period preceding the initial survey.

[8]The word "apparent" is used, because achievement motives and personal competencies may be correlated with selection into training programs and these personality characteristics may independently influence posttraining success. As will be seen below, however, the LGS data permit some of these variables to be controlled.

longitudinal character of the data, have several clear advantages. The most obvious is simply the fairly long time span afforded for estimating some of the benefits of manpower programs. Ideally, of course, it is lifetime benefits that are to be estimated, and the longer the time span covered by a study, the more confidently can such estimates be made. Secondly, the fact that the data are being collected periodically means that they are probably more accurate than if the entire five-year period were covered in a single retrospective interview.[9]

The Dependent Variables in the LGS

Among the most useful aspects of the LGS for purposes of generating control groups for the evaluation of manpower programs is the wide variety of data the surveys make available.[10] The LGS studies yield measures of virtually every aspect of labor market status that might be used as a criterion of the effectiveness of a manpower program. Among these, for example, are labor force and employment status in the week of the survey, number of weeks worked in the twelve-month period preceding each survey, number of weeks unemployed, and number of weeks out of the labor force; occupation (in terms of Census three-digit code and Duncan index of socioeconomic status) of each job held, current hourly rate of pay, number of hours *actually* worked in the survey week and number of weekly hours *usually* worked during the 12-month period, annual earnings, and annual income from other sources (including separately identified transfer payments).

In addition to these more-or-less commonplace measures, there are others that have been far less commonly used in evaluations of manpower programs. For instance, there are measures of job satisfaction in each survey that provide at least a crude basis for assessing changes in psychic income over time. Also, there are data on the amount and kind of work activity of all other members of the respondent's family who live in the household. If comparable information is collected for the experimental group, such data for a control group selected from one of the LGS samples will permit the use of a broader array of criteria than has been typical in assessing the contributions of manpower programs.

Explanatory or Control Variables

In the absence of a random dichotomization of the applicants for a manpower program, there is no way of guaranteeing a statistically unbiased control group

---

[9]This may actually be a disadvantage, however, by introducing an element that destroys comparability if the experimental group has not also been interviewed periodically.

[10]For a more detailed description, see the reports on the initial survey of each of the cohorts: Parnes, et al. (1970b, 1970c) and Shea, et al.

whose experiences can be compared with those of the experimental group for purposes of arriving at confident measures of the effects of the program. The attempt must be to make the two groups as comparable as possible in all characteristics that may be expected to be related directly to labor market success or to the efficiency of the program. The Longitudinal Surveys are admirably suited to this purpose because they provide measures of a substantial number of characteristics that are related to labor market success and that are also likely to be related to the probability of an individual's applying for and being accepted into a manpower program. Some of these are fairly commonplace: occupation, educational attainment, extent of unemployment in some base period, prior work experience, prior training, and physical and health condition. Some, however, are considerably more subtle and have less frequently been used as control variables in manpower evaluations. Among these are several social-psychological measures that are available for one or more of the LGS cohorts.[11]

Thus, if comparable information is collected for the group whose exposure to the manpower program is to be evaluated, the LGS provide a basis for developing a rather carefully matched sample. Moreover, by introducing such explanatory variables into a multivariate analysis of the experience of both the experimental and control groups, one would be able to go farther toward isolating the independent effects of the manpower program than most studies that have not been able to use random control groups.

Conclusions

For retrospective evaluations of manpower programs conducted in the last half of the 1960s, the National Longitudinal Surveys offer a fruitful source of control groups. The value of the LGS data would be particularly pronounced for studies of programs completed in the early part of this period, since these would allow a longer period of postprogram experience to be evaluated. The data would also be especially valuable for studies of such youth programs as NYC and the Job Corps, since virtually all of the participants in these programs fall within the universe represented by two of the LGS samples—the boys and the girls.

The chief value of the LGS data lies in the richness of both the labor market variables and the explanatory variables that the studies employ. Especially im-

---

[11] These include, for instance, a measure of commitment to work, which has been used in the surveys of the men and women and is to be introduced into the final surveys of the boys and girls. Another, used in the surveys of women and girls, measures the respondent's attitude toward the propriety of labor market activity on the part of married women with children. Third, is the married woman's perception of her husband's attitude toward her working. Still a fourth is a measure of the extent of the respondent's labor market information, which is most fully developed in the interview schedules for the boys and girls. A fifth is a measure of alienation based upon an abbreviated version of the Rotter Internal-External Scale. And as a final example, for the boys and girls there are measures of the quality of the high schools they attended as well as of the respondent's mental ability.

portant among the latter are certain social-psychological measures that are designed to represent such characteristics as work commitment, alienation, and innate ability. Naturally, for the LGS data fully to serve their purpose, identical or similar measures would have to be collected for the experimental group.

These advantages should not obscure certain severe limitations of the LGS data, the most obvious of which is that they cannot be used for programs whose participants do not fall within the four age-sex cohorts represented. Nor can they be used to evaluate programs that are yet to begin.[12] The latter difficulty is perhaps not so serious, for one would hope that superior research designs will be built into the planning of future programs and will make the construction of ex-post control groups unnecessary. This has rarely been done with respect to the programs of the past five years, however; and for evaluating these retrospectively, the LGS data appear to be especially useful.

---

[12] Sometime in the future, benchmark data and a model of period-to-period *change* in labor force and employment status may emerge from the surveys. While speculative at this time, such a model with its estimated coefficients may be of some use to those evaluators who are forced to use before-and-after data.

17 The Uses of Social Security Administration Data

Robert N. Heller

There are many ways to measure the impact of manpower programs. I will focus on assessments of the success of specific programs—the kind of study that starts with a list of people. The researcher knows that some of the people were in a program, some were not, he has some other facts about them, and he wants to compare changes.

After many talks with experts in measuring the impact of manpower programs and a little reading, I have developed a concept of the "ideal study." It should cover many years after the program and should yield its findings within a month after the program ends. It should use a huge sample at low cost to pinpoint the effect of many variables on many groups and it needs the kind of information that can only be gotten by interviewing. It should have accurate data and a high rate of response to those interviews of people who have not been contacted for many years. I am told that this ideal is a real challenge.

Social Security Administration (SSA) data can contribute to some of these goals, but we can't help you reach them all. SSA data can measure impact in terms of earnings and employment. We can provide the data for a long-term follow-up, for large samples at modest cost with a very high rate of response and accurate recall for 20 years. Even the ideal study based on SSA data has some elusive aspects. Some researcher's ideal study would give him data for individuals to run on his own computer but our records are confidential. It should use earnings by quarter and data on geographic and industrial mobility which we have in SSA records but we resist developing for your sample because it takes a tremendous amount of clerk-time which we can't spare and we won't let your clerks into our confidential files, even if they could find their way.

We have been experimenting for five years to build workable methods of providing sophisticated statistics for your sample without breaching confidentiality and without using too much SSA manpower or interfering with Social Security program administration. We have made real progress.

Available Data

At this point, I'd like to step back and review the most relevant Social Security Administration resources. For each of 200 million Social Security numbers ever issued, we maintain on magnetic tape a summary earnings record. Given a Social Security number, the summary earnings record is easy for us to access through ongoing SSA systems. Among the items of information in the summary earnings record now, 92 are most pertinent to measuring the impact of manpower programs. For each of the 20 years from 1951 through 1970, the record has the amount of taxable earnings. For each of the 72 calendar quarters starting with 1953, the record also tells whether the individual did or did not have $50 or more from nonfarm wages or salaries. That's about all that matters. Other SSA information either duplicates what you typically know, such as age, or is not machine-readable. Not much information perhaps—no occupation, no hours worked. But I have read that earnings are probably the most important measure of the effects of manpower programs, both from the viewpoint of the individual and the public.

More information is available from the Social Security Administration's Continuous Work-History Sample (CWHS). It could be useful to analyze the broad impact of manpower programs, although it is not a prime medium for evaluations concerned with specific sets of trainees. It is a one-percent sample. If you had a study population of 100,000 so that the 1,000 expected to fall in our one-percent sample might be enough, then the CWHS could be something to consider. As yet, it has not been used this way.

The CWHS has unique value when external identification or linkage are not needed. Its "LEED" file, with a 10-year wage history, provides geographic and industrial data, including mobility, and other details not available in the summary earnings record, such as estimates of total wages (going above the Social Security maximum).

Problems in Using SSA Data

What are the weaknesses and problems of SSA data? For each year, there is only one earnings amount. Then, too, we don't get total earnings, just taxable earnings up to the maximum. The summary earnings record is admittedly not ideal for a study of high-wage workers. It allows no good way of estimating a worker's total wages. But the maximum does not seem a serious limitation for most studies of manpower programs.

When MDTA was enacted in 1962, the maximum was $4,800. In 1966, it went up to $6,600; in 1968, to $7,800; in 1972, it will be at least $9,000 and our Advisory Council has recommended that it go to $12,000 in 1974 with automatic increases thereafter.[1] In 1965, about three-quarters of wages and salaries under the $4,800 maximum were covered. By 1969, under the $7,800 maximum it was over four-fifths. But most workers never reach the maximum so all their

---

[1] Legislation passed by the House of Representatives in June 1971 would raise it to $10,200 in 1972 and provides for automatic adjustments.

earnings are in the record. It is true that in some past years most regularly employed men earned more than the maximum, but manpower program clients are not average regularly employed men. The typical manpower program deals with people for exactly the reason that their employment and earnings are below par. Further, the median or certain other measures avoid the problem.

In one rather extreme group, we found 3 percent with maximum earnings of $6,600 in 1967, which I estimated biased the mean earnings by less than 4 percent. A year later with a higher maximum, it was 2 percent.

As to timeliness, I readily concede that we cannot contribute to the quickie study that has to be done just after training. There is a built-in lag until wage data can be had from the summary earnings record. We in SSA keep learning, partly through communications with manpower researchers, better ways of helping to confront manpower program evaluation studies. One thing we have learned is to emphasize the importance of the season. Records can be read out at any time, but some times are better than others. Wage data can first reach the summary earnings record about six months after each quarter. A few wage reports are filed or processed late. In rough terms, the first chance brings in about 90 percent of a quarter's reports and the second chance brings in another 6 percent. For the year as a whole, the records are about 97 percent complete after the October-December quarter has had its first chance the following June, but the shortage has a seasonal bias. I usually recommend waiting until October to tap data for the previous year. By October, nonfarm wage and salary data are about 99 percent complete. Farm and self-employment data move a little slower, but are often unimportant for manpower studies.

For a specific study, certain aspects of the Social Security law or records system may constitute limitations. For example, the summary earnings record includes military wages without a label.

The SSA statistical output has to be reviewed for possible disclosures and small cells have to be withheld. Incidentally, this means that large samples are better than small samples because they tend to have fewer small cells and there is likely to be less loss of data.

Maybe the greatest weakness if having to deal with bureaucrats and their red tape. Then there is always the likelihood of delay when SSA staff and computers have heavy workloads, as just after legislation. Delay can be reduced when a project is thoroughly thought out, planned and organized in advance by both of us. Also, if you cannot provide Social Security numbers for your sample, there can be a major hangup. If you can provide good identifying information for us to use in searching our files for Social Security numbers, there can still be a hangup because this is a clerical search and we can hire only so many clerks. If your identifying information for the individuals in your sample is incomplete, we are likely to advise you that the chances of successful results are so small we don't want to waste your money or our time on it.[2]

I have not talked yet about how you can get records for individuals to take home and look at or put on your own computers. Perhaps the best answer is that you can't, but many of you already know that an individual has the right to authorize disclosure of certain data from his own record under certain conditions. Some researchers have solicited such releases from their samples, with uneven success. The Social Security Administration does not encourage researchers to solicit releases, for various reasons. The process tends to lose one of the great advantages of Social Security data by reducing the response rate through the people you can't find and those who will not sign on the dotted line. We can't help you find people for interviewing. I can't recommend releases because I have heard too many tragic stories about 50 percent response rates. Also, we normally set a one-year limit on authorizations so that they cannot be used for long-term follow-up studies (there is no time limit on the statistics we can compile). Nevertheless, some have used released data to their satisfaction.[3]

Advantages of SSA Data

Social Security data also have many advantages. The records cover 90 percent of paid employment under nationally uniform laws and procedures and are centralized. You don't have to find the subject, persuade him to answer your questions, and rely on his memory. Wages are reported by employers. Our computerized systems allow us to handle large volumes with relative ease and a lot cheaper than field interviews. The difference in cost of the same statistical product from SSA between a 100-case sample and a 10,000-case sample would be perhaps $2,000. The response rate can be extremely high (e.g., over 98 percent) since it depends only on the accuracy of the Social Security numbers or other identifying information that you provide.

Access to the Data. One of the objectives of the Social Security Administration is to contribute through the effective development of our unique record resources to the improvement of the federal statistical system and to the sources of knowledge of the economy. This includes encouraging the linkage of these

---

[2] In discussing strengths and weakness, I come to one point I'm not sure how to classify. The researcher is forced to do a lot of advance thinking and planning. We will provide a certain amount of background literature and advice, mostly about how the obscure features of the Social Security records and systems may affect your plans. We can't plan your study for you and I doubt that you would want us to. I can't yet point to a prior use of SSA data as a model for all future studies. Maybe it exists and I just didn't know it. One plan that has impressed me would use SSA statistics for 10,000 supplemented by interview data for a few hundred.

[3] Another proposition I'd like to head off goes like this: the researcher says to us, "Now here I have some Social Security numbers and all I want you to do is get out your earnings records for them, take off the Social Security numbers, give me the linked records, and I won't be able to identify the individuals." I will just say that the assumptions are false and the proposition does not pass our current criteria for maintaining confidentiality.

data with other bodies of statistical information and making data available for research uses by other organizations, subject always to careful safeguarding of the confidentiality of information relating to individuals. To this end, we developed the standardized statistical program described in a little guide pamphlet called "Some Statistical Research Resources Available at the Social Security Administration," published in 1967.

Most of the basic principles described in that pamphlet remain unchanged, but we have advanced to more flexible programs, mainly by developing or adapting canned programs. We can now compile frequency distributions giving you the choice of intervals, means, medians, sums of squares, variances, and regressions. We can use the AID (Automatic Interaction Detector) program. We can accept as input up to 35 digits of codes from your own sources to be linked with summary earnings record data for the statistics you specify. For example, we can compile SSA earnings data before and after training according to your information about the kind of training and so forth.

As to procedures for getting data, the SSA prepares a standard contract with cost estimates after we have received a letter describing the proposal. I recommend that a number of things be done before you try to write a formal request for a contract. If you are not already thoroughly familiar with Social Security data, read some of our literature, especially the guide pamphlet. If you're still not sure, get in touch with us by phone or in person so that we can talk over briefly what you have in mind. We may be able to suggest alternatives or bring out obscure but pertinent facts to help you.[4]

---

[4] A technical bibliography, designed to lead a prospective user to more thorough treatments of points I have touched on only briefly, is available from the Office of Research and Statistics, Social Security Administration, Baltimore, Maryland, 21235.

18 The Uses of Unemployment Insurance Wage Data

Dwight Kelley[1]

The wage reports of the unemployment insurance system appear to be a useful source of earnings information for manpower evaluation studies but they have been used in only a few instances. Recent legislation will eliminate some of the coverage exclusions which limited their usefulness, heretofore, so it seems timely to review the advantages and disadvantages of these reports in comparison with other sources of earnings information.

Coverage

Thirty-six states, the District of Columbia and Puerto Rico collect wage information from all employers covered by the unemployment insurance laws. The information is required by statute and is taken from payroll records by employers so it is generally more accurate than data obtained by personal interviews. Moreover, the earnings information for each state is stored at a central point arranged by Social Security number on punch cards or magnetic tape so it is quickly available at a low cost.

However, some workers are excluded from coverage and the exclusions vary among the states. The incomplete coverage is, no doubt, the major cause for the limited use of the reports. Generally the state programs exclude farm, railroad and domestic workers, self-employed persons, employees of nonprofit organizations and most government workers. Some states exclude firms with fewer than four employees.

The Employment Security Amendments of 1970 (Public Law 91-373) will extend coverage to about 4,750,000 additional jobs, beginning January 1, 1972, the largest single increase in coverage since the beginning of the unemployment insurance program. The major additions will be employers with one or more employees, nonprofit organizations which employ four or more persons, and state hospitals and institutions of higher education. Several of the states which have

---

[1] Since this paper was prepared for a panel discussion on Sources of Economic Data in Manpower Evaluation Studies, it is a review of the readily available information about one source of such data, not a report of extensive research on the subject. The paper is largely an extension and updating of a report by Michael E. Borus [1970].

already passed legislation required to conform with the provisions of the federal law have adopted coverage provisions going beyond the requirements of the federal act. Some of the states which have not yet enacted conforming legislation are also likely to extend coverage beyond the federal requirements.

Unpublished national data available from the Current Population Survey shows an estimated 65% of employment in 1968 in covered industries. Ideally, of course, earnings information covering all types of employment is desired, but coverage may be higher for those who have participated in manpower training programs. The exclusions which will continue after 1972 seem likely to be less serious omissions. The major categories not covered will be farm workers, domestic workers, self-employed and most government employees. The exclusion of farm and domestic jobs should not affect postprogram earnings very much although preprogram earnings may be affected more significantly. The exclusion of government workers is a significant limitation particularly for training programs in the clerical and service occupations.

On the whole, it seems more meaningful to compute coverage in relation to jobs on nonagricultural payrolls rather than all jobs. Nationally, 74.7% of employees on nonagricultural payrolls were covered by state unemployment insurance programs in 1969. In the states which cover employers with one or more employees, 77.2% of the employees on nonagricultural payrolls were covered. The additional coverage described above should bring the proportion of nonagricultural jobs covered by the program to approximately 80% beginning in 1972.

Reliability and Availability

Compared to obtaining earnings information directly from trainees, unemployment wage reports are more reliable, more readily available and less expensive. The wage reports are not subject to the response errors usually associated with personal interviews because they are required by legislation and are compiled by employers from payroll records. In most states, the reports are filed within three months after the end of the quarter so the earnings information is available without an excessive lapse of time. Since the wage information is used regularly by the state agencies in computing benefits, all of the information for a state is filed in a central file by Social Security number on punch cards or magnetic tape and so may be recovered quickly and inexpensively. In contrast, locating individuals for personal interviews is a long and expensive process.

The unemployment insurance reports are similar to the Social Security Administration records which have been more widely used by researchers as a source of wage information, but in some respects the state wage files are superior to the Social Security records. Because they are more comprehensive, the Social Security records are usually considered first but, in some instances, a lack of knowledge about the state wage files may have led to their having been overlooked as a source of earnings data.

The unemployment insurance reports are available more promptly because they are collected quarterly and are usually filed within three months after the end of the quarter, whereas the Social Security reports are filed annually and are not useable until 10 months or more after the end of the year. Thus, the unemployment insurance reports are available at least 6 months earlier than are those of the Social Security. The six months additional time lapse is a minimum which applies to data for the last quarter of the year, data for the first quarter are not available until 15 months later than the unemployment insurance data.

Another advantage of the state wage files is that only a few states limit the amount of earnings to be reported, whereas only the first $7,800 is now reported for Social Security.[2] However, existing law provides for increasing this base and further increases have been proposed.

I suspect that the state reports may be more complete for the categories that are covered, although I have no statistics to verify this hypothesis. Use of the records in the claims process uncovers a substantial number of errors and failures to report. Social Security records are not ordinarily exposed to a check of this kind until the individual nears retirement age.

Limitations

The wage reports have some significant limitations including especially the limited coverage. The 14 states which do not require wage reports include some of the largest industrial states, notably New York, New Jersey, Michigan, and Ohio. As mentioned above, about 75% of the employees on nonagricultural payrolls were covered in 1969. Coverage will increase to about 80% in 1972 when the additional coverage required by the Employment Security Amendments of 1970 become effective.

Another limitation is that access to the data for research purposes may be restricted by statutory provisions designed to assure that confidential information is not divulged. All state unemployment insurance laws contain such provisions, but the language of the legislation and interpretation of the provisions differ among the states.

A more important limitation for some projects is that information collected by each state includes only the employers in that state. For some manpower programs, the probability of employment outside the home state of the program may not be significant. For others, the prospect may be quite significant. Wage record files in other states could be searched but this would probably increase the cost and complicate the search sufficiently to rule out the use of this source of data in those studies where many of the participants are likely to have worked outside the state in which the program was conducted.

A fourth limitation of the state wage reports is that most states retain records

---

[2]The states which limit the amount of earnings which must be reported are: Connecticut, New Hampshire - $7,800; Texas - $4,800; Delaware - $3,600 and Oklahoma - $3,000.

for eight quarters only so that longitudinal studies would require repeated searches of the files which would, of course, increase the cost.

To summarize, state wage records have significant limitations, but for some purposes they may constitute a useful source of data at low cost. Where the need for early evaluation outweighs the need for complete coverage, wage reports are the only available source of information. In addition, wage reports will be helpful for other research purposes or to supplement data from other sources.[3]

[3] For specific limitations of the data in a particular state and to request permission for use of wage reports, the researcher should contact the Administrator of the Employment Security Agency or the Director of Research and Statistics in the particular state with which he is interested in working. The addresses of these agencies can be found in any issue of *Area Trends in Employment and Unemployment.*

Sources of Economic Data in Manpower Evaluation Studies: Comment

Robert S. David

Life for us manpower evaluators will be considerably less frustrating when we reach the happy state of affairs suggested by the preceding papers. We'll be able to call the Office of Manpower Management Data Systems and get complete and current data on any or all of our manpower programs at any level of government.[1]

Under the data system of the future, we'll be able to find out if some group of people is better off than they otherwise would be because of manpower services. We'll get the follow-up data on the group and pull out a Parnes-type study to see if our study group did as well as a comparable group of people who did not receive manpower services.

If we want to trace the employment history of a group of people for a long period of time, we can check with Social Security or the Unemployment Insurance Service or the Internal Revenue Service. By then their records will be complete and available. We shall have solved the technical problems and broken the security barrier. Moreover, we shall have learned how to use these sources of data intelligently for management and policy purposes, as suggested by John Fischer of the Job Corps.

We manpower evaluators in the Department of Labor are working on many fronts to hasten the happy day. I can assure you we'll know when that day arrives. In almost every one of our in-house and contract evaluations, we test the data system. And the results are generally disappointing. Like farmers who always complain about the weather, manpower evaluators always complain about data problems. At times they overdo it a bit to cover failures.

After we solve our data problems, we still will be unable to answer our most basic manpower problems unless we improve our ability to integrate the data and relate it to the real, live world. Too many of our manpower evaluations are backward looks at isolated pieces of dead issues. We'll never be able to solve our basic manpower problems on a continuing basis unless we drop our backward, segmented and categorical thinking.

Comprehensive data systems are absolutely essential to rational manpower planning aimed at keeping unemployment at a tolerable level and developing a

---

[1] In sharp contrast, Garth Mangum and a very competent crew have been working for a couple of years to gather comprehensive manpower data for four cities. This has proved far more difficult than anybody expected. They've had to extricate the data in bits and pieces from thousands of scattered sources. Soon we'll see how successful they were in building total manpower pictures for Boston, Denver, San Francisco and Oakland.

competent and flexible labor force capable of meeting the growing and changing needs of industry. Such planning should take place on a regular basis at every level of government. In my view, it should focus mainly on local areas. To develop and carry out effective plans for full employment, local leaders will have to look ahead to potential manpower imbalances—unneeded workers and skill shortages—and then mobilize manpower programs to prevent these imbalances. This will call for the kinds of data promised by the preceding contributors to this volume. In addition, it will call for accurate projections of labor-force growth and the manpower needs of industry. Perhaps what we'll need most of all is an analytical framework for an entire local labor market. Then we can plug in the data to give us a total view of our current and prospective manpower problems.

The Urban Institute has done an excellent study for us along these lines—*An Evaluation System to Support Planning, Allocation and Control in A Decentralized, Comprehensive Manpower Program.*[2] This study stresses the need for two-way flows of information from the bottom up and from the top down. Under decentralization, according to the Institute, we shall need information to support an evaluation system that will be able to cope with the following functions:

At the Prime Sponsor Level

1. analysis for the development of a comprehensive plan
2. allocation of resources among services
3. administrative monitoring of contracts and projects

At the Regional Office Level

1. assessment of prime sponsors' plans
2. allocation of resources among prime sponsors
3. administrative monitoring of prime sponsors

At the National Office

1. program development
2. development of manpower goals and objectives
3. allocation of resources among regions
4. administrative monitoring of the program on a state and regional basis.

---

[2] Also see the paper by Scanlon, Nay and Wholey in this volume.

Sources of Economic Data in Manpower Evaluation Studies: Comment

Edward Prescott

From my experience with the government, the types of questions asked by administrators and policy-makers are as follows: 1) what would be the effect of increasing the number of MDTA trainees by 20 percent under current labor market conditions? 2) what would be the effect of reallocating training between the OJT and Institutional programs? or 3) how effective would a given program be in training 25,000 female welfare recipients with dependent children? To answer questions such as these, models (i.e., sets of relationships) must be constructed. Manpower analysts have not been successful in developing such models to predict the effect of alternative manpower strategies, the principle reason being the lack of access to the needed data. The government does collect and store the needed information but it is extremely difficult to use it. Part of the problem arises because of confidentiality requirements, but a more serious problem is that the data items have not been brought together and an efficient system has not been developed to access them.

What is needed is a government agency (this avoids the confidentiality problem) to develop and maintain the system. The paper by Martin Koenig indicates his office in the Department of Labor is making progress in this regard. For problems of analysis, the system should include enrollee files containing demographic, termination, and short-run follow-up information plus project codes. In addition, a project file with labor market code is needed which specifies the nature of training. Both these are part of the Manpower Data System. The enrollee files should be supplemented by longitudinal earnings information. Because of its national coverage, Social Security Administration data appear to be the most useful. Unlike data from the Internal Revenue Service, there is not a low-income cut-off or the problem of joint returns. Possibly Unemployment Insurance wage report data could be obtained by OMMDS from the 36 states where individual earnings are recorded. However, these data are not available for a number of states and currently only two years of data are available.

This data system should be augmented by a file specifying conditions for each of the labor markets for clearly local labor market conditions affect the impact of training. Possibly, it might be useful to supplement the system by survey data such as provided by the National Longitudinal Surveys, or the Current Population Survey. It seems that these sources should provide some benchmarks with which to compare the posttraining employment experience of the trainees. Developing these benchmarks is as yet an unsolved problem and would constitute a challenging research project.

The system must be efficient in providing the pretraining and posttraining earnings and short-run follow-up indicators for groups of individuals. Suppose there were six variables each with four levels and the analyst wished to estimate the first and possibly second-order interaction. There are 4^6 or 4,096 cells, but a sample of only 4,096 should be sufficient for accurate estimation. One merely selects one individual for each cell and the information for this sample of 4,096 is drawn from the data system. Because of the balanced experimental design, one can deal with each variable separately and have 1,024 observations per reported cell. Alternatively, if second-order effects are of interest, the cell size would fall to 256. This is still a large number and confidentiality of individual earnings is preserved. Observe this is a simpler and more efficient method of obtaining the results than say regression analysis.[1] This example is illustrative of what can be done using moderate size samples and cross-tabulations. With data for a number of years, both cross-sectional and time series analyses could be performed.

In summary, if manpower economics is to progress, a manpower data system, such as the one suggested here, is needed. Only then will we be able to develop models to forecast the effect of alternative manpower policies in much the same way macroeconomists use their models to forecast the effects of alternative monetary and fiscal policies. We could then estimate the marginal or incremental impacts, which are relevant in decision-making, rather than the average figures currently provided by most manpower studies.

---

[1] When dealing with unbalanced experimental design and moderate sized samples, regression analysis is a useful technique. From the tape with information drawn from the data system, cross-product matrixes could be constructed. They could be given to the evaluator who could then run regressions using any subset of the variables. This is possible because the cross-product matrix is a sufficient statistic containing all the relevant information. From the cross-product matrix, identification of an individual is impossible.

Sources of Economic Data in Manpower Evaluation Studies: Comment

William R. Tash

The long-range follow-up of individuals who have received manpower training is both a difficult and costly undertaking. Cost estimates per average person interviewed 6-12 months after training, for example, ranged between $50 and $150 on several national surveys. Completed interview rates on national surveys frequently are less than 80% for experimental groups and considerably less for control groups. Both cost per completed interview and nonresponse rates increase as the time since training increases. In fact, no national study has even attempted to interview terminees two or more years after training. Consequently, it is critical that the major manpower evaluation efforts have access to and utilize existing data sources which may support their collection systems.

Even granting the limitations in each of the sources of data outlined by our speakers, the advantage of having relatively accurate information, on nearly all participants, and for surprisingly little cost is unmistakingly great. Given these advantages, it's therefore, quite disturbing to find the absence of any major report or national study which has used Internal Revenue Service (IRS), Social Security Administration (SSA) or Unemployment Insurance (UI) data. While it has been noted that the Job Corps staff has used IRS data, and the Manpower Administration staff SSA data—the results of their efforts have not been made available even for the professionals in the field of manpower evaluation. My question, then, is why not and when can we see such results in reports?

While the SSA system undoubtedly offers the most complete data for a national study as well as the most complete report on individual earnings, the UI and IRS data offer advantages frequently overlooked. In those states where UI data is available, it may be accessed more readily and provide information not available on the SSA record. The IRS data are probably the least desirable, yet they could still provide an excellent source for verifying data, as well as supplementary information on family income. All the described data sources appear to be a "steal" at the going rate of 10 or 15 cents per record. Since the speaker from the Social Security Administration cautioned researchers on the problem of confidentiality, I would suggest that manpower participants be asked at entry to training to give a release of their SSA files for evaluation purposes. This would assure the SSA of willing acceptance by participants, and permit freer access by evaluators.

The possible use of the five-year longitudinal data as a control group is an intriguing alternative to collecting control information relative to individual projects. In those manpower programs where it would be unfeasible to use a *randomly* selected control group, performance could be measured in relation to the longitudinal comparison data. Perhaps the notion of a national control group or comparison group which resembles the disadvantaged populations entering manpower programs might well be reconsidered as an integral part of a national evaluation system in the future.

When one considers that well over $5 million a year are spent on man power evaluations and nearly $13 million on manpower data systems, the need to interrelate efforts and utilize alternative sources of cheap data become imperative. Hopefully, the Manpower Administration will be able to initiate such systems during the coming year.

Part Seven:
Measuring Secondary Labor
Market Effects of Manpower
Programs

19

Some Externalities in Program Evaluation

Sherwin Rosen[1]

This paper deals with some broad issues concerning secondary or external labor market effects that might be considered in analyzing and evaluating government sponsored training programs. The discussion is centered on the likely influence of technological and pecuniary second-order effects of training in the labor market rather than on such things as its influence on community health and crime rates, also involving external effects, but outside of the labor market; and which are discussed by other authors in this volume. The framework of analysis rests on the conditions under which conventional cost-benefit evaluation is valid; namely, that training creates productive resources that were not known to exist prior to graduation from training programs. On this view, social benefits of a program are related to the increased range of future production possibilities available to society as a whole due to the creation of labor resources through training. Social costs are discounted consumption alternatives foregone from diverting resources into training programs rather than to some other use. For the most part, the discussion is focused on some conceptual issues relating to the measurement of social benefits on the basis of market prices or incomes, a problem which has a long history in welfare economics [see Mishan]. The first part of the paper is devoted to introducing the concept of training as resource creation. The main discussion that follows identifies two genuine technological externalities and how they would be treated in program evaluation. Finally, the last part of the paper notes some issues for evaluation arising in connection with pecuniary or monetary externalities that would likely emerge from widespread training programs.

Training as Resource Creation

In a market economy, a person's income (excluding transfer payments) is defined by the resources he owns and their market prices. Hence, individuals with low incomes are either poor in resources, or own resources that are not highly valued in the market, or some combination of the two. Since most income of the nonaged poor derives from their labor, it may be said that their labor resources

---

[1] I have benefited from the discussion and criticism of Stanley Engerman and Glen Cain on several issues, though they do not necessarily agree with all views presented in the paper.

are either low in quantity or are held in forms that do not command high prices in the market. Recent developments in the theory of labor economics have suggested that, for some purposes, it is useful to think of labor resources as analogous to physical capital. It is the services of a person's skills and knowledge that have market value, and the rental value of these skills can be associated with wage income. Highly skilled workers exhibit high wage rates, because they have more services to sell than the lesser skilled. Thus, skills and knowledge embodied in people are the source of labor income, and can be treated for analytical purposes as a kind of capital. Of course, the major difference between this kind of capital and other types is the absence of markets for ownership claims for embodied knowledge or skill. All transactions take place in the rental market as it were; that is, in the labor market. Curiously enough, the market situation for physical capital is almost the reverse of that for skills. With the major exception of certain kinds of real estate, rental markets for many types of physical capital are too "thin" to be warranted in practice, and only assets are traded. Hence, most firms own large portions of their physical capital rather than rent it.

As an accounting matter, all asset prices can be converted to corresponding rental prices and conversely. Indeed, in those cases where firms own their capital stock, rational decision-making requires the imputation of annual rentals, in the form of depreciation and interest expenses, to be charged against operating expenditures, for only in that way can costs attributable to current ouput be reckoned correctly. In the case of skills, it is quite possible to reverse the process and calculate implicit capital values from observed annual rentals or income.

More specifically, let h denote the quantity of skill of a certain type possessed by a person. For example, salesmen's skills should be differentiated from those of skilled craftsmen. Suppose further, that embodied skills of the type under consideration deteriorate at rate δ per annum. Now δ represents the sum of two forces: (1) embodied skills depreciate due to aging, since the human body as a productive agent at some point slows down with age; and (2) knowledge available to society in various activities changes from time to time, changing production techniques and usually making older skills of certain types obsolete. Suppose the person under consideration is currently t years of age and expects to retire from work activity at age N (e.g., N might be 65 years of age). Let R denote an implicit rental price per unit of skill per annum. Ignoring variations in time worked per year, current labor (wage and salary or self-employment) income is defined by Rh. For expository convenience, assume δ is positive (depreciation rather than "appreciation") and constant over time. Then if R remains unchanged from year to year, income next year will be $Rh(1-\delta)$, since the person will have 100δ percent less skill next year. If the individual does not plan to accumulate or learn additional skills in the future, either for replacement or for other purposes, his income stream may be capitalized to obtain an implicit stock value, V_t, as follows:

$$V_t = \frac{Rh}{(1+r)} + \frac{Rh\,(1\text{-}\delta)}{(1+r)^2} + \frac{Rh\,(1\text{-}\delta)^2}{(1+r)^3} + \ldots + \frac{Rh\,(1\text{-}\delta)^{N\text{-}t\text{-}1}}{(1+r)^{N\text{-}t}}$$

which can be simplified to read

$$V_t = Rh/(r + \delta)a_t \tag{1}$$

where r is a rate of discount and $a_t =$

$$a_t = [1 - [(1\text{-}\delta)/(1+r)]^{N\text{-}t}]^{-1}$$

is a correction to the gross discount factor $(r+\delta)$ to account for finite lifetime. Therefore, $Rh = (r+\delta)a_t V_t$. Annual labor earnings, Rh, can be defined as a percentage gross return, $(r+\delta)a_t$, on the implicit present or asset value of embodied skills and knowledge, V_t. Dividing through by h and noting that V_t/h has the dimensions of a price per unit, the unit flow or rental price of labor is seen to be the amortized value of the implicit unit stock price, where the amortization factor includes a return on investment in the form of an interest charge plus provision for depreciation-obsolescence, along with a correction for finite life.[2]

These identities suggest that some important determinants of labor earnings are likely to include the magnitudes of r, δ and h. Thus, a major technological innovation rendering some skills obsolete can be treated as an unexpected decrease in rental price, R, or a comparable increase in δ. Both result in decreases in V_t, or in capital losses. If r and δ are constant for an individual, then labor earnings depend on h, or on the pattern by which skills evolve over the course of working life. There are two major factors to be considered here: (1) exogenous events and decisions made by the person prior to the time he enters the labor market; and (2) decisions regarding the augmentation of skills during working life. The first category includes such things as natural ability and participation in full-time school activity; while the second includes learning activities that occur through work experience in the labor market. In fact, many training programs can be characterized as attempts to increase h either through vocational-type school activity or by on-the-job training programs.

It is apparent that a person's skill and knowledge is not fixed once and for all at the time he enters the labor market. For example, it is a well-documented fact that earnings typically rise with age.[3] Though there are many institutional arrangements in the labor market that might account for these earnings patterns, such as seniority systems, there are reasons to believe that most labor market activity in the United States is not so "tradition directed" and noncompetitive as

---

[2] This formulation is identical to that for physical capital, with the exception of the finite life adjustment factor [see Jorgenson].

[3] Cross-section data are presented by Hanoch and Thurow, while cohort earnings patterns through time are shown in Miller and Hornseth.

to institutionalize higher pay for older workers if their productivity did not systematically rise with labor market experience. How does this come about?

Externalities and Firm-Specific Skills

The literature distinguishes between two types of skill and knowledge that have labor market value. Some skills are firm-specific and have no alternative uses outside the firm. Other skills are more general and have uses in firms other than the worker's present place of employment.[4] In the latter group are skills that may be specific to the industry in which the worker is employed (e.g., continuous mining machine operators, baseball players, etc.) and those that are more general and cut across industry lines (e.g., machinists, welders, etc.). As will be seen below, it is also useful to identify the productive function of skill and knowledge more precisely.

Viewing skills as relating to vocational knowledge, i.e., the ability to perform certain mental or physical tasks of a stated type, the extent of firm-specific skill in the economy would appear to depend on the form of industrial organization in product markets. In competitive industries, it is common to assume that all firms have access to the best available technology. If so, then all firms operate with similar types of machines and methods of production, and, in a reasonably well-informed market with no serious transactions costs, it is difficult to see how firm-specific skills of any magnitude could arise. Of course, it need not be true that all firms are exactly alike. For example, layouts of physical plants may differ, so that familiarity with locations of various work and other activities makes a given amount of time on the job more productive. Yet, as a first approximation, such knowledge might be supposed to be minor, compared with the general skills necessary to operate the plant at all.

It may be argued that many product markets display significant departures from competitive organization. Even so, as long as there exist several firms in the same labor market area, there is little reason to expect large differences in production techniques among them. Again, slight differences in that regard would imply some firm-specific knowledge embodied in workers. For example, in the railroad industry, tracks run over terrain that differs from firm to firm. Knowledge of the particular terrain allows an engineer to run his train with greater safety and less delay. But surely the main skills embodied in engineers is their ability to operate trains of various types, independently of terrain. Thus, we are left with cases of pure monopoly, which converts all industry specific skills into firm-specific ones, and also with firm-specific skills arising from transactions costs in the labor market. Few would argue that thorough-going product monopoly is so widespread in the economy as to generate significant amounts of firm-specific skill on that account alone, though transaction cost may not be an insignificant source.

[4]This distinction is due to Becker.

There is another concept of firm-specific skill, not clearly identified in the literature, that requires a rather broader perspective than the narrower view of labor as so many units of productive input. Certainly, one thing that all the detailed labor market studies have indicated is that, for many problems, workers cannot be considered to be homogeneous bundles of labor. Advanced economic organization that achieves high productivity through extensive division of labor and specialization of function necessarily implies a great deal of interdependencies and interactions within various broad categories of resources we choose to label labor inputs of various types in aggregate production functions. In particular, when production tasks are highly specialized and workers are not homogeneous, the output attributable to any one worker depends very much on what other workers are doing and how he *personally* relates to them. This fact is perhaps the most important thing that differentiates labor as productive input from capital. In a relevant sense, there is a true technical externality among workers— in the same way that bee-keeping and neighboring apple orchards benefit from each other's existence [see Meade]. One might be tempted to label it a kind of downstream effect, which captures a particular essence of the situation. However, such a label would be too narrow, precluding two-way simultaneous interactions, or genuine team effects. Thus, a worker becomes more productive when he learns the routines and particular characteristics of his fellow workers, and how to take advantage of them in pursuing his own tasks. By the same token, other workers become more productive when learning his particular work habits. This is knowledge that is firm-specific and cannot be of use to other firms, for the identity of workers is different in those firms.

Though a technological externality is involved here, no case can be made for social losses or divergence from ideal output due to its existence. The reason revolves around the fact that it is the role and social function of the entrepreneur to internalize all such externalities within the firm. Indeed, the nature of the firm is to take certain transactions out of the market altogether.[5] Clearly, given the kind of technological spillovers postulated here, markets in *all* transactions (i.e., each worker acting as his own firm) would be inefficient and result in loss of social output, for technical externalities would not be properly accounted for. By internalizing production externalities within the firm, the entrepreneur receives a return on his organizational abilities that at the same time leads to socially optimal output. Though the magnitude of the total return to this type of activity is uniquely determined, the entrepreneur's share is not. For once the production organization has been put together and is running as an integrated unit, it is possible for coalitions to form and attempt to claim the entire organizational rent. For example, once a worker gains the knowledge of his fellow workers' work habits and is an integral part of the production team,

---

[5]On this, see Coase (1951), who discusses the impact of transactions costs on the nature of firms. The notion of "internalizing externalities" is also associated with Coase (1960), among others.

he can threaten to quit, imposing economic losses on the entrepreneur, who would have to undertake expenditures (in terms of foregone output) necessary to get someone else up to the same level of productive efficiency.[6]

Suppose that FEPC laws, trade unionism, moral pressures, or simply good personnel management practices dictate equal pay for equal work within establishments. Then, it is apparent that the methods by which employers take account of production externalities among workers is through a type of specialization. Personnel managers will seek out individuals who can be expected, *a priori*, to work well together, and assemble a work force in which workers complement each other through a compatible set of personality and other traits. Once a production team is formed and is working at maximum efficiency, replacements due to retirements and people quitting, or expansions in the work force due to increased demand will be sought out from the pool of potential employees with similar attributes. Applicants for jobs who do not possess these characteristics will be rejected, since their wage rate is greater than the marginal product of employing them, and they must apply elsewhere. It is evident that the costs of assembling a cohesive work force within the firm depend very much on the personal characteristics of individual workers. Other things equal, potential trouble-makers will be avoided.

Another factor that is likely to be important in these decisions is the perceived reliability of a prospective employee with respect to both potential length of employment and rate of absenteeism, for both create external diseconomies in production.[7] Indeed, if this is the case, a set of equalizing wage differentials

---

[6]The problem here is very similar to one that occurs in the economics of zoning. In a free land market, there are natural forces giving rise to the emergence of distinct neighborhoods, between which land-use patterns are quite different and within which they are very similar. Thus, if individuals in their residential decisions place premiums on the avoidance of noise, smoke and traffic patterns associated with industrial uses of land, there will be a tendency for residential areas and industrial areas to arise in separate locations. In this way, total land value is maximized, and the difference between that maximum value and the value that would occur if the pattern of land use was totally random is the social value of avoiding external diseconomies by specialization of land use. However, once neighborhoods have formed, any single owner can attempt to expropriate a larger share of the surplus by threatening to alter the use of his property to a less preferred alternative; e.g., by threatening to build a shanty in a neighborhood with $100,000 houses. Moreover, every owner of land in the neighborhood can do the same, and the situation has much in common with an *n*-person noncooperative game. By prohibiting this kind of extortion threat, zoning laws represent one possible solution to the problem. Several of these aspects of externalities problems have been pointed out in an interesting paper by Davis and Whinston.

[7]An interesting attempt at modeling a related problem is made by Pencavel. Also, see Hamermesh and Goldfarb, and Ehrenberg. The importance of turnover in conjunction with firm-specific investments in workers is emphasized by Becker and some applications of the concept along those lines are given in Oi, Rosen (1968) and in the literature on short-run production functions. In all those works (including Becker), the nature of firm-specific human capital is not precisely specified, and so far as it is, seems to be related to transaction costs (e.g., search, hiring and perhaps worker orientation costs) rather than firm-specific knowledge of the sort put forth here. However, note that a related concept has been put forth in an excellent paper by Welch, though the emphasis and development is quite different than is done here.

should arise, in which production team assembly costs are shifted backwards to workers and those who are thought to generate greater external diseconomies are paid lower wage rates.[8] Basically, this is the reason why differences in pay between different groups do not automatically and necessarily imply market discrimination between them. The magnitude of these differentials in the market depends on relative costs of organizing and maintaining integrated labor production units as well as on the alternatives available to workers in various types of employment and the extent to which job specialization and worker complementarities are related in production elsewhere. For example, if workers exhibiting high rates of absenteeism have good chances of finding jobs not requiring extensive interaction and coordination with others, the effects of absenteeism on wage rates will not be very pronounced.

The magnitude of total rents due to internalization is determined by the possibilities of new entry (of firms) into the industry. If there is free entry, long-run equilibrium requires that the rate of profit from entrepreneurial activity of this type be zero at the extensive margin (that is, for a potential entrant). Firms possessing great organizational talent will produce a surplus, or pure rent, which may be shared with employees in the form of wage premiums or other prerequisites, or may not be, depending on labor supply conditions in the market.

Though retraining programs are unlikely to have significant effects on the creation of firm-specific skills in the vocational sense, a number of authors have pointed out their effect for changing work habits and attitudes of trainees, e.g., studies in Somers (1968). Graduation from a training program may very likely certify a worker as more reliable and thereby enable him to enter the pool of potential workers exhibiting high external economies and therefore higher wage rates. This is a real social gain attributable to the program, which is reflected by the fact that when the supply of such individuals is increased, production possibilities of society are shifted outward, since production is rendered easier and more efficient. Moreover, if labor markets are working efficiently, social gain is measured for cost-benefit analysis by the increased wage rates received by trainees, reflecting their greater productivity. Technological spillovers of the type under consideration need be considered no further, since they were already taken into account by firms in organizing their work forces, resulting in equalizing wage differences among various types of workers in the first place.

It is often claimed that retraining does not really improve worker productivity, but merely serves to filter the most able and best motivated workers through the program, for they are the only ones with enough incentives and staying

---

[8]If information is imperfect, information costs may be shared with workers in the form of wage differentials between new workers and established ones during trial employment periods. It is in fact a common practice for union security clauses to be waived during a 30-day trial period after hiring. Also, if external effects tend to rise with employment experience in the firm, more experienced workers will be paid more to reflect that fact, giving rise to natural seniority systems. The latter is consistent with the phenomenon of "competitive unionism" as analyzed by Lewis.

power to take retraining seriously [see Sewell and Somers (1968)]. This argument certainly has merit and would affect the manner in which benefits of training are to be measured. For example, unqualified use of control groups from the ranks of program dropouts would be called into question.[9] However, all this is really beside the conceptual point in question. Retraining can actually alter work incentives and the ability of trainees to work efficiently in production assemblies on the one hand, or it may merely certify that graduates have these attributes on the other. In the former case, real capital is increased directly. In the latter case, training provides valuable information services to society. Real capital is increased in an indirect manner; in exactly the same way that real wealth is created when prospecting yields discoveries of mineral or oil deposits. In either case, workers are able to increase their income, which measures the real social product of the program.

If in fact training serves merely as a certification device, it is arguable that there may be other means of providing that service at less social cost. Though there are many informal mechanisms producing labor market information [see Rees and Shultz], the absence of private agencies in the certification business itself suggests that alternative methods are not readily available. It is probably true that certification is best accomplished through prior work or other experience such as schooling. Moreover, such an argument stands on the same footing as one that asserts that program managers do not produce skills in trainees according to the best available techniques. That is, if training provides skills directly, are training programs run "on" their production functions or at maximum feasible productivity? It may be noted that there is little reason to expect efficient production, since government agencies are typically not run as profit-making ventures. An implication is that there may be something to be gained by diverting programs through profit-making enterprises by use of wage subsidies or tax credits, rather than direct provision of training through nonprofit institutions.

Finally, it can now be seen why wage subsidies or tax incentives are necessary to induce employers to provide this kind of training within firms. Employers do not hire workers whose expected external economies (within the firm) are less than the average amount being generated by current employees, for output attributable to that worker does not rise sufficiently to cover his cost. The subsidy is necessary to compensate for the external diseconomy, that is, the slightly lower output achieved by other workers if he (or she) is hired. Thus, the subsidy required to induce employment must be sufficient to compensate for the marginal reduction in output that occurs when the going production team is disrupted by this type of trainee. Cases where the necessary minimum payments might be very large are not difficult to envision, but that is an empirical matter that in principle can be determined one way or another. In any event, this analy-

---

[9] Several methodological problems involved in program evaluation are discussed by Cain and Hollister (1969b).

sis suggests some tendency toward segregation of trainees away from regular assembly workers within the firm if subsidies are used and are set at *less* than appropriate amounts (i.e., the amounts necessary to compensate for the *entire* external diseconomy), for external diseconomies can be avoided in that manner. It may be surmised that segregation reduces training program output (in terms of altered trainee work incentives, etc.) per dollar of public expenditure, compared to what would result if segregation did not occur, making it imperative that sufficiently large subsidies be used.

Externalities and General Skills

On the basis of the logic above, general skills might be associated in the main with vocational knowledge of one sort or another. Here there is the result that costs of skill acquisition are generally borne by parties to whom returns accrue [see Becker]. This is obvious in the case of most full-time school enrollment (with qualification due to various scholarships and third-party payments), but is far less obvious for knowledge that is acquired on the job and through learning experience. One condition for Pareto optimality in the absence of technical externalities, or where such externalities have been internalized by market forces (as above), requires that marginal internal rates of return on various types of investment be set equal to "the" rate of interest. Can it be claimed that this result will automatically occur in the case of embodied skills acquired in the labor market? If so, by what means? If not, what are the possible sources of market failure?

To attempt to answer some of these questions, consider a simple model of skill accumulation in the labor market.[10] Begin with the hypothesis that learning, or gross acquisition of skill and knowledge embodied in workers, is a joint-product (or by-product) of work activity. That is, workers learn by doing and as an automatic consequence of working. Basically, that is the reason why skill (or h in equation (1) above) and therefore labor earnings are expected to grow with labor market experience. Work activities and learning are strictly complementary in this formulation of the problem. However, the ratio between the two varies from job to job. For purposes of illustration, think of the differences between dead-end jobs and jobs with a future. Very little activity is devoted toward enhancement of worker knowledge and skill in the one case, whereas a great deal of ostensible work effort is devoted to learning activities in the other. This view implies that labor markets can be characterized by sets of two-way, simultaneous transactions. Both services of skill *and* opportunities to accumulate additional skills are traded in the market. Workers offer the services of their skill to employers, but also receive in return fixed opportunities to learn something, depending on the character of the job chosen. On the other side of the bargain,

---

[10] Details and further analysis can be found in Rosen (1971).

firms employ various skills possessed by workers as productive inputs, but also produce opportunities for workers to learn, depending on how production is organized. Thus, the analysis can be carried out by constructing a conceptual or implicit market for learning (i.e., investment) that is dual to the market for jobs.

Demand for jobs with learning content derives from the fact that skill has market rental value (R in terms of equation (1)), so that workers are willing to pay for opportunities to learn. Supply of jobs with learning content is based on the fact that their provision involves opportunity costs to firms in terms of marketable output foregone. The organization of production and the nature of work activities within firms can be structured in alternative ways to produce various chances for employees to learn. Thus, costs stem from foregone output due to allocating productive resources of workers' time and services of physical capital toward instructional purposes rather than to current output. Instruction in this connection should be interpreted in its broadest possible context, for most learning due to work experience occurs in very informal ways.

If provision of jobs with learning content is costly, firms will not choose to provide them unless production costs can be covered. The manner in which this is done is by, in effect, selling those jobs to employees. Again, a set of equalizing wage differentials must arise in the labor market, in which (for a person of given skill) jobs offering large learning opportunities pay lower wages than those offering lesser possibilities. In fact, these equalizing wage differentials can be regarded as implicit prices for investment in embodied skill and knowledge. In equilibrium, these prices clear the implicit market for learning options.

In a market system, the presence of technical externalities in production requires appropriate taxation and subsidization policies for the achievement of Pareto efficiency. A standard textbook example of technical economies of production involves the training of labor. For example, the following appears in a leading economics text:

If one glass-blowing firm on the island of Murano expands its operations, it may have to train more glass blowers who are potentially available for employment by its competitors, and those competitors will incur no training costs if they recruit any of those workers. [Baumol; pp. 368-369]

As it stands, here is a clear case of divergence between social and private marginal products. If investment in the acquisition of skills was organized in this way, equilibrium would establish a wedge between the marginal social internal rate of return and the rate of interest, requiring subsidization of this type of investment to achieve economic efficiency. But it is obvious that the source of market failure in the quotation is due to the peculiar financial arrangement of investment, since those bearing the cost do not reap full social returns. Certainly, there is no reason in principle for this to be the case. Moreover, an explicit mechanism whereby investment costs can be shifted to workers (who capture the returns) has been demonstrated above. Again, the market internalizes such externalities.

Workers pay for learning by the emergence of equalizing wage differentials, allowing them to receive lower wages than they could otherwise earn in exchange for learning. In sum, there is no reason to expect market failure in allocating resources to human investment on this account alone. Furthermore, the social benefit of training is the wealth so created, again measured by discounted increased future earning power in the market.

This is *not* to say that government has no role in the provision of training. The economic case for government intervention in the learning market is based on at least three considerations: (1) Existence of ubiquitous "capital market imperfections." (2) Market discrimination makes the supply price of learning opportunities higher to some workers than to others, and effectively prices members of the former group out of the market for high learning-content jobs. Similarly, discrimination can produce differences in rental values (R) on services of skills between groups, resulting in inefficiency. Subsidies "buy off" discrimination of these types. (3) Anything producing wage floors or rigidities can prevent wage differentials (of both types—across workers and across jobs) from equalizing, very seriously constraining choices available to some workers, especially the low skilled. Some important factors here are likely to be legislated or social minimum wages and trade union restrictions. Both wage subsidies and direct provision of skill overcome these barriers.[11]

If in fact costs of investment are fully shifted to recipients, the existence of widespread externalities associated with skill and knowledge of the type under consideration is very unlikely. Knowledge available to society at large is a public good, implying that private allocation of resources to increase society's stock of available knowledge will be less than optimal in the absence of government incentives to the contrary. But human investment of the type discussed here is hardly related to additions to overall knowledge. Rather, most learning activity in the labor market and in vocational training programs is concerned with acquisition of a portion of the existing stock of knowledge and technique. Though one person's acquisition does not in any sense preclude the possibility of another person learning the same thing, lack of exclusion yields no difficulties for economic efficiency, for learning is not costless to the person engaging in it and skill has economic value only when it is embodied in workers. Finally, the process of innovation is one of the least understood problems in the social sciences. Though employee suggestion boxes are probably not an insignificant source of invention, program evaluation is justified in ignoring the undoubtedly trivial effects on overall knowledge available to society due to manpower programs.

A rather different source of market failure arises in discussions of investment, particularly with respect to less developed areas [see Scitovsky]. Under static conditions, competitive markets are efficient because market prices convey all socially relevant information. However, correct investment decisions not only require knowledge of current prices, but of future prices as well, and the latter are

---

[11] See Rosen (1971) for elaboration on these points.

generally not known with certainty. Investment projects can have unforeseen consequences with alteration of subsequent prices in ways that, had they been known at the time of project initiation, would have implied a different course of action. Thus, training a labor force in a relatively small, isolated labor market area may attract industry there, raise the demand for labor in the area and necessitate further training of workers. If the initial scale of the project was designed around expected increased trainee earnings based on preproject industry location, less than the optimal number of trainees would have been put through the program in the first instance. In cases such as this, there is a divergence between the optimal rate of investment and the actual rate. If any investment occurs at all, the market eventually will grope its way to long-run (stationary) equilibrium. At that point, there is no reason to expect the marginal social product of skill embodied in workers not to equal marginal social cost of acquisition of skill. Hence, the long-run stock will be socially optimal. Only the rate at which the steady-state stock is approached is nonoptimal. Evidently, sufficiently centralized investment planning could (in principle) make the rate of investment socially optimal as well.

At least since the time of Marshall's *Principles*, economists have recognized that decisions to acquire skill and knowledge are made under conditions of great uncertainty and imperfect information. Therefore, such decisions are bound to be subject to error, *ex post*. But what role can government play here? Certainly, if government bureaus have access to information that is not available to otherwise interested economic units, that information should be widely disseminated. However, it is not clear that government possesses systematically greater information concerning the market for skills than is possessed by other parties. Two examples will suffice to illustrate the point: (1) Not too many years ago, a portion of governmental resources was devoted to the training of agricultural labor. (2) The much discussed shortage of scientists and engineers in the late fifties and early sixties (never clearly verified) led to decisions which, when viewed in light of current market conditions, were hardly optimal. This too might argue for the potential efficacy of wage subsidies in going firms rather than direct provision of training services, but only if firms providing training have greater information regarding potential markets for skills than other parties.

Pecuniary Externalities: The Income Distribution Effects of Training

The discussion so far has been confined to potential technical externalities involved in human investment decisions. There is another class of secondary effects having to do with changes in product and factor prices—or pecuniary externalities—that have no significance for welfare economics (narrowly defined).[12] Price changes do have significant effects on the distribution of income,

---

[12] Basically, the reason is that price changes have no effect on present and future production possibilities functions. Varying income distributions and distributions of initial endowments certainly affect the actual locations chosen on these functions, however. For an excellent exposition of these important differences, see McKean.

however, which probably accounts for their concern in the manpower literature. After all, a primary goal of manpower programs is to raise market incomes of trainees. To illustrate the nature of this issue, consider the following examples.

Suppose cost-benefit analysis indicates it is socially desirable to train farm labor, and training programs are established to that end. If the increase in supply of workers is large enough, wage rates of agricultural workers (or R in equation (1)) will fall. Hence, earnings of workers who were in the market prior to the program will fall and they will suffer capital losses. Some will apply for jobs elsewhere. If demand for agricultural labor is inelastic, total earnings paid to all farm workers as a group will actually fall. In any event, a large fraction of farm workers are officially classified as poor, and, though training raises incomes of trainees, the problem of rural poverty overall might be exacerbated.

Concern over this question is legitimate. But why stop here? There are other effects to be considered. If demand for agricultural products is sufficiently inelastic, the fall in price of farm labor will reduce the demand for farm capital, reducing its price as well (at least in the short run). Manufacturers of farm machinery, whose factories were geared to higher rates of production at the old prices, will suffer capital losses, borne by shareholders in these companies in the form of falling security prices. No doubt some of the more aged poor ultimately derive income from such securities. Also, when the farm equipment industry contracts, some of the first to be fired will be low-skilled, low-income workers. On the other hand, reduced food prices increase the real income of everybody, but help the poor relatively more than others, since they spend a larger fraction of their money income on those goods. The reduction in food prices will also increase demand for complementary goods. For example, the restaurant business will probably expand, increasing the demand for many low-skilled workers, such as short-order cooks, bus boys, dishwashers and car hikers.

Now consider another example. In spite of greatly increased demand for medical services in recent years, the doctor-population ratio has not risen very much. Solely for the sake of argument, suppose there exists a genuine economic shortage of doctors, which would imply that the social rate of return to training additional doctors exceeds the going rate of return on investment elsewhere. If an extensive policy was adopted to greatly increase medical school enrollments and to reduce practice restrictions on foreign-educated M.D.s, the effects would be very similar to those mentioned above for farm workers. In particular, doctors' incomes (per unit of effort) would tend to fall, stock prices in the drug industry might rise, etc. In principle, there is no real difference between the two cases. Yet there is a big practical difference: It is difficult to believe that an objective policy-maker (ignoring pressure from the medical lobby) would seriously take account of capital losses imposed on existing practitioners of medicine due to increased supply, for doctors as a group are one of the highest paid professions in our society; whereas he would be prone to do so in the case of farm labor.

Conclusion

It is worth emphasizing once again that, as a matter of logic at least, questions of economic efficiency can be separated from ethical questions having to do with distribution. In the first problem, we seek the conditions under which discounted utility of consumption of all members of society can be maximized, given total initial resources and available technical production knowledge. On the production side, we wish to know how total wealth of society can be maximized, which reflects these future consumption possibilities. If the discounted net social return on a potential investment exceeds its social cost, that investment is justified and real wealth is increased by undertaking it. The difference between returns and costs is the social profit due to the investment. Moreover, there exists an income (or, more precisely wealth) distribution that would make no person worse off over his lifetime with the investment than without it and that would make at least one person better off. Otherwise, returns could not exceed costs. We have seen above, that under a well-functioning market system, the social benefit of investment in the acquisition of skill through manpower programs is always measured by the increased earning power of trainees, since externalities tend to be internalized by wage differentials in the market. Purely on grounds of economic efficiency, if benefits to trainees exceed costs, then training should be provided independently of subsequent windfall gains and losses in the economy due to the program.[13] Furthermore, gains and losses elsewhere should not be added or subtracted from benefits to trainees for purposes of program evaluation. This is obvious in the second example above: it would clearly be erroneous to subtract capital losses from benefits or add them to costs in calculating net social benefit from increased supply of practitioners. Moreover, if an increase in supply was warranted, the price of medical care would fall, raising real incomes of all members of society by sufficient amounts to *more* than compensate existing practitioners' capital losses if necessary.

The real point is that there are two problems to be considered. One is to design economic policies that help develop and utilize human resources as efficiently as possible. The other is to achieve an equitable distribution of income. In addition, there is more than one policy instrument available for these purposes, for incomes of the poor can be raised directly by use of transfer payments of various types. Viewed entirely as a redistributive mechanism, training programs must surely come off as second-best by comparison with real transfer policies, even though there exists no practical mixtures of transfer payment pro-

---

[13] Note that the existence of unemployment in the economy is automatically captured in cost-benefit analysis, since opportunity costs of trainees' time while in the program as well as measured gross benefits in terms of future income prospects are altered. Given the view presented in this paper, training is properly considered as a resource-creating device, rather than as a policy aimed entirely at reducing unemployment. Of course, given a certain configuration of other policies, unemployment may be reduced as well. See Cain and Stromsdorfer for a discussion of related issues.

grams that have no consequences for the aggregate supply of work effort. Thus, there is likely to be a trade-off between maximum average lifetime consumption per capita (efficiency) and the variance around that average (equity). Efficient policies are those combinations that achieve their objectives at minimum social cost, i.e., that are located on the efficiency-equity frontier. Furthermore, transfer payments are likely to interact with human resource development. For example, availability of income maintenance may have effects on the motivation of potential trainees that affect cost-benefit calculations of training programs. In any event, it is incorrect to consider both efficiency and equity implications of a particular training program in isolation of other policies. If benefits to trainees exceed social costs, there is a presumption that training is warranted, so long as appropriate transfer payment mechanisms exist.

20 The Secondary Effects of Manpower Programs

Daniel S. Hammermesh[1]

America's manpower programs have been aimed primarily toward increasing the skills embodied in disadvantaged workers and enabling them to find useful employment. Recent research has endeavored to evaluate the effects on the disadvantaged of the two billion dollars spent each year on these programs. A full evaluation of their political and economic effects must, however, also take into account their effects on other population groups.

Certain secondary effects should be considered in calculating the benefits to be used in any benefit-cost calculation for training programs.[2] Perhaps the most important of these occur because of the change these programs cause in the structure of private economic decision-making. On the supply side of the labor market, training subsidies shift the relative flows of new workers toward those occupations in which training is offered. On the demand side, there is an incentive for individual firms to alter their wage and hiring policies in order to reach a new profit-maximizing position given the new factor-price structure implied by the subsidies.

This paper considers three such secondary effects of training programs. On the negative side, a very important secondary impact of training programs is what is known as the displacement problem. Unless workers are trained for jobs in which vacancies exist, the subsidies given to firms to employ disadvantaged workers result in the displacement of other, nonsubsidized workers from employment. Estimates of benefit-cost ratios which ignore displacement will thus be biased upward, as the employment and income losses of displaced workers are left out.[3]

---

[1] Robert Goldfarb, Albert Rees, and Michael Taussig made helpful comments which contributed to the analysis. The research on which this paper is based was financed by the Ford Foundation through its grant to the Princeton Industrial Relations Section for the study of urban labor markets.

[2] We will not treat here certain secondary effects such as the rise in morale among disadvantaged trainees who find employment and the generational effects upon the children of successful trainees. Secondary and other economic effects of manpower programs are discussed in detail in my book, *Economic Aspects of Manpower Training Programs: Theory and Policy*. This paper summarizes part of the material in that volume.

[3] Secondary effects are important not only for policy evaluation; they may also result in unexpected political repercussions upon the very programs designed to help the disadvantaged. For example, if some program hurts or helps groups other than that at which it is aimed, these latter groups will either lobby against or for the continuation and expansion of the particular program. If the effects are negative, and the second group is successful in its lobbying efforts, the existence of the program itself may be threatened by what are seemingly only secondary effects.

In addition to the displacement effects of training, the secondary effects of job matching programs must also be analyzed. In its role in improving the short-run trade-off between inflation and unemployment, job matching may have important secondary effects on firms' employment decisions, and these may confound the original purposes of the program. Finally, because on-the-job training is inextricably linked to mobility patterns through its effects on firms' wages, changes in the training process induced by government subsidies will automatically produce changes in the amount of mobility in the labor market. Whether these effects are beneficial or detrimental to the efficiency of the labor market should also be an important criterion to use in deciding on the merits of training and job information programs.

The Displacement Problem

We define the percentage employment displacement effect of a training subsidy as:

$$(1) \qquad \left(1 - \frac{E_1 + E^* - E_0}{E^*}\right) \cdot 100 , \qquad (1)$$

where E_0 is initial employment, E_1 is the employment of nonsubsidized workers after the training subsidy has been given and E^* is some positive number of disadvantaged, subsidized workers employed. Its magnitude can range between zero (no displacement) and one hundred percent (the only effect of the training program is to substitute disadvantaged for nonsubsidized workers). Displacement could be measured within a single firm, within a single occupation in an entire labor market, or for all employment in a labor market, although the exact details would have to differ depending on the application. Our measure concentrates on employment and ignores income changes among the trainees and other workers; these income shifts are much more difficult to analyze.

The nature of displacement. It is essential that the displacement effect be calculated between two short-run equilibria, i.e., that intermediate adjustments be allowed time to work themselves out. The firm's immediate response to any subsidy will not be to lay off currently employed, nonsubsidized workers. This type of *direct displacement* is highly unlikely, for the firm has a large investment in the training of these workers which will generally be unprofitable to forego merely to reap some profit on the hiring of subsidized, disadvantaged trainees. In the short run in which capital is fixed but nonsubsidized workers retire, quit or fail to return from layoff, the firm has an incentive to hire subsidized disadvantaged workers over nonsubsidized potential new hires. Since quit rates are usually greater than one percent per month, this indirect effect will occur rapidly as firms replace nonsubsidized quits by subsidized new hires. This type of *indirect displacement* is clearly the one which must be analyzed.

Only if the firm operates in a labor market for an occupation whose supply is completely inelastic will the displacement problem be nonexistent. In this case, the increase in the number of trained workers shifts the vertical portion of the supply curve outward and to the right, thus decreasing each subsidized firm's incentive to raise wages to attract labor from other firms. In this case of true shortage, the displacement effect will be zero. If, however, the supply curve has some nonzero elasticity, the provision of disadvantaged, subsidized trainees to the firm will result in the indirect displacement of nonsubsidized workers either in this firm or in other firms employing workers in the same occupation. Displacement is likely to occur in cases in which the occupations for which training is offered are not those in which shortages of workers exist. For example, in the postwar period lower-skilled occupations, those which require little prior training and little on-the-job training, have not been characterized by shortages.[4] Training programs which provide subsidized, disadvantaged trainees in these occupations are likely to result in substantial displacement or prospective low-skilled employees who are not receiving the subsidy. Similarly, in times of high aggregate unemployment, when there is no general shortage of labor, training subsidies are also likely to produce a fairly large displacement effect in nearly all occupations.

Unfortunately, it is currently impossible to measure the amount of displacement caused by any local manpower program. There are no data on equilibrium employment in individual firms receiving the subsidy, and data on factors affecting employment which might be used in some econometric model of employment decisions by all firms in the labor market also are not available. Data on such variables as changes in each firm's product demand, changes in local unemployment rates by occupation and the flows of labor into the labor market would all be needed to isolate the firms' decisions about their profit-maximizing employment. Our only data are on the number of trainees placed; using (1), we can easily see that these data are insufficient for the estimation of the displacement effect.

The importance of the displacement problem for evaluation and the current impossibility of even attempting to estimate it suggest that additional data should be collected. As part of the regular monitoring of trainees in OJT programs, their employers should also be required to report total employment in each occupation which contains some subsidized workers. While we still would be unable to estimate labor marketwide displacement, there would at least be some hope of isolating the behavior of firms receiving the subsidy and removing part of the bias in the estimated benefit-cost ratios.

---

[4] At no time during this period has the unemployment rate of craftsmen exceeded that of nonfarm laborers or operatives.

A model for the simulation of displacement. Because we cannot now estimate displacement effects empirically, we resort instead to constructing a theoretical model and simulating it using approximations to real-world parameters. We assume that no shortage of nonsubsidized workers exists and that each worker requires some amount S of training before he can produce. Furthermore, each disadvantaged worker requires an additional investment in training, so that the total investment required to enable him to participate in the production process is $S + g_i$, where i refers to the individual worker. The magnitude of g_i will vary within the disadvantaged group. Some workers will require only small amounts of extra training to bring them up to par with nonsubsidized workers, while for others the investment would have to be truly immense to enable them to participate in production. Since we assume no shortage of nonsubsidized workers, unless the firm receives a subsidy for training and hiring disadvantaged workers, it will never pay it to employ these individuals.

We assume, therefore, that the government wishes to see some employment of disadvantaged workers and offers a subsidy for this purpose. This subsidy, which is in reality fixed by the nature of the job for which training is offered, is assumed to be of an amount g^*. For any disadvantaged worker for whom $g_i > g^*$, the firm will never undertake training. If it were to do so, it would be making less money on training him than it would on the nonsubsidized worker for whom the profits of training are assumed to be zero. Only those disadvantaged workers for whom g_i is less the g^* will be hired and trained and the firm makes an extra profit of $g^* - g_i$ on training the i'th disadvantaged worker.

This simple model can be used to explain the existence of "creaming," the frequently observed phenomenon in which employers attempt to pick the best qualified of those workers classified as disadvantaged. The firm has an incentive to drive g_i down to zero if it can in order to maximize the extra profits of training. It does this by picking from the group of workers qualifying for the subsidy those for whom the additional training costs are lowest.[5]

In our model, we assume that the firm combines untrained employees with some amount of training per capita and some amount of physical capital to produce homogeneous output for sale in a competitive market. The firm takes the wage of untrained labor as given, but it sets some additional wage premium in order to minimize the costs of turnover. The actual magnitude of this premium depends upon the responsiveness of the firm's quit rate to changes in the

---

[5]The very existence of "creaming" is an excellent example of the operation of profit-maximizing behavior by employers. If one postulated that employers were not profit-maximizers, but rather trained workers out of altruism, one would expect the least qualified disadvantaged workers to be hired. In that way, the entrepreneur would be maximizing his contribution to charity by employing those people who need help the most. That this does not occur is a good justification for the use of economic theory in analyzing the operation of manpower training programs. Even the JOBS program, designed to enlist business cooperation through subsidies to hire and train disadvantaged workers, appears to be characterized by substantial "creaming."

premium as well as on the amount of training the firm offers.[6] The firm's revenue is thus determined by these three factors of production and the price it receives from selling output. Its costs consist of the wage costs of employment, the ordinary costs S of training each worker times the number of quits each period and a negative cost, the extra profits it makes on training subsidized workers. This last component is a function of the quit rate of subsidized employees and the average magnitude of $g^* - g_i$.

We can then assume that the firm has in mind four profit-maximizing conditions based upon inputs of capital, ordinary training, employment and on the wage premium which it sets to minimize its turnover costs. The firm's decisions are also determined by various parameters which it faces: 1) the capital intensity of production; 2) the training intensity of production; and 3) the responsiveness of the quit rate to changes in the wage premium. If we assume a three-factor Cobb-Douglas style production function, we may conclude that the employment intensity of production is one minus the sum of the capital and training intensities. We can then use the four profit-maximizing conditions of the firm to estimate its response to a subsidy for training disadvantaged workers under various assumptions about the magnitudes of these three parameters. In particular, we can estimate its equilibrium employment in the unsubsidized case and compare that to its employment of subsidized and nonsubsidized workers in the case in which the subsidy is offered. We can thus estimate the magnitude of the displacement effect of the subsidy program and the conditions when it will be greater or smaller under the assumption that nonsubsidized firms do not change their employment. This last provision is completely consistent with the assumption that the supply curve of nonsubsidized labor in this surplus occupation is horizontal where it is intersected by the market demand curve. These simulations are made with varying assumptions about the relation between S and g^* in order to allow greater training allowances for jobs in which even the nonsubsidized worker requires more training.

One would expect, and we do observe that the existence of the simulated subsidy program encourages firms to lower their wage premium and increase the amount of turnover they face. Other things equal, the amount the firm gains from training disadvantaged workers is increased when the number of disadvantaged workers it trains rises. In the new equilibrium, therefore, the firm has an incentive to turn over workers more rapidly than before in order to increase its profits.

The most pervasive general result in our simulations is that there exists, under our assumption of no shortage of nonsubsidized workers, a trade-off between the number of disadvantaged workers placed in a firm and the percentage displacement of nonsubsidized trainees. Given a fixed budget for training, the government has a choice in the case of labor surplus of either increasing the number of disadvantaged workers placed and simultaneously increasing the percentage

---

[6] See Hamermesh, p. 48.

displacement of nonsubsidized workers, or decreasing this displacement but also placing fewer disadvantaged trainees. This is clearly a very difficult dilemma to face, and it points out again the need to concentrate training in those occupations and at those times in which shortages are proven to exist.

Variations in the factor intensities of capital and training have no uniform effect on the magnitude of displacement. Depending upon the assumptions about the relationship of S to g^*, variations in these parameters have different effects on displacement. We may thus conclude, that, aside from the effects on output which might exist if the subsidy is given to more labor-intensive firms, there is no reason to concentrate subsidies in firms having production functions characterized by different distribution parameters if each firm's output is fixed.

The only one of the three parameters which has a definite effect on the magnitude of displacement is that representing the responsiveness of the quit rate to changes in the wage premium. In the firms in which quits are more sensitive to this variable, a fixed-budget subsidy produces fewer disadvantaged trainees employed but also substantially less displacement both in absolute and percentage terms. If, but only if, training subsidies are given in occupations which are not in shortage, this result suggests that funds be concentrated in those firms in which the quit rate is rather large and the workers are relatively low skilled.

Even in times of labor surplus, some intelligent application of the training subsidies may serve to minimize the displacement which they cause. If, for example, they are concentrated in firms in which production is relatively labor intensive, this policy should in the long-run shift output toward these firms and result in an increase in employment in the economy, when other factors are held constant. Whether this policy is desirable in terms of its effects on long-run economic growth is another question.

One other alternative is that the provision of the training subsidies might have a positive effect on total production through the increase in the government deficit which must in the short-run accompany any expansion of training appropriations.[7] Deficit-financing has the clearly beneficial effect of mitigating the amount of displacement in the short-run in occupations in which the employment is less than full. One must doubt, however, whether in the long-run it could have any effect. Given legislative pressure for a balanced budget, any increased deficit induced by expenditures for the training program will after some period of time have to be wiped out through increased taxes. Only if one believes that the taxes come from individuals with relatively low propensities to consume and the subsidies are given to individuals whose propensities to consume are large, can one believe that the aggregate demand effect is likely to be important.

Policy implications of the results. Perhaps the most important implication of our discussion is the essentiality of concentrating training in occupations in

---

[7] This possibility is discussed at length in Cain and Stromsdorfer, pp. 333-335.

which shortages exist and at times of general labor market shortage. If high-skilled occupations are in shortage, they should be the ones in which the government subsidizes training. Furthermore, training should be given when aggregate unemployment is low. Only in this way can the government avoid facing the dilemma of either training more workers and causing a higher percentage displacement or providing fewer jobs for the disadvantaged and causing less displacement.

These considerations suggest the appropriateness of a strategy of upgrading currently employed low-skilled workers. In general, upgrading would be concentrated on training low-skilled workers for more highly skilled jobs in which shortages exist. Such a strategy would thus avoid the displacement likely to arise from training currently unemployed workers for entry-level vacancies. Moreover, the government's cost per trainee of such a policy may well be less than the cost incurred under direct subsidies which train the disadvantaged for entry-level jobs.

If the displacement effect of some subsidy program is large, one must conclude that its major effect is merely distributional. It transfers jobs and income from the least qualified workers who are ineligible for this subsidy to the best qualified workers who are eligible. While this may be beneficial under certain assumptions about the shape of a social welfare function, it has the very serious negative effect of causing substantial dissatisfaction among those workers who lose under this policy. Indeed, these dissatisfactions may well be an important cause of the so-called blue-collar revolt. Favoritism for disadvantaged workers in hiring and promotion, and government programs designed to help these workers have been cited both in the report by Assistant Secretary of Labor Rosow and in a number of newspaper articles discussing the plight of the blue-collar worker.[8]

Even if the displacement problem is obviated by concentrating training funds in shortage occupations and at times of low aggregate unemployment, the creaming problem will still be very important under the current regulations for the administration of manpower subsidies. As we have shown, there exists an incentive for the profit-maximizing firm to do as much creaming as it can within the regulations issued by the government. If it wishes to circumvent this difficulty, the government could link reimbursements for training not only to the characteristics of the job for which the trainee is given training, but could also include in its reimbursement schedule some measure of his personal characteristics. A points system could be used, so that for identical jobs firms would receive a larger subsidy for training workers with greater skill deficiencies than for those who do not have these deficiencies. While it is difficult to guess the appropriate set of points to be given for each disability (educational, age, etc.), one could pick an initial set of these point allocations and observe how the market reacts

[8]The Rosow memorandum, "The Problem of the Blue-Collar Worker," was issued on April 16, 1970. The evidence on the increasing discontent of the blue-collar worker is cited in greater detail in Hamermesh, pp. 39-40.

to them. If certain workers are then selected to a much greater extent than others, the government could change its point allocations to put disadvantaged workers with different qualifications on an equal footing. Using this iterative scheme, the government could then arrive at an allocation of workers which completely ends the creaming problem. If the government is interested in doing so, this scheme would enable it to help those workers who need help the most.

As is apparent from the discussion of our simulation results, the displacement effect is likely to impart a substantial upward bias to the estimated benefit-cost ratios of individual training programs. Although most benefit-cost analysts recognize the existence of this problem, they usually ignore its effects in computing their ratios and discussing the implications of their computations for manpower policy. This problem is especially serious in those studies using data from the period 1962 through 1965, when the aggregate unemployment rate was fairly high and thus displacement may have been quite large.[9] Given the high unemployment of the last eighteen months, the bias has undoubtedly increased in its importance for evaluation. There is very little one can do actually to adjust benefit-cost estimates to account for the displacement problem. The researcher should, however, recognize that the upward bias of these estimates will be greater in times of high unemployment and in programs which train for entry-level jobs and should modify his conclusions accordingly.

Shifting the Short-Run Phillips Curve through Job Matching and Training

The main implication of our discussion of the displacement problem is that manpower training should be concentrated in shortage occupations. Not only will this help to mitigate the displacement of nonsubsidized workers, it will also help to shift the short-run trade-off between inflation and unemployment. We view this trade-off as resulting from excess demand for labor in some labor markets combined with surpluses in others, and assume also that wages are sticky and training takes time. Training of new entrants into the labor force for those occupations which are in shortage should have the result of evening out these imbalances and preventing upward pressure on wage rates from employers competing for labor which is not available.

Improved man-job matching may also have the same beneficial effect on this trade-off. Indeed, some writers concentrate upon this in their discussion of appropriate manpower measures for use in shifting the Phillips curve.[10] The

---

[9]Levitan and Mangum recognize that the importance of the displacement effect varies inversely with the business cycle, p. 33.

[10]Holt, et al., (1971) offer an extremely sanguine view of the role of job matching in producing a better short-run trade-off between inflation and unemployment.

argument is that as employers' searching becomes more efficient, they will have greater success in finding workers who fit the qualifications for the vacancies which exist in their firms. There is thus less of an incentive for them to raise wages, for at equal rates of aggregate unemployment, the shortage of workers they perceive is not so great as before the job information program was started. Similarly, on the supply side, workers will avoid searching through vacancies which are unsuitable for them and will thus be unemployed for a shorter period of time. In this way, the amount of frictional unemployment in the labor market will be decreased.

In terms of the Phillips curve, after a job matching policy is instituted at any unemployment rate, there exist fewer vacancies in the labor market because employers can search more efficiently through those prospective employees who present themselves at the gate. This is translated into a downward shift in the short-run trade-off between the rate of inflation and unemployment. Since at any unemployment rate there are fewer vacancies, employers need not raise their wage rates as much as they had previously in order to attract the necessary labor. If we assume that product prices reflect factor costs, this decline in the rate of wage inflation at any unemployment rate is translated into a decline in the rate of price inflation.

This shift in the Phillips curve is the primary effect of a successful job matching program. We must also, however, consider an important secondary effect. There exists a long literature which suggests that, as the profit-maximizing employer's marginal costs of training and search in any time period rise, it pays him to increase the lag in his adjustment of employment to changes in product demand.[11] Some estimates suggest even that this lag may have a half-life of nine months, while the best estimates are that its duration is three to five months.[12] Whatever the empirical estimates, the theory explicitly states that costs of adjustment can be linked to the duration of the lag in adjustment of some factor of production to changes in product demand.

This adjustment lag has a clear-cut effect on changes in measured labor productivity and has been proposed as the reason for observed decreases in productivity during cyclical recessions.[13] At these times, output drops and employment also drops, but the latter still remains above its equilibrium level. We assume, therefore, that employers engage in labor hoarding and thus do not work their employees up to full capacity. True employment is thus less than measured employment, so that output falls more than would be expected by observing measured employment.

The job matching program lowers the costs of search for individual em-

---

[11] This is discussed in Charles Holt, et al., (1960), Chapter 2.

[12] Much of the empirical evidence on the average lag of adjustment of employment to output is discussed in Fair, Chapter 2.

[13] Kuh and many others have made this connection.

ployers. If the lag in the adjustment of employment to output arises because of costs of adjustment, we should expect that the length of this lag will decrease after the job matching program is put into effect. Intuitively, if it becomes easier for employers to adjust employment because the marginal cost of information acquisition decreases, we should expect them to be more willing to lay off workers during recessions because it is easier for them to find other qualified workers when product demand recovers. We should therefore expect there to be more fluctuation in measured productivity in an economy with no job matching program as compared to another, otherwise identical economy with one. This result occurs because employment fluctuations will be less in the first economy than in the second. In terms of Figure 20-1, we might postulate that in the first economy cyclical output fluctuations cause movement along P_O between points A and B. In the second economy, in which the job matching program helps to shift the curve, policy-makers can choose both lower unemployment and lower rates of inflation. However, unless this choice is consciously exercised through macroeconomic measures, the economy may well move over a wider range of unemployment, for example between points C and D. Although this economy is better off in that its rate of inflation is lower at any unemployment rate, one may well observe in it higher rates of unemployment than in the economy in which the Phillips curve has not been shifted by job matching programs.

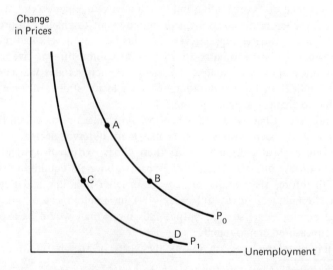

Figure 20-1. The Short-Run Phillips Curve and the Effects of Job-Matching Programs.

While we can say *a priori* that a job matching program could result in wider fluctuations in employment, we cannot state that the observed unemployment rates will necessarily be higher than those which existed before the program was instituted. This result depends upon the policy choices of macroeconomic planners between remaining at the high rates of unemployment they had chosen previously or picking lower rates of unemployment and foregoing decreases in the rate of inflation. Our result suggests that there exists a possible need for adjustments in macroeconomic policy in order to avoid higher unemployment rates which may result from the change in the structure of firms' employment decisions induced by the institution of programs designed to disseminate labor market information.

If macro policy is adjusted and planners take advantage of the improved short-run trade-off to achieve lower unemployment, future training programs should be able to avoid much of the displacement characterizing today's training. Just as efforts to minimize displacement by concentrating training in shortage occupations help to improve the short-run inflation-unemployment trade-off, so job matching programs may produce the useful secondary benefit of decreasing the amount of displacement of nonsubsidized workers.

Mobility and Training

For purposes of our discussion, we use the practical definition of mobility and equate it to a firm's turnover. While most sociologists and economists would wish to attach a normative connotation to the term mobility, in reality it is extremely difficult to be sure that all job moves raise the status or occupation of the individual making the move.[14] We assume for the moment that all turnover occurs because of the desire of workers to improve some aspect of their compensation or working conditions. Whether this is socially desirable is another question and will be discussed below.

The theory of training suggests that the amount of training a firm offers affects its turnover. In particular, if training is specific to a given firm, the firm has an incentive to raise a worker's wage above that he could receive in other firms in order to avoid incurring the costs of training a new worker when the current employee quits. Given identical responses of quit rates to changes in the real wage, as the amount of training per worker which the firm must undertake increases, the profit-maximizing wage increases and the turnover rate in the firm decreases.

Subsidies which affect the amount of training and hiring costs incurred by the firm will therefore affect its turnover rate and indirectly the total amount of mobility within a local labor market. This secondary effect of programs designed

---

[14] Reynolds contains a detailed discussion of the nature of labor mobility and presents some evidence on reasons why individuals quit their jobs.

to increase job mobility or to subsidize training may be beneficial or detrimental depending upon the circumstances. For example, in the case of an upgrading subsidy, the firm is given an incentive to increase the duration of employment of workers whom it hires at entry-level occupations. Rather than filling vacancies for its higher-skilled positions by hiring from the outside, firms on the margin will shift toward promoting workers from entry-level jobs. Thus, an upgrading subsidy has the effect of decreasing turnover in a labor market, both because entry-level workers in the firm have an incentive to remain and because skilled workers elsewhere will not be bid away by firms seeking to fill high-skilled vacancies.

Retraining subsidies have the opposite secondary effect on the amount of mobility in the labor market. If these are offered to workers who feel themselves locked into jobs which do not pay as well as others but which they cannot leave because of the large foregone earnings necessary to undergo retraining, workers on the margin will leave their jobs and shift to other employment which will in the future pay them a higher wage. A retraining subsidy which is offered not just to unemployed workers but to currently employed workers who are dissatisfied with their conditions of employment will thus induce some individuals to quit for more attractive positions.

Successful job information programs may have both accentuating and attenuating secondary effects on the amount of mobility in a labor market. On the other hand, workers who are dissatisfied with their current employment but who now become aware of more attractive jobs elsewhere in the labor market will have an incentive to quit. Other workers, who had quit in the expectation of finding more attractive employment but who became disappointed, would remain in their current jobs when job information improves. The net effect of programs designed to increase job information on the amount of mobility in a labor market is thus unclear. What is true, however, is that information programs necessarily improve the functioning of labor markets and move mobility closer to some optimum. On the one hand, the resource loss resulting from the unemployment of workers who quit because of overly optimistic job expectations is obviated. On the other hand, workers who remain locked into unsatisfactory jobs have an incentive to move toward employment which makes them better off.

It is much more difficult to evaluate whether the secondary effects of training subsidies on mobility are detrimental or beneficial. This depends upon whether the socially desirable degree of mobility is greater than or less than that currently observed in labor markets. There is no general consensus on what constitutes an optimal rate of mobility. (For example, most economists would argue that mobility is insufficient, while most employers would disagree.) For purposes of discussion, however, we shall assume society has fixed on a desired rate of mobility. If this rate is above that currently observed, retraining subsidies, which increase the amount of mobility, move society closer to an optimum; upgrading subsidies, which decrease the amount of mobility, move it further away from that optimum. If the consensus is that mobility is too high, the opposite result holds. Upgrading subsidies are then more desirable, for they lower the amount of labor market mobility down to the social optimum. Whatever the consensus, it is important that these effects be recognized in program construction and their implications for evaluation be studied further.

Conclusions

We have argued that it is essential that secondary effects of training and other manpower programs be analyzed to arrive at a correct evaluation of these subsidies. While some of these secondary effects are detrimental to the achievement of the primary goals (for example, the displacement of other workers by disadvantaged workers), others may be beneficial. Labor market information programs, which may have the detrimental effect of increasing fluctuations in employment, have a beneficial effect on labor market mobility.[15]

Manpower programs are one of the most important tools available for helping disadvantaged workers to improve their economic position and enabling the labor market to function more efficiently. It is essential that the success of these programs not be jeopardized by negative secondary effects and that their positive secondary effects be considered among their benefits. Our discussion suggests that secondary effects may well be secondary in name only. They may be of primary importance for the evaluation, operation and eventual success of the programs which induce them.

---

[15] Similarly, training for jobs in public employment, although its main purpose is to provide relief for unemployed and disadvantaged workers, has the effect of increasing the amount of government services provided. Many people would regard this last consideration as a strong additional argument in favor of job training in the public sector.

Secondary Labor Market
Effects of Manpower
Programs: Comment

Glen G. Cain[1]

The papers of Hamermesh and Rosen examine indirect labor market effects of manpower training programs. These are effects which stem from or impinge upon nonparticipants in the training program—mainly on other workers, although employers, stockholders, and consumers are sometimes mentioned. The modifying phrase "labor market" is used because neither paper considers effects of training programs on variables other than employment and earnings—although Hamermesh mentions political attitudes once and Rosen briefly mentions non-labor prices and quantities. But if one did not already know that this restricted topic is complicated enough, he would have been so convinced by a reading of these papers.

I view these papers as at minimum pointing to variables and issues that need to be investigated in analyzing indirect effects of manpower programs and at maximum as offering a useful theoretical framework for analysis. The hard job of quantifying these effects remains to be done and neither paper offers this nor, in my opinion, much that is useful for immediate empirical application.

Rosen's paper provides a straightforward and clear exposition of the human capital approach to examining manpower programs. He extends the concept of a worker's human capital to include skills in contributing to coworkers' productivity and notes the externalities of this extension. I agree with Rosen's approach, and indeed, I will draw upon it in expressing my general disagreement with Hamermesh's paper. My comments on Rosen's paper will mainly consist of the problems I see in it for practical applications and empirical work.

A serious problem of estimating the determinants of a worker's human capital (Rosen's equation (1)) is that the deterioration-obsolescence factor, δ may at times be negative as well as positive and in any case is not constant. The already tough problem in distinguishing between firm-specific and general training is made more complicated by the heterogeneity of technology within even competitive industries. I do not believe Rosen's assumption of homogeneity is tenable.

The proposition that a worker may be counterproductive just because he generates prejudicial, negative attitudes on the part of employers, coworkers, or

---

[1] To avoid lengthening an already long comment, I will make a number of assertions without supporting argument or citations. Any reader who wishes to see a longer version of the comment is invited to write to me at The Department of Economics, University of Wisconsin, Madison, Wisconsin, 53706.

customers is not new, but surely the challenge we face is to know when this response carries such large social external diseconomies that governmental intervention is called for—as it so obviously is concerning discrimination based on color. Rosen's analysis does not help us to decide when intervention is efficient, let alone when it is equitable.

I am unhappy with the sanguine views expressed that seem to equate the certification of workers as skilled with the actual teaching and inculcating of skills. Although search services constitute a socially useful output, we have reason to be skeptical that full-fledged training programs lasting months are cost-effective ways of performing this service. Contrary to Rosen's belief, many private agencies like employment agencies, training institutes, and schools provide varying types of certification services. Nor should we forget that the informal channels of word-of-mouth may be more efficient than private and governmental agencies.

Rosen emphasizes the trainees' wage gains from whatever source—certification, social skill improvement, or job skill improvement—as a measure of the real social product of the program. I agree, but how do we know when such gains are the result of a *mere* transfer payment (say, an outright wage subsidy) in contrast to when they stem from a real increase in the worker's human capital? If the subsidy goes to the firm and there is not competition for the subsidy among firms, then the transfer payment may show up as increased profits (or rents) to the recipient firm. Maybe this is an efficient (if not an equitable) subsidy, but how do we find out? Surely, these questions find answers in the design of an evaluation analysis. In principle, we would like to have a treatment and control group for each type of training program; those which merely certify, those which teach social skills, and those which teach job skills. Control groups are crucial, and without them we cannot hope to evaluate the real net social gain. For this reason, I wince when Rosen states that the measurement problem (involving control groups and all that) is "beside the point," even though this statement is correct for the point he is making.

Among Rosen's few explicit policy proposals, his suggestion to turn training programs over to private industry is not appealing to me. It runs into the equity problem occasioned by "creaming" (as Hamermesh points out), and, after witnessing the performances of Boeing, Lockheed, and General Dynamics, I wonder about the presumption of efficiency. An alternative device to decentralize governmental training is to grant a training subsidy-voucher to individual workers directly—something akin to the GI bill.

On the matter of pecuniary externalities, Rosen makes clear that a full general equilibrium model is called for, but it is also clear, I believe, that we will have to be satisfied with estimating the major first- and second-order effects, at best. We have not adequately learned how to do this yet, but Rosen's paper is a help.

Rosen's analysis of training does not deal with the business cycle. In one sense, it applies to a full employment economy; in another, it may be said to abstract over the business cycle—applying to normal times or to an average point in time or to the long run. In each application, the assumption is that good times and bad times are averaged out insofar as they affect the numerical values of the variables and the parameters in the model, which does, let us recall, stress present values of human capital formation. The present value criterion clearly takes into account as many years in the future as the analyst deems necessary, but it does, at least in its conventional usage, take market prices as *guides* for constructing the ingredients for the present value computation. Realistically, *current* market prices *are* our guides for determining future market prices and for obtaining the shadow prices of commodities and services transacted in the nonmarket sector, such as home goods, leisure, schooling time, and search efforts of the unemployed.

If unemployment is so extensive that we can no longer accept market prices as guides, then the conventional benefit-cost analysis is in trouble. In the extreme case of the Great Depression, for example, many resources were nearly costless and almost any expansionary governmental activity had a favorable benefit-cost ratio.

A sympathetic interpretation of Hamermesh's paper is that it attempts to grapple with the problems of conventional analysis over the business cycle and, in particular, to examine the performance of training programs under conditions of shortages or, conversely, of abnormally high unemployment. I do not think the attempt is successful. His model is neither more realistic nor superior analytically to the more conventional approach exemplified by Rosen's paper.

Trouble begins on his first page and continues throughout the first section. He states:

Unless workers are trained for jobs in which vacancies exist, the subsidies given to firms to employ disadvantaged workers result in the long run displacement of other, nonsubsidized workers from employment. Estimates of benefit-cost ratios which ignore displacement will then be biased upward . . .

The statement is misleading in three respects. First, in general, vacancies *do* exist in the long run since, in general, demand curves slope down and there is an increase in employment in response to the increase in supply. Second, even if vacancies exist, displacements can still occur. Third, the losses to the displaced workers do not in general lead to biases in the benefit-cost ratio.

I can accept the proposition that short-run demand curves are perfectly inelastic (even though I doubt that they are for the aggregate of all firms which are potential employers of the graduates of training programs) or that wages are rigid in the short run for the jobs in these firms. These conditions would fix the quantity of jobs, and any placement of a trainee must be offset by the displacement of an existing worker. It is a "lump-of-labor" situation. Even here, the displaced worker would presumably shift to the next best alternative use of his time, and at the margin, this equals (or is just below) his prevailing wage. To the extent that he takes a wage cut in moving to another full-time job he is worse off, but his loss is the new employer's gain, and there is no loss to society as a whole—only a transfer from the displaced worker to his new employer.

If, however, all firms which are potential employers have inelastic demand curves and all wages are rigid, then the displaced worker becomes unemployed, or drops out of the labor force. There is a loss to him (unless the nonmarket uses of time are valued at his old wage level) and there will, in general, be a loss to society because there is no offsetting gain to anyone else. The same proposition holds if the displaced employee finds some job in another market that utilizes only part of his effort—assuming that his full efforts have not simply become obsolete. This partial loss is not offset by anyone else's partial gain, either.

But if we are to evaluate programs in their complete time-setting, this short-run scenario is a markedly inferior model to that of the conventional analysis in which demand curves slope down, supply curves slope up, and wages and prices can change—particularly if we consider the flexibility offered by all the non-pecuniary components of wages and prices and by the context of generally rising money wages and prices.

In a more conventional analysis and over the longer run, displacement can certainly occur. If the supply of workers to an occupation is increased sufficiently, this will decrease the wages of workers in the occupation, and the latter will suffer a capital loss. And, although total employment will expand, there will be a process of adjustment in which *some* workers will leave this occupation as the wage falls below that of their best alternative. Just as important, there will be some additional workers who *would have* entered this occupation if the trainees had not entered, and these potential entrants will now go elsewhere, and they will probably end up earning lower wages than if there had never been a training program. Hamermesh would have us believe, I think, that these wage losses by the displaced and the potentially displaced workers should be offset against the wage gains of the placed trainees when computing benefit-cost ratios for the training program. This is 99 percent wrong for the simple reason that Hamermesh is confusing these losses, which amount to negative pecuniary externalities, with real-resource negative externalities.[2] This is exactly what Rosen has told us not to do, and if you want other authorities, I can cite Viner and Mishan. That distributional changes are involved is, obviously, not in question, and if someone were computing a super-efficiency, benefit-cost ratio that incorporates such distributional gains and losses, then these pecuniary externalities would need to be included.

What is the one percent of Hamermesh's view that is valid? It is that in the nitty gritty of the process of adjustment there is likely to be some dead-weight losses, because workers will not always smoothly adjust from one equilibrium

---

[2] Briefly, the proposition is that wage declines in an occupation are accompanied by lower prices (and, in the short run, higher profits), so that the worker's loss is offset by the consumer's (and employers') gain.

point on their labor-nonlabor "curve" to another point. Transitory unemployment among workers "forced" to make the adjustments constitute external costs that can be technological in nature. To be somewhat melodramatic, the influx of new workers can be likened to a storm that hits and results in permanent damage.

But I do not think the analogy of a storm or some other such shock is apt. I believe that the workings of training programs are more appropriately compared with the way the educational system works. Do we need to consider the externalities of displacements when college graduates increase and take jobs away from those with high school degrees who might otherwise have obtained them? What about each new high school graduate or immigrant who first enters the labor force? Is each displacing an already employed worker? Unless we are adopting the lump-of-labor view of the market, they are not, and neither is the graduate of a training program. The externalities that we must consider are the pecuniary externalities that arise in tracing the distributional impact of these actions and not the technological externalities that must be weighed in a benefit-cost analysis of the efficiency question. If, however, we have reason to believe that the labor market cannot make sufficiently smooth adjustments to the changing composition of the labor force, then it is necessary to consider the technological externalities, but Hamermesh's paper gives us no help in making this judgment.

It is easy to say that the ideal benefit-cost calculation should trace the pattern of market and nonmarket earnings for all affected workers and compare this pattern with the situation that would have existed without the program in a world in which every imperfection in adjustments is calibrated. Indeed, the real world is characterized by a vast amount of job heterogeneity, by wage dispersion for even the same or similar jobs, by complex search behavior by both workers and employers, and by an impressively large amount of job mobility and movement in and out of the labor force. This complexity reveals the likelihood for some technological externalities in adjustment processes, but it also suggests to me many sources of flexibility and adjustment possibilities. We can see, incidentally, that this sort of technological eternal diseconomy of a training or educational program exists, in principle, for any change in the economy which calls for a response or adjustment which may not be perfectly smooth. To incorporate these effects in manpower analyses requires an exceeding degree of refinement and precision in cost-benefit analysis, and, I believe, is asking too much at this stage. Certainly Hamermesh gives us no help in this extraordinarily difficult task.

Hamermesh advocates training programs primarily for shortage occupations. To the extent that shortage connotes a high rate of return of the investment because of favorable earnings for the trainees, this is perfectly reasonable—almost tautalogical. But to the extent that this advocacy stems from the displacement criterion, it is on shaky ground. A shortage conventionally refers to a situation in which wages or other forms of employee benefits will be rising, thus attracting new workers until an equilibrium is achieved. Now, if graduates of training programs are hired instead of these potential hirees among nontrainees, what happens to the latter group? Presumably, they will go elsewhere. And will not the same problems of displacement (as Hamermesh uses the term) arise there—the same, that is, as those arising if the trainees were sent there to begin with? Perhaps some model of labor force behavior can be constructed to demonstrate that those technological externalities produced by the frictions of adjustments are less if trainees instead of nontrainees enter shortage occupations, but I do not see this model in Hamermesh's paper.

Given his particular and, I believe, peculiar view of the displacement problem, it is not surprising that Hamermesh calls for concentrating training programs in periods of low unemployment. He makes it appear obvious that training programs should be undertaken procyclically. He overlooks the argument for a countercyclical program based on the availability of free resources from currently unemployed factors of production (especially workers), which may make the opportunity costs so low during periods of high unemployment that training becomes a profitable investment in the light of the long-run payoffs when the business cycle turns up.[3]

In the second part of the paper, there is a discussion of the relation of the Phillips curve to training programs which leaves out some basic issues. On the one hand, any training program with a high rate of return indicates that more output will be forthcoming from the existing resources. Other things the same, this ought to be deflationary—more goods being chased by the same amount of money, to use an old-fashioned expression. On the other hand, any training program which taxes employed workers and uses the revenue to employ unemployed workers in a training program can shift the Phillips curve leftward—if the taxed workers do not reduce their work effort. But what is the benefit-cost ratio of this exercise? Perhaps it is very low. Unfortunately, I see no guide to policy from these considerations, except the trivial one of adopting training programs when their rate of return justifies their adoption.

I question Hamermesh's conclusion that a job matching program is likely to produce wider fluctuations in employment. It seems to me that if the program succeeds in matching compatibility traits between employers and employees, turnover rates would decline. I am reminded of Boulding's remark that "the labor market is like the marriage market." [(1951), p. 254]. Will computer dating increase divorce rates? That's one question. Maybe yes, maybe no. But even if it did, who is to say this is not optimal?

The same point can be made regarding the broader question of the relation between job mobility and subsidies for training and job information. Such sub-

---

[3]I do not mean to endorse the common, and often cynical, advocacy of training programs to cure unemployment, since they are at best an extremely ineffective tool to reduce overall unemployment. The diseconomies of raising false hopes and then dashing them from this strategy *ought* to be measured.

sidies can lower the costs of turnover and encourage job mobility—Hamermesh's point—but they can also raise the benefits of job stability by promoting optimal matching to begin with. Nevertheless, the important consideration, as I see it, is not whether mobility increases or decreases, but whether whatever effects the subsidies have will result in a favorable or unfavorable benefit-cost verdict. I certainly disagree with Hamermesh's bald assertion that: "... information programs necessarily improve the functioning of labor markets and move mobility closer to some optimum." This simply assumes away the whole question of evaluation.

I conclude by saying that although Hamermesh is addressing some tough questions that Rosen bypassed, and although he provides here and there some useful insights in the economics of training programs, the paper is more valuable pedagogically for what is wrong about it than what is right.

Secondary Labor Market
Effects of Manpower
Programs: Comment

Lester C. Thurow

In his paper on "The Secondary Effects of Manpower Program," Daniel Hamermesh lists a number of categorical imperatives for manpower programs. While I am in sympathy with the broad thrust of his remarks and conclusions, I am confused about their details and how they are to be made into universalizable rules.

Categorical Imperative (1): Every replacement trained leads to an equal and opposite displacement unless training is concentrated in labor shortage areas.

I suspect that this categorical imperative is more universal than the author realizes. If macroeconomic policies are being set in terms of target unemployment rates (as they were in the Kennedy-Johnson administrations and are in the Nixon administration), every training program is simply a program for reshuffling employment or unemployment and not a program for reducing unemployment. Unemployment will only fall if the Phillips curve happens to improve and policy-makers decide to alter their unemployment target. As a result, the conditional clause can be discarded in the first categorical imperative.

This is not to say, however, that training policies are worthless. A manpower program that succeeded in reshuffling employment to reduce the dispersion in the distribution of earned incomes or succeeded in equalizing the probability of being unemployed would be a bright success. A recession where each of us were unemployed 6.2% of the time would not have serious welfare consequences. I would argue that the prime goal of manpower programs should be such a reshuffling.

Leaving the benefits of reshuffling aside, however, I am puzzled as to when a labor shortage exists. Does it exist when vacancies exceed unemployment, when money wages are rising, when real wages are rising, when actual output is less than desired output because of an inability to hire labor at the prevailing wage, or when the rate of return on training is above the social rate of time preference? The author does not tell us his definition, but rate-of-return calculations are certainly the correct method for telling whether training should or should not occur. Unfortunately, normal definitions of labor shortages, such as vacancies exceeding unemployment, provide no information about the desirability of expanding training.

Categorical Imperative (2): If each firm's output is fixed, there is no reason to concentrate subsidies in firms having production functions characterized by different distribution parameters.

I would have thought that it would pay to concentrate training on those skills where the rate of return is above the social rate of time preference and where the elasticity of substitution between these skills and other factors of production is low.

Categorical Imperative (3): In general, upgrading should be concentrated on training low-skilled workers for more highly skilled jobs in which shortages exist.

I suspect that this categorical imperative runs against the grain of any internal labor market. The employee teamwork that Rosen talks about in his paper would be nonexistent. Even more importantly, the informal on-the-job training that takes place among employees would vanish as new workers were jumped over old workers.

The big manpower problem is not employing the unemployed—this can only be done with adequate macro-policies—but reducing the dispersions in the distribution of earned income. Forgetting to upgrade those already employed is hardly a method for reducing these dispersions. Over six million individuals work full time (over 35 hours per week and 50 weeks per year) and still make less than $3,000 per year. These workers have all of the industrial discipline that seems to be so hard to instill yet they have not had the opportunities to advance either because of lack of cognitive job skills or because of discrimination. Instead of being ignored, they should be the prime target of manpower programs. At the very least, those who subscribed to the mores of the system should be helped by the system.

Categorical Imperative (4): Thou shalt not "cream."

While I sympathize with the welfare motives behind this principle, I disagree with it as a matter of political economy. To start with those hardest to help and to then move up to those easier to help is to condemn manpower programs to permanent failure and an early demise. If manpower programs are to have a future, they must at some early point demonstrate success. By starting with those easiest to help (it should be noted that this group is still in need of help and is not easy to help on any absolute standard), programs may be able to succeed, may learn something that will be of use in helping those harder to help, and may be able to build up the political base that will allow them to survive the inevitable failures in helping those hardest to help.

In addition, the principle runs into the rank order equity problem. In most activities, it is permissible for governments to reduce welfare differentials, but it is not permissible to alter rank orders overtly. There is no reason why we should subscribe to the principle of rank order equity or horizontal equity for that matter, but we do. To overtly alter rank order incomes is to invite the most vigorous of backlashes.

Categorical Imperative (5): Focus job training and information programs on labor shortage areas in an effort to improve the Phillips curve.

Such an improvement is supposed to occur since employers will no longer find it as necessary to raise wages to shorten employee search times. First, I know of no empirical evidence that shortening employee search times will improve the Phillips curve. Second, equally impressive theoretical arguments can be made in the reverse direction. Shortening the employer's employee search time also shortens the employee's job search time. This may lead to an increase in the quit rate large enough to increase the employer's total search time even though his search time per employee falls. Employers may be forced to adjust wages faster with shorter search times than they would with longer search times. More mobility may also interfere with the teamwork necessary for high productivity.

Categorical Imperative (6): Be agnostic about the socially desirable degree of mobility.

Somehow I feel that economists should not only be defining the socially desirable degree of mobility, but should be attempting to quantify it. The Japanese may demonstrate the conflict between optimum mobility in a static society and optimum mobility in a dynamic society. With their industrial tenure and lack of static mobility, they may have less than the optimum degree of static mobility, but this same lack of mobility seems to lead to a readiness to accept new techniques of production that is unknown in our more mobile society. If you can only advance in your present position and firm and cannot be laid off, both you and your employer have a strong interest in maximizing technical progress. If you can switch jobs and can be laid off, you maximize your own welfare by resisting advances that may lead to unemployment and by jumping to a better job—not by upgrading your existing job.

Implicitly, the paper by Sherwin Rosen—"Some Externalities in Program Evaluation"—is arguing that manpower programs should be concentrated on distributional objectives since private market mechanisms will push the economy close to its efficiency frontier. I agree with the implicit conclusions, but I think that Rosen is too sanguine about the efficiency of the private labor market.

In reality, the Becker model, upon which Rosen bases his work, is too simplistic. First, individuals must invest in their human capital subject to two budget constraints, time and financial resources. While improvements in the capital markets can remove the financial constraint, there is no mechanism for relieving the time constraint. Consequently, many if not most income-maximizing individuals will not drive the rate of return on their human capital down to the marginal social rate of time preference. They simply will not have time to do so. Second, each individual's human capital production function is different or at least we each have different fixed amounts of natural resources (IQ, etc.) with which to work. Both of these factors lead to large "rental payments." This means the whole notion of a market equilibrium is much more complex than either Becker or Rosen realize. Third, when government training programs are under consideration, marginal analysis is inappropriate. Nonmarginal changes are being contemplated. When such nonmarginal changes are contemplated, there is a fundamental externality in any economy. In almost all production functions, the returns to each factor of production depend upon the quantity of other factors of production that are in use. Thus, the returns to physical capital will be dependent upon the quantity of human capital with which it works. Yet, workers who are investing in their human capital will not take into account the increases in the marginal product of physical capital. As a result, even in a perfectly functioning labor market, governments may need to intervene to ensure that the right nonmarginal changes occur.

I also disagree with the simplistic notion that what occurs in the market must be rational. Rosen maintains that seniority wage payments prove that productivity rises with age and that the absence of private certification firms proves that education cannot be serving a certification function. Such statements of faith would put the most illiterate totum worshiper to shame. Any time a theory has reached the point where there is no evidence that can possibly lead you to modify it, something is wrong with the theory. Unfortunately, Rosen's belief in the perfection of the market mechanism seems to have reached such a state.

Good reasons exist for both of these phenomena. Seniority wage payments may be necessary to facilitate informal on-the-job training. Without them, older workers might be unwilling to help younger workers. Certification is an area where private firms cannot exist since certification can only be done by looking at past actions. There are no simple tests for determining work habits and motivation.

Finally, Rosen discusses the effect of team effort and the extra returns to a team as opposed to a collection of individuals. It seems to me that this opens Pandora's box as far as the perfection of private markets is concerned. Individual marginal products no longer exhaust the total product and some other theory of distribution has to enter the system. When it does, however, all of the neat efficiency axioms of the marginal productivity theory go out the window. Unfortunately, Rosen suggests no replacements.

References

References

Aller, Curtis C. "Lessons Learned from Vocational Training Programs Given in a Prison Setting." In *Education and Training in Correctional Institutions.* Center for Studies in Vocational and Technical Education, The University of Wisconsin, 1968.

Anderson, Darrell and John A. Niemi. *Adult Education and the Disadvantaged Adult.* ERIC Clearinghouse on Adult Education, 1969.

Anderson, O.W. "The Utilization of Health Services." In *Handbook of Medical Sociology,* edited by H.E. Freeman, S. Levine and L.G. Reeder. Prentice-Hall, 1963.

Avnet, H. *Physician Service Patterns and Illness Rates.* Group Health Insurance, Inc., 1967.

Baldwin, S. *The Impact of Government Programs on the Employability of Youth in the Seattle Labor Market.* University of Washington, 1968.

Barth, Peter S. "An Assessment of Four Manpower Programs." Paper presented to the Operations Research Society of America, 5 May 1971. Mimeograph.

Baumol, William. *Economic Theory and Operations Analysis.* 2d Edition, Prentice-Hall, 1965.

Becker, Gary. *Human Capital.* National Bureau of Economic Research, 1964.

Bickner, R.E. "Measurements and Indices of Health." In *Outcomes Conference I-II: Methodology of Identifying, Measuring, and Evaluating Outcomes of Health Service Programs, Systems, and Subsystems,* edited by C.E. Hopkins. Department of Health, Education and Welfare, Public Health Service, Health Services and Mental Health Administration, 1969.

Block, J. *The Challenge of Response Sets.* Appleton, 1965.

Blum, Zahava D., Nancy L. Karweit and Aage B. Sorensen. *A Method for the Collection and Analysis of Retrospective Life Histories.* The Johns Hopkins University, July 1969.

Bortner, R.W. and D.F. Hultsch. "A Multivariate Analysis of Correlates of Life Satisfaction in Adulthood." *Journal of Gerontology* 25 (Jan. 1970): 41-47.

Borus, Michael E. "A Benefit-Cost Analysis of the Economic Effectiveness of Retraining the Unemployed." *Yale Economic Essays* 4 (Fall 1964): 371-429.

Borus, Michael E. "Using Unemployment Insurance Wage Reports As a Data Source." *Monthly Labor Review* 93 (July 1970): 66-68.

Borus, Michael E., John P. Brennan and Sidney Rosen. "A Benefit Cost Analysis of the Neighborhood Youth Corps." *Journal of Human Resources* 5 (Spring 1970): 139-59.

Borus, Michael E. and William R. Tash. *Measuring the Impact of Manpower Programs: A Primer.* Institute of Labor and Industrial Relations, The University of Michigan-Wayne State University, 1970.

Boulding, Kenneth E. In *The Impact of the Labor Union,* edited by David McC. Wright. Kelley and Millman, Inc., 1951.

Boulding, Kenneth E. "Fun and Games with the Gross National Product—The Role of Misleading Indicators in Social Policy." In *The Environmental Crisis*, edited by H.W. Helfrich, Jr. Yale University Press, 1970.

Bowlby, Roger L. and William R. Schriver. "Nonwage Benefits of Vocational Training: Employability and Mobility." *Industrial and Labor Relations Review* 23 (July 1970): 500-09.

Bradburn, N.M. and D. Caplovitz. *Reports on Happiness*. Aldine, 1965.

Bright, M. "Tracing a Longitudinal Sample Over Time." *Journal of Chronic Diseases* 20 (Sept. 1967): 707-16.

Britton, J.H. "Living in Rural Pennsylvania Community in Old Age." In *Patterns of Living and Housing of Middle-Aged and Older People*, edited by F.M. Carp and W.M. Burnett. Publication No. 1496, Public Health Service, U.S. Department of Health, Education and Welfare, 1966.

Brodman, K. "Cornell Medical Index-Health Questionnaire." In *Contributions Toward Medical Psychology*, edited by A. Weider, vol. 2. Ronald Press, 1953.

Brown, G.W. "The Experiences of Discharged Chronic Schizophrenic Patients in Various Types of Living Groups." *Milbank Memorial Fund Quarterly* 37 (April 1959): 105-31.

Brunner, G.A. and S.J. Carroll. "The Effect of Prior Telephone Appointments on Completion Rates and Response Content." *Public Opinion Quarterly* 31 (Winter 1967-68): 652-54.

Bureau of National Affairs. *Manpower Information Service*. March 24, 1971, 318-20.

Buss, A. *The Psychology of Aggression*. John Wiley, 1961.

Bylund, H. *Social, Cultural, and Educational Factors Associated with Relative Vocational Success of Navajo High School Graduates*. Utah State University, 1970.

Cain, Glen G. and Robinson G. Hollister. "Evaluating Manpower Programs for the Disadvantaged." In *Cost-Benefit Analysis of Manpower Policies*, edited by Gerald G. Somers and W. Donald Wood. Industrial Relations Centre, Queens University, 1969, pp. 119-51, (a).

Cain, Glen G. and Robinson G. Hollister. "The Methodology of Evaluating Social Action Programs." In *Public-Private Manpower Policies*, edited by Arnold R. Weber, Frank H. Cassell, and Woodrow L. Ginsburg. Industrial Relations Research Association, 1969, pp. 5-33, (b).

Cain, Glen G. and Ernst W. Stromsdorfer. "An Economic Evaluation of Government Retraining Programs in West Virginia." In *Retraining the Unemployed*, edited by Gerald G. Somers. University of Wisconsin Press, 1968, pp. 299-335.

Campbell, D.T. "Reforms as Experiments," *American Psychologist* 24 (1969): 409-29.

Campbell, Donald T. and Julian C. Stanley. *Experimental and Quasi-Experimental Designs for Research*. Rand-McNally & Co., 1969.

Cannell, C.F., G. Fisher and T. Bakker. *Reporting of Hospitalization in the Health Interview Survey*. Public Health Service Publication No. 1000–Series 2–No. 6, National Center for Health Statistics, 1961.

Cantril, H. *The Patterns of Human Concerns*. Rutgers University Press, 1965.

Carroll, Adger B. and Loren A. Ihnen. *Costs and Returns of Technical Education: A Pilot Study*. Department of Economics, North Carolina State University, 1966.

Clyde, D.J. "Self Ratings." In *Drugs and Behavior*, edited by L. Uhr and J.G. Miller. John Wiley, 1960.

Coase, Ronald. "The Nature of the Firm." *Economica* 4 (Nov. 1937): 386-405.

Coase, Ronald. "The Problem of Social Cost." *Journal of Law and Economics* 3 (Oct. 1960): 1-44.

Cobb, S., G.W. Brooks, S.V. Kasl and W.E. Connelly. "The Health of People Changing Jobs: A Description of a Longitudinal Study." *American Journal of Public Health* 56 (Sept. 1966): 1476-81.

Cobb, S., J.R.P. French, R.L. Kahn and F.C. Mann. "An Environmental Approach to Mental Health." *Bulletin of the New York Academy of Science* 107 (May 22, 1963): 596-606.

Cobb, S., P. Hunt and E. Harburg. "The Intrafamilial Transmission of Rheumatoid Arthritis. II. An Interview Measure of Rheumatoid Arthritis." *Journal of Chronic Diseases* 22 (Sept. 1969): 203-15.

Cobb, S. and S.V. Kasl. "Some Medical Aspects of Unemployment." In *Employment of the Middle-Aged: Papers from Industrial Gerontology Seminars*, edited by G. Shatto. C.C. Thomas, 1971, in press.

Cobb, S., D. McFarland, S.V. Kasl and G.W. Brooks. "On the Relationship Among Variables in a Longitudinal Study of People Changing Jobs." In *Proceedings of The Fifth Scientific Meeting of the International Epidemiological Association*. Belgrade: Savremena Administracija Publishing House, 1970.

Conley, Ronald W. "A Benefit-Cost Analysis of the Vocational Rehabilitation Program." *Journal of Human Resources* 4 (Spring 1969): 226-52.

Conrad, John P. *Crime and Its Correction*. University of California Press, 1965.

Coopersmith, S. *The Antecedents of Self-Esteem*. W.H. Freeman, 1967.

Corazzini, Arthur. "The Decision to Invest in Vocational Education." *Journal of Human Resources*. Supplement: Vocational Education. 3 (1968): 88-120.

Croog, S. "Ethnic Origins, Educational Level, and Responses to a Health Questionnaire." *Human Organization* 20 (1961): 65-69.

Crowne, D.P. and D. Marlowe. *The Approval Motive*. John Wiley, 1964.

Davis, M.S. and R.L. Eichhorn. "Compliance with Medical Regimens: A Panel Study." *Journal of Health and Human Behavior* 4 (Winter 1963): 240-49.

Davis, Otto A. and Andrew Whinston. "Externalities, Welfare and the Theory of Games." *Journal of Political Economy* 70 (June 1962): 241-62.

Dohrenwend, Barbara, John Colombotos and Bruce Dohrenwend. "Social Distance and Interviewer Effects." *Public Opinion Quarterly* 32 (Fall 1968): 410-22.

Dohrenwend, B.P. and B.S. Dohrenwend. "The Problem of Validity in Field Studies of Psychological Disorder." *Journal of Abnormal Psychology* 70 (Feb. 1965): 52-69.

Drotning, J.E. and D.B. Lipsky. *Interviewing Jet Trainees: Early Field Experience*. Survey Research Center, State University of New York at Buffalo, 1969.

Dunn, J.P. and S. Cobb. "Frequency of Peptic Ulcer Among Executives, Craftsmen, and Foremen." *Journal of Occupational Medicine* 4 (July 1962): 343-48.

Eckland, B.K. "Retrieving Mobile Cases in Longitudinal Surveys." *Public Opinion Quarterly* 32 (Spring 1968): 51-64.

Ehrenberg, R.G. "Heterogeneous Labor, the Internal Labor Market and the Dynamics of the Employment-Hours Decision." *Journal of Economic Theory* forthcoming, 1971.

Elinson J. and R.E. Trussell. "Some Factors Relating to Degree of Correspondence for Diagnostic Information Obtained by Household Interviews and Clinical Examination." *American Journal of Public Health* 47 (March 1957): 311-21.

Fair, Ray. *The Short-Run Demand for Workers and Hours*. North Holland Publishing Company, 1969.

Freeman, H.E. and O.G. Simmons. "Mental Patients in the Community: Family Settings and Performance Levels." *American Sociological Review* 23 (Feb. 1958): 147-54.

Freeman, H.E. and O.G. Simmons. *The Mental Patient Comes Home*. Wiley, 1963.

French, J.R.P. and R.L. Kahn. "A Programmatic Approach to Studying the Industrial Environment and Mental Health." *Journal of Sociological Issues* 18 (July 1962): 1-47.

Friedman, H.J. and H.W. Martin. "A Comparison of Self and Physician's Health Ratings in an Older Population." *Journal of Health and Human Behavior* 3 (Fall 1963): 179-83.

Geismar, L.L. and M.A. LaSorte. "Research Interviewing with Low-Income Families." *Social Work* 8 (April 1963): 10-13.

Gibbard, Harold A. and Gerald G. Somers. "Government Retraining of the Unemployed in West Virginia." In *Retraining the Unemployed*, edited by Gerald G. Somers. University of Wisconsin Press, 1968, pp. 17-124.

Glaser, Daniel. *The Effectiveness of a Prison and Parole System*. Bobbs-Merrill, 1964.

Glass, Gene V. "Pay-off Evaluation of Title I." Paper delivered at the Annual Convention of the National Council on Measurement in Education, New York City, 5 February 1971.

Glueck, Sheldon and Eleanor Glueck. *500 Criminal Careers*. Alfred A. Knopf, 1930.

Goldfarb, Robert S. "The Evaluation of Government Programs: The Case of New Haven's Manpower Training Activities." *Yale Economic Essays* 9 (Fall 1969): 59-104.

Greenleigh Associates, Inc. *Field Test and Evaluation of Selected Basic Education Systems*. Greenleigh Associates, Inc., 1966.

Greenleigh Associates, Inc. *Inventory of Federally-Funded Adult Basic Education Programs*. Greenleigh Associates, Inc., 1968, (a).

Greenleigh Associates, Inc. *Participants in Four Basic Education Systems*. Greenleigh Associates, Inc., 1968 (b).

Gurin, G. *Inner-City Negro Youth in a Job Training Project*. Institute for Social Research, University of Michigan, 1968.

Gurin, G., J. Veroff and S. Feld. *Americans View Their Mental Health*. Basic Books, 1960.

Haberman, P.W. "The Reliability and Validity of the Data." In *Poverty and Health*, edited by J. Kosa, A. Antonovsky, and I.K. Zola. Harvard University Press, 1969.

Hamermesh, Daniel S. *Economic Aspects of Manpower Training Programs: Theory and Policy*. D.C. Heath and Company, 1971.

Hamermesh, Daniel S. and Robert S. Goldfarb. "Manpower Programs in a Local Labor Market." *American Economic Review* 60 (Sept. 1970): 706-09.

Hanoch, Giora. "An Economic Analysis of Earnings and Schooling." *Journal of Human Resources* 2 (Summer 1967): 310-29.

Hansen, W. Lee, Burton A. Weisbrod and William J. Scanlon. "Schooling and Earnings of Low Achievers." *American Economic Review* 60 (June 1970): 409-18.

Hardin, Einar. "Benefit-Cost Analyses of Occupational Training Programs: A Comparison of Recent Studies." In *Cost-Benefit Analysis of Manpower Policies*, edited by Gerald G. Somers and W. Donald Wood. Industrial Relations Centre, Queens University, 1969, pp. 97-118.

Hardin, Einar and Michael E. Borus. "An Economic Evaluation of the Retraining Program in Michigan: Methodological Problems of Research," in *Proceedings of the American Statistical Association, 1966, Social Statistics Section*. American Statistical Association, 1966, pp. 133-37.

Hardin, Einar and Michael E. Borus. *The Economic Benefits and Costs of Retraining*. D.C. Heath and Co., 1971.

Harmeling, M. *Social and Cultural Links in the Urban Occupational Adjustment of Southern Appalachian Migrants*. Fordham University, 1969.

Havens, B.J. "An Investigation of Activity Patterns and Adjustment in an Aging Population." *The Gerontologist* 8 (Autumn 1968): 201-06.

Havinghurst, R.J. "The Leisure Activities of the Middle Aged." *American Journal of Sociology* 63 (Sept. 1957): 152-62.

Havinghurst, R.J. and K. Feigenbaum. "Leisure and Life Style." *American Journal of Sociology* 64 (Jan. 1959): 306-404.

Heyman, D.K. and F.C. Jeffers. "Effect of Time Lapse on Consistency of Self-Health and Medical Evaluations of Elderly Persons." *Journal of Gerontology* 18 (April 1963): 160-64.

Hinkle, L.E., Jr. "Measurement of the Effects of the Environment upon the Health and Behavior of People." Unpublished manuscript, The Division of Human Ecology, Cornell University Medical College, 1971.

Hochstim, J.R. "Health and Ways of Living." In *The Community as an Epidemiologic Laboratory*, edited by I.I. Kessler and M.L. Levin. The Johns Hopkins Press, 1970.

Holt, Charles, et al. *Planning Production, Inventories and Work Force*. Prentice-Hall, 1960.

Holt, Charles, C. Duncan MacRae, Stuart O. Schweitzer and Ralph E. Smith. *The Unemployment—Inflation Dilemma: A Manpower Solution*. The Urban Institute, 1971.

Hu, Teh-wei, Maw Lin Lee, Ernst W. Stromsdorfer and Jacob J. Kaufman. *A Cost-Effectiveness Study of Vocational Education: A Comparison of Vocational and Nonvocational Education in Secondary Schools*. Institute for Research on Human Resources, Pennsylvania State University, 1969.

Hunt, S.M., K. Singer and S. Cobb. "Components of Depression." *Archives of General Psychiatry* 16 (April 1967): 441-47.

Jahoda, M. *Current Concepts of Positive Mental Health*. Basic Books, 1958.

Johnston, James. *Econometric Methods*. McGraw-Hill, 1963.

Jorgenson, Dale. "Capital Theory and Investment Behavior." *American Economic Review* 53 (May 1963): 247-59.

Kasl, S.V. and S. Cobb. "Some Psychological Factors Associated with Illness Behavior and Selected Illnesses." *Journal of Chronic Diseases* 17 (April 1964): 325-45.

Kasl, S.V. and S. Cobb. "Health Behavior, Illness Behavior, and Sick Role Behavior." *Archives of Environmental Health* 12 (April 1966): 531-41.

Kasl, S.V. and S. Cobb. "Blood Pressure Changes in Men Undergoing Job Loss: A Preliminary Report." *Psychosomatic Medicine* 32 (Jan/Feb 1970): 19-38.

Kasl, S.V. and S. Cobb. "Changes in Reported Illness and Illness Behavior Related to the Termination of Employment." Paper presented at the 6th International Scientific Meeting of the International Epidemiological Association, Primosten, Yugoslavia, 1971.

Kasl, S.V., S. Cobb and G.W. Brooks. "Changes in Serum Uric Acid and Cholesterol Levels in Men Undergoing Job Loss." *Journal of the American Medical Association* 206 (Nov. 11, 1968): 1500-07.

Katona, George. "Expectations and Decisions in Economic Behavior." In *The Policy Sciences*, edited by Daniel Lerner and Harold D. Lasswell. Stanford University Press, 1951.

Katz, S., A.B. Ford, R.W. Moskowitz, B.A. Jackson and M.W. Jaffe. "Studies of Illness in the Aged. The Index of ADL: A Standardized Measure of Biological and Psychosocial Function." *Journal of the American Medical Association* 185 (Sept. 21, 1963): 914-19.

Kaufman, J.J. and M.V. Lewis. *General Education or Job Training for Dropouts?* The Institute for Research on Human Resources, The Pennsylvania State University, (in press).

Koos, E.L. *The Health of Regionville*. Columbia University Press, 1954.

Korn, Richard R. and Lloyd W. McCorkle. *Criminology and Penology*. Holt, 1959.

Kosa, J., J.J. Alpert and R.J. Haggerty. "On the Reliability of Family Health Information." *Social Science and Medicine* 1 (July 1967): 165-81.

Kuh, Edwin. "Cyclical and Secular Labor Productivity in U.S. Manufacturing." *Review of Economics and Statistics* 47 (Feb. 1965): 1-12.

Kutner, B., D. Fanshel, A.M. Togo and T.S. Langner. *Five Hundred Over Sixty*. Russell Sage Foundation, 1956.

Langner, T.S. "A Twenty-Two Item Screening Score of Psychiatric Symptoms Indicating Impairment." *Journal of Health and Human Behavior* 3 (Winter 1962): 269-76.

Lawton, M.P. and E.M. Brody. "Assessment of Older People: Self-Maintaining and Instrumental Activities of Daily Living." *The Gerontologist* 9 (Autumn 1969): 179-86.

Levine, Robert A. "Policy Analysis and Economic Opportunity Programs." In *The Analysis and Evaluation of Public Expenditures: The PPB System*. Compendium of papers presented to the Subcommittee on Economy in Government of the Joint Economic Committee, vol. 3, part IV, Government Printing Office, 1969, pp. 1181-96.

Levitan, Sar and Garth Mangum. *Federal Training and Work Programs in the Sixties*. Institute of Labor and Industrial Relations, University of Michigan-Wayne State University, 1969.

Lewis, H. Gregg. "Competitive and Monopoly Unionism." In *The Public Stake in Union Power*, edited by P.D. Bradley. University of Virginia Press, 1959.

Lewis, M.V., E. Cohn and D.N. Hughes. *The Retention of Participants in a Concentrated Employment Program and Their Subsequent Employment*. The Institute for Research on Human Resources, The Pennsylvania State University, (in press).

Lord, Frederic M. "Problems in Mental Test Theory Arising From Errors of Measurement." *Journal of the American Statistical Association* 54 (June 1959): 472-79.

Lord, Frederic M. "Large-Sample Covariance Analysis when the Control Variable is Fallible." *Journal of the American Statistical Association* 55 (June 1960): 307-21.

Madansky, A. "The Fitting of Straight Lines When Both Variables Are Subject to Error." *Journal of the American Statistical Association* 54 (March 1959): 173-205.

Maddox, G.L. "Some Correlates of Differences in Self-Assessment of Health Status Among the Elderly." *Journal of Gerontology* 17 (April 1962): 180-85.

Maddox, G.L. "Activity and Morale: A Longitudinal Study of Selected Elderly Subjects." *Social Forces* 42 (Dec. 1963): 195-204.

Main, Earl D. "A Nationwide Evaluation of M.D.T.A. Institutional Job Training." *Journal of Human Resources* 3 (Spring 1968): 159-70.

Mandel, Nathan G., et al. *Crime Revisited*. Department of Corrections, State of Minnesota, 1963.

Mandell, W., S. Blackman and C.E. Sullivan. *Disadvantaged Youth Approaching the World of Work*. Wakoff Research Center, 1969.

Mandler, G., J.M. Mandler and E.T. Uviller. "Autonomic Feedback: The Perception of Autonomic Activity." *Journal of Abnormal Social Psychology* 56 (May 1958): 367-73.

Marks, J., J. Stouffacher and C. Lyle. "Predicting Outcome in Schizophrenia." *Journal of Abnormal Social Psychology* 66 (Feb. 1963): 117-27.

McClelland, David and David Winter. *Motivating Economic Achievement*. New York Free Press, 1969.

McDonnell, John J., et al. *An Evaluation of MDTA Training in Correctional Institutions*. Final Report to the U.S. Department of Labor, (3 volumes), Abt Associates, 1971.

McKean, Roland. *Efficiency in Government Through Systems Analysis*. John Wiley and Sons, 1958.

Meade, James E. "External Economies and Diseconomies in a Competitive Situation." *Economic Journal* 62 (March 1952): 54-67.

Mechanic, D. *Medical Sociology*. The Free Press, 1968.

Mechanic, D. "Illness and Cure." In *Poverty and Health*, edited by J. Kosa, A. Antonovsky and I.K. Zola. Harvard University Press, 1969.

Miles, G.H., W.F. Henry and R.N. Taylor. *Optimizing the Benefits of Neighborhood Youth Corps Projects for Rural Youth*. North Star Research and Development Institute, 1969.

Miller, Herman and Richard Hornseth. "Cross-Sectional vs. Cohort Estimates of Lifetime Income." Paper presented at American Statistical Association Meetings, Detroit, Michigan, 1970.

Miller, R.W. and F.A. Zeller. *Social Psychological Factors Associated with Responses to Retraining*. Appalachian Center, West Virginia University, 1967.

Mishan, E. "The Postwar Literature on Externalities." *Journal of Economic Literature* 9 (March 1971): 1-28.

Mott, P.E., F.C. Mann, Q. McLaughlin and D.P. Warwick. *Shift Work: The Social, Psychological and Physical Consequences*. University of Michigan Press, 1965.

Neugarten, B., R.J. Havinghurst and S. Tobin. "The Measurement of Life Satisfaction." *Journal of Gerontology* 16 (April 1961): 134-43.

Norman, W.T. "On Estimating Psychological Relationships: Social Desirability and Self-Report." *Psychology Bulletin* 67 (April 1967): 273-93.

Oi, Walter. "Labor as a Quasi-Fixed Factor." *Journal of Political Economy* 70 (Dec. 1962): 538-55.

Olendzki, M.C. "Welfare Medical Care in New York City: A Research Study." Ph.D. dissertation, University of London, 1965.

Organic, H.N. and S. Goldstein. "The Brown University, Rhode Island Population Laboratory: Its Purposes and Initial Progress." In *The Community as an Epidemiologic Laboratory*, edited by I.I. Kessler and M.L. Levin. The Johns Hopkins Press, 1970.

Osgood, C.E., G.J. Suci and P.H. Tannenbaum. *The Measurement of Meaning.* University of Illinois Press, 1957.

Oswald, Ian. *Sleep.* Penguin Books, 1966.

Palmore, E.B. "The Effects of Aging on Activities and Attitudes." *The Gerontologist* 8 (Winter 1968): 259-63.

Parnes, Herbert S., Belton M. Fleisher, Robert C. Miljus, Ruth S. Spitz and Associates. *The Pre-Retirement Years.* vol. 1, Manpower Research Monograph No. 15, U.S. Department of Labor, Government Printing Office, 1970, (a).

Parnes, Herbert S., Robert C. Miljus, Ruth Spitz, and Associates. *Career Thresholds.* vol. 1, Manpower Research Monograph No. 16, U.S. Department of Labor, Government Printing Office, 1970, (b).

Parnes, Herbert S., John R. Shea, Ruth S. Spitz, Frederick A. Zeller, and Associates. *Dual Careers.* vol. 1, Manpower Research Monograph No. 21, U.S. Department of Labor, Government Printing Office, 1970, (c).

Parsons, T. "Definitions of Health and Illness in the Light of American Values and Social Structure." In *Patients, Physicians, and Illness*, edited by E.G. Jaco. The Free Press, 1958.

Pencavel, John. "Wages, Specific Training, and Labor Turnover in U.S. Manufacturing Industries." Institute for Mathematical Studies in the Social Sciences, Stanford University, 1971.

Pownall, George A. *Employment Problems of Released Prisoners.* Manpower Administration, U.S. Department of Labor, 1969.

Rees, Albert and George Shultz. *Workers and Wages in an Urban Labor Market.* University of Chicago Press, 1970.

Regelson, Lillian. "Applications of Cost-Benefit Analysis to Federal Manpower Programs." Paper presented at the 1969 Joint National Meeting of the Operations Research Society of America and the American Astronautical Society.

Reynolds, Lloyd. *The Structure of Labor Markets.* Harper and Brothers, 1951.

Ribich, Thomas I. *Education and Poverty.* The Brookings Institution, 1968.

Riley, M.W. and A. Foner. *Aging and Society. Vol. I. An Inventory of Research Findings.* Russell Sage Foundation, 1968.

Robin, Gerald D. *An Assessment of the In-Public School Neighborhood Youth Corps Projects in Cincinnati and Detroit, with Special Reference to Summer-Only and Year-Round Enrollees.* Final Report to the Manpower Administration, Contract No. 81-40-66-18. National Analysts, 1969.

Robinson, J.P. "Social Change as Measured by Time Budgets." *Journal of Leisure Research* 1 (1969): 75-77.

Robinson, J.P., R. Athansiou and K.B. Head, editors. *Measures of Occupational Attitudes and Occupational Characteristics*. Institute for Social Research, University of Michigan, 1969.

Rodgers, C.H., R.D. Artis, L.J. Hausman, C. Green and W.R. Parker. *Teenage Unemployment in Two Selected Rural Counties in the South*. Center for Occupational Education, North Carolina State University, 1969.

Roomkin, Myron. "An Evaluation of Adult Basic Education Under the Manpower Development and Training Act in Milwaukee, Wisconsin." Ph.D. dissertation, University of Wisconsin, 1971.

Rosen, Bernard. "Race, Ethnicity, and the Achievement Syndrome." *American Sociological Review* 24 (Feb. 1959): 47-60.

Rosen, Sherwin. "Short-Run Employment Variation on Class-I Railroads in the U.S." *Econometrica* 36 (July-Oct. 1968): 511-30.

Rosen, Sherwin. "Learning and Experience in the Labor Market." Forthcoming, 1971.

Rosenstock, I.M. "Prevention of Illness and Maintenance of Health." In *Poverty and Health*, edited by J. Kosa, A. Antonovsky and I.K. Zola. Harvard University Press, 1969.

Rosow, I. "Adjustment of the Normal Aged." In *Processes of Aging*, edited by R.H. Williams, C. Tibbitts and W. Donahue.Vol. II, Atherton Press,1963.

Roth, J.A. "The Treatment of the Sick." In *Poverty and Health*, edited by J. Kosa, A. Antonovsky and I.K. Zola. Harvard University Press, 1969.

Sanders, B.S. "Have Morbidity Surveys Been Oversold?" *American Journal of Public Health* 52 (Oct. 1962): 1648-59.

Sanders, B.S. "Measuring Community Health Levels." *American Journal of Public Health* 54 (July 1964): 1063-70.

Scanlon, John W., Garth N. Buchanan, Joe N. Nay, and Joseph S. Wholey. *An Evaluation System to Support Planning, Allocation and Control in a Decentralized, Comprehensive Manpower Program*. The Urban Institute, 1971.

Schlingensiepen, W. and S.V. Kasl. "Helpseeking Behavior of Male College Students with Emotional Problems." *Social Psychiatry* 5 (Jan. 1970): 25-34.

Schmale, A.H. "Object Loss, 'Giving Up,' and Disease Onset. An Overview of Research in Progress." In *Symposium on Medical Aspects of Stress in the Military Climate*. U.S. Government Printing Office, 1965.

Scitovsky, Tibor. "Two Concepts of External Economies." *Journal of Political Economy* 62 (April 1954): 143-51.

Scott, Loren C. "The Economic Effectiveness of On-the-Job Training: The Experience of the Bureau of Indian Affairs in Oklahoma." *Industrial and Labor Relations Review* 23 (Jan. 1970): 220-36.

Seeman, M. "On the Meaning of Alienation." *American Sociological Review* 24 (Dec. 1959): 783-91.

Sells, S.B., editor. *The Definition and Measurement of Mental Health*. Department of Health, Education and Welfare, Health Services and Mental Health Administration and National Center for Health Statistics, 1968.

Sewell, David. "A Critique of Cost-Benefit Analysis of Training." *Monthly Labor Review* 90 (Sept. 1967): 45-54.

Shanas, E. *The Health of Older People*. Harvard University Press, 1962.

Shanas, E., P. Townsend, D. Wedderburn, H. Friis, P. Milhj and J. Stehouner. *Old People in Three Industrial Societies*. Atherton Press, 1968.

Shea, John R., Roger D. Roderick, Frederick A. Zeller and Associates. *Years For Decision*. vol.1, Manpower Research Monograph No. 24, U.S. Department of Labor, Government Printing Office, 1971.

Shekelle, R.B., H.L. Klawans, A.M. Ostfeld, H.M. Tufo, S.W. Kimble, J.D. Waxman, J.M. MacLean and M.A. Erlich. "A Screening Procedure for Stroke." *American Journal of Public Health* (in press), 1971.

Sheppard, Harold L. "Discontented Blue-Collar Workers—A Case Study." *Monthly Labor Review* 94 (April 1971): 25-32, (a).

Sheppard, Harold L. *New Perspectives on Older Workers*. W.E. Upjohn Institute, 1971, (b).

Sheppard, Harold L. and Harvey Belitsky. *The Job Hunt*. Johns Hopkins University Press, 1966.

Shosteck, Hershel. "Survey Research in the Inner City." Unpublished paper, Spring 1971.

Snedecor, George W. *Statistical Methods*. Iowa State University Press, 1956.

Social Security Administration, Office of Research and Statistics. "Some Statistical Research Resources Available at the Social Security Administration." Social Security Administration, 1967.

Solie, Richard J. "Employment Effects of Retraining the Unemployed." *Industrial and Labor Relations Review* 21 (Jan. 1968): 210-55.

Somers, Gerald G., editor. *Retraining the Unemployed*. University of Wisconsin Press, 1968.

Somers, Gerald G., (in Cooperation with Bureau of Social Science Research, Inc.). *The Effectiveness of Vocational and Technical Programs: A National Follow-up Survey*. Center for Studies in Vocational and Technical Education, University of Wisconsin, 1971.

Somers, Gerald G., and Ernst W. Stromsdorfer. *A Cost-Effectiveness Study of the In-School and Summer Neighborhood Youth Corps*. Industrial Relations Research Institute, University of Wisconsin, 1970.

Srole, L., T.S. Langner, S.T. Michael, M.K. Opler and T.A.C. Rennie. *Mental Health in the Metropolis*. McGraw-Hill, 1962.

Stahl, S.M. "Illness Among the Aged: A Study of the Determinants of the Perception of Levels of Health in an Indigent Urban Population." University of Illinois, Ph.D. dissertation, 1971.

Sternbach, R. and B. Tursky. "Ethnic Differences Among Housewives in Psychophysical and Skin Potential Responses to Electric Shock." *Psychophysiology* 1 (Jan. 1965): 241-46.

Stoeckle, J.D., I.K. Zola and G.E. Davidson. "On Going to See the Doctor: The Contributions of the Patient to the Decision to Seek Medical Aid." *Journal of Chronic Diseases* 16 (Sept. 1963): 975-89.

Stromsdorfer, Ernst W. "Determinants of Economic Success in Retraining the Unemployed: The West Virginia Experience." *Journal of Human Resources* 3 (Spring 1968): 139-58.

Suchman, E.A., B.S. Phillips and G.F. Streib. "An Analysis of the Validity of Health Questionnaires." *Social Forces* 36 (March 1958): 223-32.

Sullivan, D.F. *Conceptual Problems in Developing an Index of Health.* Public Health Service Publication No. 1000–Series 2–No. 17, National Center for Health Statistics, May 1966.

Thurow, Lester. *Poverty and Discrimination.* The Brookings Institution, 1969.

Tobin, S.S. and B.L. Neugarten. "Life Satisfaction and Social Interaction in the Aging." *Journal of Gerontology* 16 (Oct. 1961): 344-46.

U.S. Department of Commerce. *Mobility of the Population of the U.S., March 1968 to March 1969.* Current Population Report, Series P-20, No. 193, December 26, 1969.

U.S. Department of Labor, Manpower Administration. *The Influences of MDTA on Earnings.* Manpower Evaluation Report No. 8. Manpower Administration, 1968.

U.S. Department of Labor, Manpower Administration. *The Neighborhood Youth Corps: A Review of Research.* Manpower Research Monograph No. 13, 1970.

van Zonneveld, R.J. "On Measuring Physical Health in the Elderly." In *Colloquium on Health and Aging of the Population*, edited by M.F. Lowenthal and A. Zilli. S. Karger, 1969.

Viner, Jacob. "Cost Curves and Supply Curves." *Zeitschrift für Nationalokonomie* 3 (Sept. 1931): 23-46.

Walther, R.G. *Methodological Considerations in Evaluative Research Involving Disadvantaged Populations.* Social Research Group, George Washington University, 1969.

Watson, C.G. and J.R. Fulton. "Treatment Potential of the Psychiatric-Medically Infirm. I. Self-Care Independence." *Journal of Gerontology* 22 (Oct. 1967): 449-55.

Webb, E.J., D.T. Campbell, R.D. Schwartz and L. Sechrest. *Unobtrusive Measures: Nonreactive Research in the Social Sciences.* Rand McNally, 1966.

Weisbrod, Burton A. *External Benefits of Public Education.* Industrial Relations Section, Princeton University, 1964.

Weisbrod, Burton A. "Preventing High School Drop-outs." In *Measuring Benefits of Government Investments*, edited by Robert Dorfman. The Brookings Institution, 1965, pp. 117-71.

Weisbrod, Burton A. "Conceptual Issues in Evaluating Training Programs." *Monthly Labor Review* 89 (Oct. 1966): 1091-97.

Weiss, Carol H. "Interviewing Low-Income Respondents: A Preliminary View." *Welfare in Review* 4 (Oct. 1966): 1-9.

Weiss, Carol H. "Validity of Welfare Mothers' Interview Responses." *Public Opinion Quarterly* 32 (Winter 1968-69): 622-33.

Welch, Finis. "Labor-Market Discrimination: On Interpretation of Income Differences in the Rural South." *Journal of Political Economy* 75 (June 1967): 225-40.

Wilensky, H.L. "Work, Careers, and Social Integration." *International Sociological Journal* 12 (1960): 543-60.

Wilner, D.B., R.P. Walkley, T.C. Pinkerton and M. Tayback. *The Housing Environment and Family Life.* Johns Hopkins Press, 1962.

Wood, V., M.L. Wylie and B. Sheafor. "An Analysis of a Short Self-Report Measure of Life Satisfaction: Correlation with Rater Judgments." *Journal of Gerontology* 24 (Oct. 1969): 465-69.

World Health Organization. "Measurement of Levels of Health." *World Health Organization Technical Report Series.* No. 137, 1957.

World Health Organization. "Constitution of the World Health Organization, Annex I." In *The First Ten Years of the World Health Organization.* World Health Organization, 1958.

Yett, Donald E., et al. *Determination of Economic Attributes of Community Health Profiles and Health Indices.* University of Southern California, Human Resource Research Center, May 1970. Mimeographed.

Zborowski, M. *People in Pain.* Jossey-Bass, Inc., 1969.

Zola, I.K. "Illness Behavior of the Working Class." In *Blue-Collar World*, edited by A. Shostak and W. Gomberg. Prentice-Hall, 1964.

Zola, I.K. "Culture and Symptoms: An Analysis of Patients' Presenting Complaints." *American Sociological Review* 31 (Oct. 1966): 615-30.

Zuckerman, M. and B. Lubin. *Manual for the Multiple Affect Adjective Checklist.* Educational and Industrial Testing Service, 1965.

About the Contributors

Marie G. Argana, Chief, Longitudinal Surveys Branch, Demographic Surveys Division, Bureau of the Census, U.S. Department of Commerce.

Hilda N. Barnes, Marketing Research Director, Decision Making Information.

Peter S. Barth, Brookings Institution Economic Policy Fellow, The Office of Research and Development, Office of Policy, Evaluation and Research, U.S. Department of Labor and Associate Professor of Economics, The University of New Mexico.

Michael E. Borus, Visiting Associate Professor, Department of Economics, and Research Associate, Center for Human Resource Research, The Ohio State University and Associate Professor of Labor and Industrial Relations, Michigan State University.

Edward C. Bryant, Co-Founder and President, Westat Research, Inc.

Glen G. Cain, Professor of Economics, University of Wisconsin.

John Cheston, Director, Office of Evaluation, Office of the Assistant Secretary for Policy, Evaluation and Research, U.S. Department of Labor.

Thomas N. Chirikos, Assistant Professor of Preventive Medicine, and Research Associate, Center for Human Resource Research, The Ohio State University.

Robert S. David, Chief of Methodology, Contract Evaluations Group, Division of Program Evaluation, Manpower Administration, U.S. Department of Labor.

John L. Fischer, Chief, Performance Analysis Division, Job Corps, U.S. Department of Labor.

Belton M. Fleisher, Professor of Economics, The Ohio State University.

Paul D. Gayer, Social Science Advisor, Evaluation Division, U.S. Office of Economic Opportunity.

Daniel S. Hamermesh, Assistant Professor of Economics, Princeton University.

Morris H. Hansen, Senior Staff Advisor and Vice President, Westat Research, Inc.

Einar Hardin, Professor, Associate Director for Research, and Chairman of Academic Studies, School of Labor and Industrial Relations, Michigan State University.

James A. Hefner, Associate Professor of Economics, Clark College.

Robert N. Heller, Special Assistant for Liaison with Users of Social Security Data, Office of Research and Statistics, Social Security Administration, U.S. Department of Health, Education and Welfare.

Celia Homans, Assistant Field Director, National Opinion Research Center, University of Chicago.

Stanislav V. Kasl, Associate Professor of Epidemiology and Public Health, Yale University School of Medicine.

Dwight Kelley, Chief of Research, Indiana Employment Security Division.

Martin Koenig, Manpower Analyst, Office of Manpower Management Data Systems, Manpower Administration, U.S. Department of Labor.

Morgan V. Lewis, Psychologist and Research Associate, Institute for Research on Human Resources, The Pennsylvania State University.

Garth Mangum, McGraw Professor of Economics and Director, Human Resources Institute, University of Utah.

John J. McDonnell, Senior Systems Analyst, Abt Associates, Inc.

David A. Miller, Chairman, Camil Associates, Inc.

Joe N. Nay, Senior Research Staff, Program Evaluation Studies, The Urban Institute.

Gilbert Nestel, Research Associate, Center for Human Resource Research, The Ohio State University.

Harold Nisselson, Assistant Director for Research, National Center for Educational Statistics, U.S. Office of Education.

Herbert S. Parnes, Professor of Economics and Associate Director, Center for Human Resource Research, The Ohio State University.

Edward C. Prescott, Assistant Professor of Economics, Carnegie-Mellon University.

R. Thayne Robson, Research Professor of Economics and Finance and Executive Director of the Division of Economic and Community Research and Services, Center for Economic and Community Development, University of Utah.

Howard Rosen, Director, Office of Research and Development, Manpower Administration, U.S. Department of Labor.

Sherwin Rosen, Professor of Economics, University of Rochester and Research Staff Associate, National Bureau for Economic Research.

John W. Scanlon, Senior Research Staff, Program Evaluation Studies, The Urban Institute.

John R. Shea, Assistant Professor of Educational Development and Research Associate, Center for Human Resource Research, The Ohio State University.

Harold L. Sheppard, Staff Social Scientist, The W.E. Upjohn Institute for Employment Research.

Gerald G. Somers, Professor and Chairman, Department of Economics, and Director, Center for Studies in Vocational and Technical Education, The University of Wisconsin.

Abraham Stahler, Chief, Division of Program Evaluation Studies, Manpower Administration, U.S. Department of Labor.

Ernst W. Stromsdorfer, Associate Professor of Economics, Indiana University.

William R. Tash, Deputy Chief, Program Analysis and Evaluation Branch, National Institutes of Mental Health.

Lester C. Thurow, Professor of Economics and Management, Massachusetts Institute of Technology and Research Associate, Kennedy School of Government, Harvard University.

Ralph S. Walker, Chief, Contract Evaluations Group, Manpower Administration, U.S. Department of Labor.

Joseph S. Wholey, Director, Program Evaluation Studies, The Urban Institute.

Index

275